A WRITER'S REFERENCE

Third Edition

Diana Hacker

BEDFORD BOOKS ❧ BOSTON

FOR BEDFORD/ST. MARTIN'S
President and Publisher: Charles H. Christensen
General Manager and Associate Publisher: Joan E. Feinberg
Managing Editor: Elizabeth M. Schaaf
Developmental Editor: Katherine A. Retan
Editorial Assistant: Andrea L. Goldman
Production Editor: Anne Benaquist
Production Assistant: Karen S. Baart
Copyeditor: Barbara G. Flanagan
Text design: Claire Seng-Niemoeller
Cover design: Richard Emery Design, Inc.

Library of Congress Catalog Card Number: 94–65166

Manufactured in the United States of America.

9   8

k

For information write: Bedford/St. Martin's, 75 Arlington Street, Boston, MA 02116   (617–426–7440)

ISBN: 0–312–17216–8

ACKNOWLEDGMENTS
Nelson W. Aldrich, Jr., from *Old Money: The Mythology of America's Upper Class.* Copyright © 1988 by Nelson W. Aldrich, Jr. Published by Alfred A. Knopf, Inc.
The American Heritage Dictionary of the English Language, from the entry "regard." Copyright © 1992 by Houghton Mifflin Company. Reprinted by permission from *The American Heritage Dictionary of the English Language,* Third Edition.
Eugene Boe, from "Pioneers to Eternity: Norwegians on the Prairie," *The Immigrant Experience,* edited by Thomas C. Wheeler. © 1971 by Thomas C. Wheeler. A Dial Press Book, Doubleday & Co., Inc.

Acknowledgments and copyrights are continued at the back of the book on page 354, which constitutes an extension of the copyright page.

How to use this book

A *Writer's Reference* has been carefully designed to save you time. As you can see, the book lies flat, making it easy to consult while you are revising and editing a draft. And the book's twelve section dividers will lead you — in most cases very quickly — to the information you need.

Here are brief descriptions of the book's major reference aids, followed by several tutorials that give you hands-on experience using the book.

The menu system

The Main Menu inside the front cover displays the book's contents as briefly and simply as possible. Each of the twelve sections in the Main Menu leads you to a tabbed divider, on the back of which you will find a more detailed menu.

Let's say you have a question about the proper use of commas between items in a series. Your first step is to scan the Main Menu, where you will find the comma listed as the first item under section P (Punctuation). Next flip the book open to the tabbed divider marked P. Now consult the detailed menu for the precise subsection (P1-c) and the exact page number.

The index

If you aren't sure what topic to choose from the Main Menu, consult the index at the back of the book. For example, you may not realize that the issue of whether to use *is* or *are* is a matter of subject-verb agreement (G1 on the Main Menu). In that case, simply look up "*is* versus *are*" in the index and you will be directed to the exact page you need.

The glossary of usage

When in doubt about the correct use of a particular word (such as *affect* and *effect, among* and *between,* or *hopefully*), flip to section W1 and consult the alphabetically arranged glossary for the word in question. If the word's correct use is more fully explained elsewhere in the book — as with *good* versus *well,* for example — you will find a cross-reference to the fuller explanation.

If the word you are looking for isn't in the Glossary of Usage, try the index instead. For example, you won't find an entry for "*I* versus *me*" in the glossary because the issue is too complicated for a short glossary entry. The index, however, will take you straight to the pages you need.

The directories to documentation models

When you are writing a research paper, there is no need to memorize all of the technical details about handling citations or constructing a list of the works you have cited. Instead, you can rely on one of the book's two directories to documentation models. If you are using the Modern Language Association (MLA) system of documentation, flip the book open to the tabbed section marked M to find the appropriate directory. If you are using the American Psychological Association (APA) system, flip to the tabbed section marked A.

List of ESL boxes

If you are a nonnative speaker of English, you will find most of the ESL (English as a second language) advice in the tabbed section marked T (for ESL Trouble Spots). Other ESL advice appears in boxed ESL notes throughout *A Writer's Reference.* For quick reference, a list of these ESL notes is given near the end of the book, after the index and before the correction symbols.

Correction symbols

Some instructors mark student papers with the codes given on the Main Menu or detailed menus, such as E1 or G3-c. If your instructor uses standard correction symbols instead, consult the list on the very last page of the book, right before the endpapers.

Brief table of contents (inside the back cover)

Readers who want a quick overview of the book will find a brief table of contents inside the back cover.

Tutorials

The following tutorials will give you practice using the book's menu system, the index, the Glossary of Usage, and the directory to the MLA documentation models. Answers to all tutorials appear on pages x–xii.

TUTORIAL 1   Using the menu system

Each of the following "rules" violates the principle it expresses. Using the menu system, find the section in *A Writer's Reference* that explains the principle. Then fix the problem. Examples:

> *has*
> A verb ~~have~~ to agree with its subject. *G1*
>   ∧
>
> *Tutors in*
> ~~In~~ the writing center,~~they~~ say that vague pronoun reference is
> ∧
>
> unacceptable. *G3-b*

1. Each pronoun must agree with their antecedent.
2. About sentence fragments. You should avoid them.
3. Its important to use apostrophe's correctly.
4. Watch out for *-ed* endings that have been drop from verbs.
5. Discriminate careful between adjectives and adverbs.
6. Be alert for irregular verbs that have came to you in the wrong form.
7. If your sentence begins with a long introductory word group use a comma to separate the word group from the rest of the sentence.
8. Don't write a comma splice, you must connect independent clauses with a comma and a coordinating conjunction or with a semicolon.
9. A writer must be careful not to shift your point of view.
10. When dangling, watch your modifiers.

TUTORIAL 2   Using the index

Assume that you have written the following sentences and want to know the answers to the questions in brackets. Use the index at the back of the book to locate the information you need, and edit the sentences if necessary.

1. Anyone taking the school bus to the volleyball game must bring in a permission slip signed by their parents. [Is it okay to use *their* to refer to *Anyone*? If not, what is the best way to fix the problem?]
2. We had intended to go surfing but spent most of our vacation lying on the beach. [Should I use *lying* or *laying*?]
3. We only looked at two houses before buying the house of our dreams. [Is *only* in the right place?]
4. In Saudi Arabia it is considered ill mannered for you to accept a gift. [Is it okay to use *you* to mean "anyone in general"?]
5. In Canada, Joanne picked up several bottles of maple syrup for her sister and me. [Should I write *for her sister and I*?]

TUTORIAL 3   Using the menu system or the index

Imagine that you are in the following situations. Using either the menu system or the index, find the information you need.

1. You are Ray Farley, a community college student who has been out of high school for ten years. You recall learning to punctuate items in a series by putting a comma between all items except the last two. In your college readings, however, you have noticed that most writers use a comma between all items. You're curious about the current rule. What does *A Writer's Reference* tell you?
2. You are Maria Sanchez, an honors student working in your university's writing center. Mike Lee, who speaks English as a second language, has come to you for help. He is working on a rough draft that contains a number of problems involving the use of articles (*a, an,* and *the*). You know how to use articles, but you aren't able to explain the rather complicated rules on their correct use. Which section of *A Writer's Reference* will you and Mike Lee consult?
3. You are John Pell, engaged to marry Jane Dalton. In a note to Jane's parents, you have written "Thank you for giving Jane and myself such a generous contribution toward our honeymoon trip to Hawaii." You wonder if you should write "Jane and I" or "Jane and me" instead. What does *A Writer's Reference* tell you?
4. You are Selena Young, an African American woman who supervises interns at a housing agency. Two of your interns, Jake Gilliam and Susan Green, have writing problems involving -*s* endings on verbs. Gilliam, an African American, tends to drop -*s* endings; Green, who is white, tends to add them where they don't

belong. You suspect that both problems stem from nonstandard dialects spoken at home.

Susan and Jake are in danger of losing their jobs because your boss thinks that anyone who writes "the tenant refuse" or "the landlords agrees" is beyond hope. You disagree. Susan and Jake are more intelligent than your boss supposes, and they have asked for your help. Where in *A Writer's Reference* can they find the rules they need?

5. You are Joe Thompson, a first-year college student. Your girl-friend, Samantha, who has completed two years of college, seems to enjoy correcting your English. Just yesterday she corrected your sentence "I felt badly about her death" to "I felt bad about her death." You're sure you've heard many educated persons, including professors, say "I felt badly." Upon consulting *A Writer's Reference,* what do you discover?

TUTORIAL 4 Using the Glossary of Usage

Consult the Glossary of Usage (section W1) to see if the italicized words are used correctly. Then edit any sentences containing incorrect usage. Example:

> *an*
> The pediatrician gave my daughter ~~a~~ injection for her allergy.

1. Changing attitudes *toward* alcohol have *effected* the beer industry.
2. It is *mankind's* nature to think wisely and act foolishly.
3. This afternoon I plan to *lie* out in the sun and begin working on a tan.
4. Everyone in our office is *enthused* about this project.
5. Most sleds are pulled by no *less* than two dogs and no more than ten.

TUTORIAL 5 Using the directory to MLA documentation models

Assume that you have written a short research paper on the debate over the use of marijuana for medical purposes. You have cited the following sources in your paper, using MLA documentation, and you are ready to type your list of works cited. Flip the book open to the tabbed section marked M and use the MLA directory to locate the appropriate models. Then write a correct entry for each source and arrange the entries in a properly formatted list of works cited. *Note:* Do not number the entries in a list of works cited.

A journal article by Gregg A. Bilz entitled "The Medical Use of Marijuana: The Politics of Medicine." The article appears on pages 117 to 135 of the *Hamline Journal of Public Law and Policy,* which is paginated by issue. The volume number is 13, the issue number is 1, and the year is 1992.

An unsigned magazine article entitled "Cross-Eyed and Painless." The article appears on page 89 of the July 6, 1991, issue of *The Economist.*

A book by Jack E. Henningfield and Nancy Almand Ator entitled *Barbiturates: Sleeping Potion or Intoxicant?* The book was published in Philadelphia in 1986 by Chelsea House Publishers.

A newspaper article by Michael Isikoff entitled "U.S. Provided Marijuana for Some AIDS Patients." The article appears on page A3 of the March 24, 1991, issue of the *Washington Post.*

A journal article by Gabriel Nahas and Colette Latour entitled "The Human Toxicity of Marijuana." The article appears on pages 495 to 497 of the *Medical Journal of Australia,* which is paginated by volume. The volume number is 156, and the year is 1992.

Answers to Tutorial 1

1. Each pronoun must agree with its antecedent. (G3-a)
2. You should avoid sentence fragments. (G5)
3. It's important to use apostrophes correctly. (P5-c and P5-e)
4. Watch out for *-ed* endings that have been dropped from verbs. (G2-d)
5. Discriminate carefully between adjectives and adverbs. (G4)
6. Be alert for irregular verbs that have come to you in the wrong form. (G2-a)
7. If your sentence begins with a long introductory word group, use a comma to separate the word group from the rest of the sentence. (P1-b)
8. Don't write a comma splice; you must connect independent clauses with a comma and a coordinating conjunction or with a semicolon. (G6)
9. A writer must be careful not to shift his or her [*not* their] point of view. *Or* Writers must be careful not to shift their point of view. (E4-a)
10. Look out for dangling modifiers. (E3-e)

Answers to Tutorial 2

1. The index entry *"anyone"* mentions that the word is singular, so you might not need to look further to realize that the plural *their* is incorrect. The second page reference leads you to section

G3-a, which suggests nonsexist strategies for revision, such as *Students taking the school bus to the volleyball game must bring in a permission slip signed by their parents* or *Anyone taking the school bus to the volleyball game must bring in a permission slip signed by his or her parents.*

2. The index entry "*lay, lie*" takes you to the Glossary of Usage and to section G2-b, where you will learn that *lying* (meaning "reclining or resting on a surface") is correct.

3. Look up "*only*" and you will be directed to section E3-a, which explains that limiting modifiers such as *only* should be placed before the words they modify. The sentence should read *We looked at only two houses before buying the house of our dreams.*

4. Looking up "*you,* indefinite use of" leads you to section E4-a, the Glossary of Usage, and section G3-b, all of which explain that *you* should not be used to mean "anyone in general." You can revise the sentence by using *a person* or *one* instead of *you,* or you can restructure the sentence completely: *In Saudi Arabia, accepting a gift is considered ill mannered.*

5. The index entries "*I* versus *me*" and "*me* versus *I*" take you to section G3-c, which explains why *me* is correct.

Answers to Tutorial 3

1. Section P1-c tells you that although usage varies, most experts advise using a comma between all items in a series — to prevent possible misreadings or ambiguities. To find this section, Ray Farley would probably use the menu system.

2. Maria Sanchez and Mike Lee would consult section T1, on articles. This section is easy to locate on the main menu.

3. Section G3-c explains why "Jane and me" is correct. To find section G3-c, John Pell could use the menu system if he knew to look under "Problems with pronouns." Otherwise, he could look up "*I* versus *me*" in the index. Pell could also look up "*myself*" in the index or he could consult the Glossary of Usage, where a cross-reference would direct him to section G3-c.

4. Selena Young's employees could turn to sections G1 and G2-c for help. Young could use the menu system to find these sections if she knew to look under "Subject-verb agreement" or "Other problems with verbs." If she wasn't sure about the grammatical terminology, she could look up "-*s,* as verb ending" or "Verb(s), -*s* form of" in the index.

5. Section G4-b explains why "I felt bad about her death" is correct. To find section G4-b, Joe Thompson could use the menu system if he knew that *bad* versus *badly* is a choice between an adjective and an adverb. Otherwise he could look up "*bad, badly*" in the index or the Glossary of Usage.

Answers to Tutorial 4

1. Changing attitudes toward alcohol have *affected* the beer industry.
2. It is *human* nature to think wisely and act foolishly.
3. Correct.
4. Everyone in our office is *enthusiastic* about this project.
5. Most sleds are pulled by no *fewer* than two dogs and no more than ten.

Answers to Tutorial 5

Bilz, Gregg A. "The Medical Use of Marijuana: The Politics of Medicine." Hamline Journal of Public Law and Policy 13.1 (1992): 117-35.

"Cross-Eyed and Painless." Economist 6 July 1991: 89.

Henningfield, Jack E., and Nancy Almand Ator. Barbiturates: Sleeping Potion or Intoxicant? Philadelphia: Chelsea House, 1986.

Isikoff, Michael. "U.S. Provided Marijuana for Some AIDS Patients." Washington Post 24 Mar. 1991: A3.

Nahas, Gabriel, and Colette Latour. "The Human Toxicity of Marijuana." Medical Journal of Australia 156 (1992): 495-97.

Preface for instructors

Response to the second edition of *A Writer's Reference* has been gratifying: Instructors across the country tell me that their students can and do use the book on their own. Because so many instructors assign the book primarily as a reference, I have worked to improve its reference features in this third edition. Here, briefly, is what's new.

More help for researchers

The research material now appears in three (instead of two) tabbed sections: Research Writing (R), MLA Documentation (M), and Alternative Styles of Documentation (A). With the MLA and APA advice in separate tabbed sections, there is no danger that students will consult the wrong models. So that students will be able to find the models they're looking for as quickly as possible, *A Writer's Reference* includes new, easy-to-find directories to both MLA and APA styles (see pages 270–71 and 306–07).

The APA section reflects changes in the fourth edition of the *Publication Manual of the American Psychological Association* (1994) and includes a new student essay that illustrates APA style.

The tabbed section Research Writing contains new material on using the library's major reference tools, including computer catalogs and databases. Also, an expanded discussion of plagiarism emphasizes even more strongly that in addition to being documented, borrowed language must be enclosed in quotation marks.

More help for ESL students

The tabbed section ESL Trouble Spots includes more on verbs and gives new advice on using the prepositions *at, in,* and *on.* In sections where nonnative speakers need extra help, ESL notes throughout the text alert students to special problems. These notes are boxed so that they can be easily skipped by students who don't need the advice and easily found by those who do. A list of these ESL boxes appears near the end of the book, right before the correction symbols.

A new section on document design

Both in the business world and in the academic world, writers are becoming increasingly interested in document design — the use of visual cues to help readers. Therefore, a new tabbed section, Document Design (D), discusses format options on word processors and the use of headings, displayed lists, and visuals (when appropriate) to make documents more accessible. Section D also contains guidelines for the preparation of academic manuscripts and business documents (formerly in the section on mechanics). A new student essay without documentation illustrates MLA manuscript guidelines. Students can consult this example instead of the sample MLA research paper when they are preparing a manuscript that is not based on written sources.

New tutorials in "How to use this book"

Even though *A Writer's Reference* is easy to use, students who are unfamiliar with its reference features may need some help learning to use the book on their own. For such students, the book now includes several tutorials at the end of the section "How to Use This Book." These tutorials give students practice using the menu system, the index, the Glossary of Usage, and the MLA directory. Instructors can have students do the tutorials in class or, because answers are given at the end of the tutorials, students can work through them on their own.

A user-friendly index

Even if they don't know grammatical terminology, students can nearly always find what they're looking for in the index. When faced with a choice between *I* and *me*, for example, students may not know to look up "Pronoun case." They are more likely to look up "*I* versus *me*." This and similar user-friendly entries appear throughout the index of the third edition.

More exercise options

If you are interested in learning about exercise options available with *A Writer's Reference*, please consult "A Note to Instructors" inside the front cover.

ACKNOWLEDGMENTS

No author can possibly anticipate the many ways in which a variety of students might respond to a text: Where might students be confused? How much explanation is enough? What is too intimidating? Do the examples appeal to a range of students? Are they free of stereotypes? To help me answer such questions, nearly two hundred and fifty professors from more than one hundred and fifty colleges and universities contributed useful insights based on their varied experiences in the classroom.

For their many helpful suggestions, I would like to thank an unusually perceptive group of reviewers:

Eleanor Agnew, Georgia Southern University
Doris Andrews, Southeastern Oklahoma State University
Peter Ashley, Baltimore City Community College
Cynthia Bates, University of California, Davis
Linda Bateman, Rowan College of New Jersey
Michael Bouland, Three Rivers Community College
Alice Brand, State University of New York at Brockport
JoAnn Buck, Guilford Technical Community College
Mary Buckalew, University of North Texas
Rick Burt, Oakland Community College
John Collins, Rowan College of New Jersey
Marilyn Collins, Rowan College of New Jersey
Kathryn Fitzgerald, University of Utah
Martha French, Fairmont State College
Judith Funston, Potsdam College of the State University of New York
Jill Grigsby, Pomona College
William Helms, James Madison University
Anne Herrington, University of Massachusetts at Amherst
Ann Higgins, Gulf Coast Community College
William Hochman, University of Southern Colorado
Bonnie Irwin, Iowa State University
Ted Johnston, El Paso Community College
Anne Maxham Kastrinos, Washington State University
Kathleen Kelly, Northeastern University

David Lang, Golden Gate University
Emory Maiden, Appalachian State University
Sharon Manassa, University of Florida
James McKenna, Pomona College
Judith Oster, Case Western Reserve University
Beverly Palmer, Pomona College
Michael Pilz, Bucks County Community College
John Ruden, Sacramento City College
Meena Sachdeva, University of Hawaii, Kapiolani Community
    College
Mary Sauder, Indiana University
Ron Shook, Utah State University
Will Tomory, Southwestern Michigan College
Nicole Tonkovich, University of California, San Diego
Daryl Troyer, El Paso Community College
Richard Tubbs, Community College of Aurora
James D. Williams, University of North Carolina
Randall Woodland, University of California, Los Angeles
Susan Yager, Iowa State University

For helping me see the strengths and deficiencies of the second edition, thanks go to the many instructors who took the time to answer a detailed questionnaire:

Corrine Adler, University of Washington; Kathleen Aguero, Pine Manor College; Peter Allen, Pomona College; Joyce B. Anderson, Millersville University of Pennsylvania; Nancy Anisfield, Saint Michael's College; Gwen S. Argersinger, Mesa Community College; Jan Armon, Temple University School of Law; Jo Baldwin, Miami University; Joseph Basso, University of South Dakota; Judith Baumel, Adelphi University; Audrey Becker, University of Michigan, Ann Arbor; Edward Blanchard, Merced College; Stanley S. Blair, Wesleyan College; Sally Blazar, Boston University; Cynthia Boland, Quinebaug Valley Community College; Elizabeth Bookser Barkley, College of Mount Saint Joseph; Peggy Borden, Willmar Community College; Bryan Bott, University of Colorado at Boulder; Muriel M. Brennan, College of San Mateo; Mary Brooks, Eastern Washington University; E. Barnsley Brown, University of North Carolina at Chapel Hill; Dianne Bruleigh, Onondaga Community College; P. B. Burke, Hartnell College; Jean Campion, Fort Lewis College; Donna M. Campbell, State University of New York at Buffalo; Marilyn A. Carlson, Augustana College; Jerome Cartwright, Utica College of Syracuse University; Susan Castagnetto, Pomona College; A. E. Cawns, Webster University; Cynthia Cawthra, Washington University; Patricia Cherpas, Kalamazoo Valley Community College; Renny Christopher, Cabrillo College; Alice Cleveland, College of Marin; Chas S. Clifton, University of Southern Colorado; Edward Copeland, Pomona College; Joan Kuzma Costello, Inver Hills Community College; John F. Cox, University of Arizona; Mary Crawback, Marymount College; Lillian Cunningham, University of Hawaii, Windward Community College; Kathleen Dale, University of Wisconsin, Milwaukee; Daniel L. Dawson, Miami University; S. Renee Dechert, Texas A&M University; B. J. Dimmick, New Hampshire Technical College at Claremont; Meghan H. Dorsett, Southwest Missouri State University; Jane Dunphy, Massachusetts Institute of Technology; Reg Dyck, Capital University; Diana Edwards, Naugatuck Valley Community Technical College; Margaret Edwards, University of Vermont; Faridoun Farrokh, Texas A&M University; Margaret Ferry, University of Baltimore; Carole S. Fickert, Holyoke Community College; Mary Floyd-Wilson, University of North Carolina at Chapel Hill; Karl Fornes, University of Minnesota, Morris; Jessica Freedman, American University; Martha French, Fairmont State College; Naomi Frucht, Cuesta College; Barry G. Fruchter, Nassau Community College; Jill Fugate, Skagit Valley College; Judith Funston, State University of New York at Potsdam; J. Ellen Gainor, Cornell University; Arthur Ganz, City University of New York City College; Frieda Gardner, North Hennepin Community College; Stephanie Gaynor, Tufts University; Jules Gelernt, City University of New York, Brooklyn College; Roger George, Bellevue Community College; Loreen L. Giese, Ohio University Main Campus; Ed Gieskes, Boston University; Phyllis Gilbert, Palomar College and Mira Costa College; Richard Gjervold, Moorhead State University; Ethan Goffman, Indiana University at Bloomington; Lee Goldwasser, Mira Costa College; Diane Gruenberg, Upsala College; Karen L. Gutmann, University of North Carolina at Chapel Hill; Ed Hack, City University of New York, College of Staten Island; Paul Hadella, Southern Oregon State College; Douglas Haneline, Ferris State University; Beverly V. Head, Atlanta Metropolitan College; Kathryn Henkins, Mount San Antonio College; Christopher Hermanns, City University of New York, Bernard M. Baruch College; Sharon Hileman, Sul Ross State University; Woodrow L. Holbein, The Citadel, the Military College of South Carolina; Kathleen Hudson, Schreiner College; Ann Humes, Long Beach City College; Nancy R. Ives, State University of New York at Geneseo; James M. Ivory, University of North Carolina at Chapel Hill; Allston James, Monterey Peninsula College; Nancy Jesser, University of North Carolina at Chapel Hill; Elizabeth Johnson, University of Minnesota, Twin Cities; Sally Joranko, John Carroll University; Roberta Kelly, Washington State University; Veronica Kennedy, Saint John's University; Pamela Kennedy-Cross, Stockton State College; Janis S. Kilmer, Baltimore City Community College; Susan Kimoto, University of California, Santa Cruz; Judith Kirkpatrick, University of Hawaii, Kapiolani Community College; Deborah Spangler Koelling, Northwest College; Walter Labonte, Lebanon Valley College; Cara Lazarus, University of San Francisco; William P. Lee, Glendale

Community College; Peter Lefkowicz, Lynchburg College; Karen L. Levenbade, George Washington University; Peg Levine, Ohio State University Main Campus; Cynthia Lewiecki-Wilson, Miami University; Norman H. Lewis, City University of New York, Queens College; Mary Libertin, Shippensburg University of Pennsylvania; Jian-Zhong Lin, Teikyo Loretto Heights University; Penny (Marcia) Liu, University of Connecticut, Stamford and Greenwich Academy; George Lober, Monterey Peninsula College; Judy Luther, Jefferson Community College; Kathleen J. Macdonald, University of Hawaii, Kapiolani Community College; Dan MacKendrick, Mesa State College; Angela M. Maloy, Muskegon Community College; Gerald Mann, University of Maryland, College Park; Maxine C. Mark, Colorado State University; Janet-Marting, University of Akron Main Campus; Mary Mathew, University of North Carolina at Chapel Hill; Howard Mayer, University of Hartford; Jerrine McCaffrey, Des Moines Area Community College; Nancie E. McCoy, University of Idaho; Lyle A. McGeoch, Ohio University Main Campus; Timothy F. McGinn, Oakland University; Shannon M. McGuire, Louisiana State University; Stephen McKenna, Catholic University of America; LeAnn McNew, University of Nebraska at Kearney; Mark McTague, Edinboro University of Pennsylvania; Darlene D. Mettler, Wesleyan College; Gary Meyer, Lower Columbia College; Linda Miles, University of Nebraska at Kearney; Lyle W. Morgan, Pittsburg State University; Sheila Fitzmorris, Monroe Community College; Sandra J. Mulryan, Jamestown Community College; Mary E. Murphy, Framingham State College; Thomas P. Murphy, Mansfield University of Pennsylvania; Catherine Nicholl, Augsburg College; Marie Nigro, Lincoln University; Elaine Norris, Syracuse University; Susan Oaks, State University of New York, Empire State College; Ellen Olson, Western State College; Jerry Olson, Middlesex County College; Regina Oost, Wesleyan College; Beverly W. Palmer, Pomona College; Marian Parish, Nassau Community College; Meta Pasternak, Contra Costa College; Robert F. Peltier, Trinity College; Joseph Pilaro, City University of New York, Borough of Manhattan Community College; Kristen J. Pool, Ohio University Main Campus; Kim Ports, University of Nebraska, Lincoln; Lois Powers, Fullerton College; Todd Presley, Southwest Missouri State University; Ann M. Rancourt, State University of New York at Brockport; Terry Rasmussen, Casper College; Ajmal M. Razak, Ball State University; Cheryl Reed, University of California, San Diego; Beth Reynders, Allegheny College; Janine Rider, Mesa State College; Deborah D. Rose, University of North Carolina at Chapel Hill; Bonnie Ross, Los Angeles Valley College; Eva Rosenn, Wesleyan College; Linda H. Ross, Sheridan College; Marsha Rutter, Southwestern College; Laurel Saiz, Onondaga Community College; Mark Sandona, Hood College; Lilia Savova, Indiana University of Pennsylvania; Leone Scanlon, Clark University; Carolyn Schneider, Guilford Technical Community College; Heidi M. Schultz, University of North Carolina at Chapel Hill; David Schmid, Stanford University; Darrell Schramm, University of

San Francisco; Robert Schrenr, Washington College; Karen Smith, Clarion University of Pennsylvania; Linda Smith, Skagit Valley College; Margery Smith, College of Saint Catherine; Thomas E. Smith, Widener University; Susan Stann, De Anza College; Alan L. Steinberg, State University of New York at Potsdam; Ginny Story, Western Maryland College; Sharon L. Stoops, Ivy Tech State College; Gregory J. Stratman, Drury College and University of Missouri, Rolla; Christel Taylor, Belleville Area College; Deborah Tenney, Yale University; Kim Tibbs, Southwest Missouri State University; Jude Todd, University of California, Santa Cruz; Diane Tomczak, Delta College; Curt Tong, Pomona College; Felicity Trueblood, University of Florida; Merrielle Turnbull, Ball State University; LeAnn McNew, University of Nebraska at Kearney; George T. Vaughn, Maysville Community College; Dorothy Voyles, Parkland College; Linda van der Wal, Arizona State University; Paul Warshawski, Fulton-Montgomery Community College; Rick Waters, Weber State University; Anita Wilkins, Cabrillo College; Lynn Wolf, Nova University; Robert Woods, Pomona College; Judy Worman, Dartmouth College; Joan Wry, Saint Michael's College; Judith Yaross Lee, Ohio University Main Campus; Nancy Yee, Fitchburg State College; Michael W. Young, Davis & Elkins College; Nancy Young, Curry College.

I am indebted to the students whose essays appear in this edition — Tom Weitzel and Karen Shaw — for giving me permission to use their work and to adapt it for pedagogical purposes. My thanks also go to the following students for permission to use their paragraphs: Connie Haley, Kathleen Lewis, Thu Hong Nguyen, Julie Reardon, Margaret Stack, and David Warren.

Several talented editors have made invaluable contributions to the book. Kathy Retan has been a superb developmental editor: intelligent, tactful, patient, and good-humored. Copyeditor Barbara Flanagan has brought consistency and grace to the final manuscript. Book editor Anne Benaquist has steered the book expertly through all stages of production. And managing editor Elizabeth Schaaf has orchestrated the production of the book and its ancillaries with unflappable calm.

Once again, designer Claire Seng-Niemoeller deserves special praise for her award-winning design. I am also grateful to DeNee Reiton Skipper for handling the page makeup; to Katie Blatt, Tara Padykula, and Barbara Sweet for their alert proofreading; and to editorial assistant Andrea Goldman and production assistant Karen Baart for fielding a variety of problems too numerous to mention.

As always, I am grateful to publisher Chuck Christensen for his bold vision and his wise and expert counsel and to general

Preface for instructors

manager Joan Feinberg for teaching me to write handbooks in the
first place and for supporting me with such loyalty over the years.

Finally, a note of thanks goes to my parents, Clair and Georgianna Tarvin, and to Joseph and Marian Hacker, Robert Hacker, Greg Tarvin, Betty Renshaw, Bill Fry, Bill Mullinix, Joyce Magnotto, Christine McMahon, Anne King, Wanda Van Goor, Bill Peirce, Lloyd Shaw, Melinda Kramer, Joyce McDonald, the Dougherty family, and Robbie and Austin Nichols for their support and encouragement; and to the many students over the years who have taught me that errors, a natural by-product of the writing process, are simply problems waiting to be solved.

Diana Hacker
Prince George's Community College

Contents

G

P

S

R

RESEARCH WRITING 247

M

MLA DOCUMENTATION 269

A

B

Online Research
and Documentation

O

Online Research and Documentation

Written in response to rapidly changing technology, the following pages contain up-to-date advice on conducting Internet research, working with online sources, and documenting online sources.

If you have access to the Internet, you may also wish to visit a useful Web site that accompanies this book: *Research and Documentation in the Electronic Age* (www.bedfordbooks.com/rd). The site contains documentation models for MLA, APA, *Chicago*, and CBE styles. In addition, it lists print sources and provides links to Internet sources for a variety of disciplines.

O1

Conducting online research

Although the Internet can be a rich source of information, some of which can't be found anywhere else, it lacks quality control. And there is no Internet librarian to help you sort through its massive collection in search of reliable sources. For these reasons, most instructors will want you to use Internet sources only to supplement — not to replace — traditional library sources (see R1-c).

Traditional libraries contain countless research-quality sources that have been carefully selected, classified, and indexed; some of these sources are poorly represented (or difficult to find) on the Internet. Also, because anyone can publish on the Internet, you should be especially careful to evaluate the reliability and potential bias of sources that exist solely online (see O2-c).

NOTE: Traditional libraries and the Internet are not mutually exclusive resources. While online, you can (and should) visit Web sites maintained by public and university libraries to browse their holdings, access some sources, and link to online reference materials. The Libraries of Purdue University have created an excellent Web site: thorplus.lib.purdue.edu/index.html.

With these cautions in mind, you may find some of the following Internet sources useful.

O1-a The World Wide Web

The World Wide Web (or Web) is a collection of documents or "pages" that can be called up on a computer by using a browser such as Netscape or Internet Explorer. Documents on the Web are often linked to other documents, and researchers can pursue the connections at the click of a mouse. Web search engines and directories make it possible to find everything from electronic books and journals to government documents, reports from special-interest organizations, and electronic discussion groups.

Search engines

Search engines such as Lycos (www.lycos.com) are programs that allow you to locate Web sites by typing in keywords. Because the programs match only the words you type in, not their synonyms, you may need to try more than one search term. Don't be surprised when keywords lead you to irrelevant sites, because it is words — not concepts — that the programs search for. For a sample search screen, see the next page.

Directories

Directories, also known as indexes, can be more useful than search engines because their compilers evaluate sites before adding them to the list. Be aware, however, that directories are only as good as their compilers. Some are updated frequently; others contain many sites that no longer exist or have moved. Some examples of well-maintained directories are WWW Virtual Library (vlib.stanford .edu/Overview.html) and Argus Clearinghouse (www.clearinghouse .net). For a sample directory screen, see the next page.

O1-b Newsgroups and listservs

Newsgroups are a means of communicating with a group of people interested in a particular topic. Rather than traveling through electronic mail, newsgroup messages are public postings that can be read by anyone. Newsgroups are classified with abbreviations such as *alt*, *rec*, *soc*, and *sci* (standing for *alternative*, *recreational*, *society*, and *science*).

A similar but less public forum is an e-mail discussion list or "listserv." You can subscribe to a list that suits your interests and receive all the mail that members send to the list. As with newsgroups, you can also post questions to the list. Answers to your questions can at times prove quite helpful to your research, giving you a sense of public opinion about your topic, for example, or providing new leads to useful sources.

SAMPLE SEARCH SCREEN

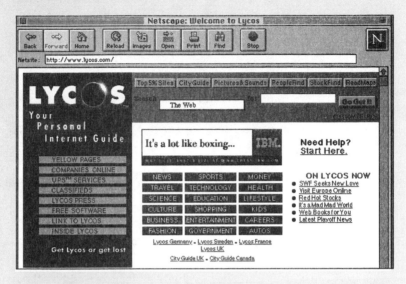

SAMPLE DIRECTORY SCREEN

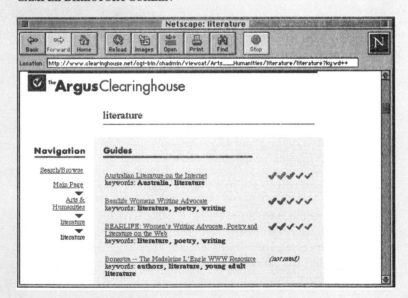

If you're looking for a newsgroup or listserv related to your topic, a good place to start is Tile.Net (www.tile.net), a searchable site that lists hundreds of newsgroups and listservs.

O1-c MUD's, MOO's, and IRC's

Through MUD's (multi-user dimensions), MOO's (MUD's, object-oriented), and IRC's (Internet relay chats), the Internet allows for real-time communication. People can send, receive, and respond to messages while they are simultaneously connected. Often participants will communicate in a space that includes several different "rooms," places where different subtopics are under discussion.

O2

Working with online sources

After you have done some initial research online, you will probably have far more sources than you will be able to use. Your challenge will be to home in on a reasonable number of sites that are worth your time and attention.

O2-a Previewing online sources

Your first step will be to determine quickly whether a source is worth further evaluation. To preview a Web site or other online source, take the following steps:

— Browse the main page of the site. Do its contents and links seem relevant to your research question?

— Consider the reputation, credibility, and motive of the site's author. Eliminate from your search those sites that have a clearly unreliable (or unnamed) author or sponsor.

— Is there a note about when the site was last updated? For a current topic, some sites may be too outdated.

If the site looks promising, add it to the bookmarks or favorites list on your browser for easy access later.

NOTE: For advice on evaluating online sources as you read them, see O2-c.

O2-b Maintaining a working bibliography

Just as you would with print sources, keep careful track of the sources you consult online. Whether you use note cards, printouts, or computer files to keep track of bibliographic information, make sure you have a record of the following items:

— Any authors, editors, compilers, or translators of the Web site and of the text of the material
— Title and subtitle of the material you want to use, as well as the title of the site
— Publishing information for any print version of the material (if readily available): city, publisher, date, page numbers, and volume and issue numbers
— Version number or other identifying number of the source
— Date of publication (or latest revision)
— Page or paragraph numbers (if available)
— Name of any sponsoring organization or institution
— Date you visited the site
— URL (address of the site)

CAUTION: Punctuation, spelling, and sometimes even capitalization must be exact to access Internet sites. To ensure accuracy, you may wish to cut and paste a site's address from your browser into a computer file.

O2-c Evaluating online sources

After previewing your online sources (see O2-a) to determine which ones seem useful and worthwhile, evaluate them using the following checklist.

Checklist for evaluating online sources

AUTHORITY

— Can you determine the author of the site? Is the author of the site knowledgeable and credible? Does the site offer links to the author's home page, résumé, or e-mail address?

OBJECTIVITY

— Who, if anyone, sponsors the site? Note that a site's domain name usually specifies the type of group hosting the site: commercial (.com), educational (.edu), nonprofit (.org), governmental (.gov), military (.mil), or network (.net).

AUDIENCE AND PURPOSE

— Who is the intended audience of the site? Why is the information available: to argue a position? to sell a product? to inform readers?

DOCUMENTATION

— On the Internet, traditional methods of documentation are often replaced with links to original sources. Whenever possible, check out a linked source to confirm its authority.

QUALITY OF PRESENTATION

— Consider the design and navigation of the site. Is it well laid out and easy to use? Do its links work, and are they up-to-date and relevant? Is the material well written and relatively free of errors?

O2-d Printing out hard copies

When researching on the Internet, you will probably find it easier to print out pages of text to work from than to take notes from a computer screen. In addition, it is useful to keep a hard copy of sources found on the Internet because they may not be accessible at a future date. Be sure that your printed materials include the site's URL, the date of access, and the full title of the site so you can include them in your list of works cited and can revisit the site if necessary. (See the next page for an example.)

SAMPLE WEB PAGE PRINTOUT

California Mountain Lion Page   http://www.sierraclub.org/chapters/ca/mountain-lion/

California Mountain Lion Page

California Wildlife Protection Coalition

Prop. 197 defeated. Thanks everyone!

Note: These web pages were written to help defeat Prop. 197 last March 1996. For up to date information on Mountain Lions, please see the **Mountain Lion Foundation's web page at** *http://www.mtn-lion.org*
- DEA 12/96.

Lobbyists from the Gun Owners of California, National Rifle Association (NRA) and Safari Club rammed Senate Bill 28 through the legislature. It appeared on the March ballot as Proposition 197, but was defeated. Without collecting a single voter signature, and hiding behind a disingenuous concern for public safety, trophy hunters convinced the politicians to delete the protections for cougars that were set into law directly by the citizens of California. They are exploiting people's concerns about public safety so they can hang mountain lions over their mantelpieces.

If you blow all the smoke away, the bottom line is that Proposition 197 was a special interest trophy hunting measure, NOT a public safety measure.

Current law allows the killing of any mountain lion that poses a threat to people. It also incorporates Department of Fish and Game (DFG) regulations that specifically allow trained state personnel to kill (or authorize others to kill) any and all lions that damage livestock, domestic animals, or other private property.

But DFG won't do their job to provide public safety. Official testimony at legislative hearings and an internal DFG memo reveal that the Department has deliberately ignored the occasions when mountain lions posed a threat. Now, the media stories that have resulted from DFG's inaction are being used to bolster a campaign to restore trophy hunting. DFG's motivation? The Department obtains much of its funding from selling licenses to trophy hunters, and relies heavily on legislative lobbying by special interest groups like NRA for their annual budget.

- Mountain Lion Background Information
- **Trophy Hunting** of Mountain Lions: A History of Deception
- Mountain Lions and **Public Safety**
- Full text of Proposition 197 (defeated)

O3

Documenting electronic sources

In citations for electronic sources, you give the same publication information as for other sources and add pertinent information about the electronic source. Because electronic sources vary so widely in format, all information may not always be available.

O3-a MLA style for World Wide Web sources

The documentation style for Web sources presented in this section is consistent with MLA's most recent guidelines, which can be found at www.mla.org.

BASIC FORMAT FOR A WEB SITE   Include as much of the following information as available, in the order given:

1. Name of the author, editor, compiler, or translator of the source.
2. Title of the work. Use quotation marks for titles of short works such as poems and articles; underline or italicize book and periodical titles.
3. Name of the editor, compiler, or translator of the text (if relevant and if not cited earlier).
4. Publication information for any print version of the source.
5. Title of the site (underlined or italicized).
6. Name of the editor of the site.
7. Version number of the source (if not part of the title) or, for a journal, the volume number, issue number, or other identifying number.
8. Date of electronic publication, of the latest update, or of posting.
9. Newsgroup or discussion list name.
10. The number range or total number of pages, paragraphs, or other sections, if they are numbered.
11. Name of any institution or organization sponsoring or associated with the site.
12. Date of access.
13. Electronic address, or URL, of the source (in angle brackets).

Gielecki, Mark. Renewable Energy Annual 1997--Volume 1.
    Energy Information Administration. 3 Nov. 1997.
    US Dept. of Energy. 4 Feb. 1998 <http://
    www.eia.doe.gov/fuelrenewable.html>.

SCHOLARLY PROJECT ON THE WEB

The Einstein Papers Project. Ed. Robert Schulmann and
    A. J. Kox. 18 Feb. 1998. Boston U. 9 Mar. 1998
    <http://albert.bu.edu>.

PROFESSIONAL WEB SITE

Blue Note Records. 22 Jan. 1998. Blue Note Records. 11
    Feb. 1998 <http://www.bluenote.com/>.

PERSONAL WEB SITE

Bansner, Phil. Home page. 2 Feb. 1998 <http://
    www.philbansner.com>.

BOOK ON THE WEB

Brown, William W. Narrative of William W. Brown, an
    American Slave, Written by Himself. London, 1849.
    Documenting the American South: The Southern
    Experience in Nineteenth-Century America. Ed.
    Natalia Smith. 1996. Academic Affairs Lib., U of
    North Carolina, Chapel Hill. 9 Feb. 1998 <http://
    sunsite.unc.edu/docsouth/brown/brown.html>.

POEM ON THE WEB

Dickinson, Emily. "Hope." Poems by Emily Dickinson,
    3rd ser. Boston, 1896. Project Bartleby Archive.
    Ed. Steven van Leeuwen. Dec. 1995. Columbia U.
    2 Feb. 1998 <http://www.columbia.edu/acis/
    bartleby/dickinson1.html#3>.

Poe, Edgar Allan. "The Raven." <u>Poets' Corner</u>. Ed.

Steve Spanoudis, Bob Blair, and Nelson Miller.

3 Feb. 1998. 4 Feb. 1998 <http://www.geocities.com/

~spanoudi/poems/poe01.html#4>.

ARTICLE IN AN ONLINE DATABASE

"Gog and Magog." <u>The Encyclopedia Mythica</u>. Ed. Micha

F. Lindemans. 2 Jan. 1998. 31 Jan. 1998 <http://

www.pantheon.org/mythica/articles/g/

gog_and_magog.html>.

ARTICLE IN AN ONLINE JOURNAL

Baucom, Ian. "Charting the Black Atlantic." <u>Postmodern</u>

<u>Culture</u> 8.1 (1997): 28 pars. Johns Hopkins UP.

3 Feb. 1998 <http://www.iath.virginia.edu/pmc/

current.issue/baucom.997.html>.

ARTICLE IN AN ONLINE MAGAZINE

Coontz, Stephanie. "Family Myths, Family Realities."

<u>Salon</u> 12 Dec. 1997. 3 Feb. 1998 <http://

www.salonmagazine.com/mwt/feature/1997/12/

23coontz.html>.

POSTING TO AN ONLINE DISCUSSION LIST

Crosby, Connie. "Literary Criticism." Online posting.

2 Feb. 1996. Café Utne. 3 Feb. 1998 <http://

www.utne.com/motet/bin/

show?-u4Lsul+it-1a+Literature+12>.

O3-b MLA style for other electronic sources

The fourth edition of the *MLA Handbook for Writers of Research Papers* (New York: MLA, 1995) includes some guidelines for citing electronic sources other than Web sites. The following models illustrate those guidelines.

CD-ROM ISSUED PERIODICALLY CD-ROM databases that are produced periodically (monthly or quarterly, for example) may contain previously published material, such as journal or newspaper articles, or material that has not been previously published, such as reports. In either case, cite such material as you would a printed source, followed by the title of the database (underlined or italicized), the medium ("CD-ROM"), the name of the company producing the CD-ROM, and the date of electronic publication.

Bohlen, Celestine. "Albania Struggles to Contain

Dissent over Lost Investments." New York Times

11 Feb. 1997, late ed.: A9. InfoTrac: General

Periodicals ASAP. CD-ROM. Information Access.

13 Feb. 1997.

Wattenberg, Ruth. "Helping Students in the Middle."

American Educator 19.4 (1996): 2-18. ERIC.

CD-ROM. SilverPlatter. Sept. 1996.

CD-ROM ISSUED IN A SINGLE EDITION Some works on CD-ROM, such as dictionaries and encyclopedias, are released in single editions that are not updated periodically. Treat such sources as you would a book, but give the medium ("CD-ROM") before the publication information.

Merriam-Webster's Collegiate Dictionary. 10th ed.

CD-ROM. Springfield, MA: Merriam, 1996.

"Picasso, Pablo." The 1997 Grolier Multimedia

Encyclopedia. CD-ROM. Danbury: Grolier, 1997.

ONLINE MATERIAL FROM A COMPUTER SERVICE Computer services such as Dialog, CompuServe, America Online, and Nexis provide a variety of databases that may be revised continually or periodically. For material from such a source, cite the publication information given in the source, the title of the database (underlined or italicized), the medium ("Online"), and the name of the computer service. In addition, give the date on which you accessed the material.

Bass, Alison. "Women Just as Spatial as Men." Boston

Globe 22 Feb. 1993, 3rd ed.: 25. Boston Globe-

File 631. Online. Dialog. 6 Feb. 1995.

```
Kleinman, Arthur, and Alex Cohen. "Psychiatry's Global

    Challenge." Scientific American Mar. 1997: 86-

    89. Atlantic Monthly Online. Online. America

    Online. 15 Mar. 1997.
```

E-MAIL   For correspondence received via electronic mail, use the designation "E-mail."

```
Romanski, Dave. E-mail to the author. 16 Apr. 1997.
```

O3-c ACW style for Internet sources

The following guidelines for documenting Internet sources are based on a style sheet produced by Janice R. Walker of the University of South Florida and endorsed by the Alliance for Computers and Writing (ACW). Check with your instructor before following these ACW models; he or she may prefer that you adhere strictly to MLA style (see O3-a). For more information on ACW style, go to www.cas.usf.edu/english/walker/mla.html.

WORLD WIDE WEB (WWW) SITES   Begin with the author's name (if available) followed by the title of the cited work, in quotation marks; the title of the complete work (if applicable), underlined or italicized; and the publication date (if known and if different from the date of access). Conclude with the URL and the date of access.

```
Tómasson, Gunnar. "Anne Hath a Way." Five Notes on

    Shakespeare. 25 Feb. 1996. http://www.globescope

    .com/ws/will4.htm (5 Jan. 1997).
```

FILE TRANSFER PROTOCOL (FTP) SITES   Include the author's name (if available) followed by the title of the work, in quotation marks; the publication date (if known and if different from the date of access); the ftp address; and the date of access.

```
Manning, Gerard. "Celas Worldwide Celtic Music Radio

    Listing." 26 Jan. 1996. ftp://celtic.stanford

    .edu/pub/radio.list (30 Jan. 1997).
```

TELNET SITES Begin with the author's name (if known); the title of the cited work, in quotation marks; the title of the complete work (if applicable), underlined or italicized; and the document date (if available and if different from the date of access). Conclude with the telnet address, the instructions for access, and the date of access.

Gelb, Lenore. "FDA Approves First HIV Home Test

    System." FDA Index. 14 May 1996. telnet://fdabbs

    .fda.gov select Road Map (6 Mar. 1997).

SYNCHRONOUS COMMUNICATIONS For a synchronous communication (such as one taking place through a MOO or a MUD), include the source cited, the address, and the date. When you have cited a particular "speaker," begin with the speaker's name and describe the type of communication (for example, "Personal interview").

University of Waterloo Campus Tour. telnet watarts

    .uwaterloo.ca7777 (3 Feb. 1997).

GOPHER SITES Begin with the author's name (if known), followed by the title of the work, in quotation marks; the publication date (if known and if different from the date of access); and any other relevant publication information, followed by the gopher address and date of access.

McGann, Jerome. "The Complete Writings and Pictures of

    Dante Gabriel Rossetti: A Hypermedia Research

    Archive." Jan. 1993. gopher://IUBVM.UCS.INDIANA

    .EDU:70/00/victoria/00000002.victoria (4 Feb.

    1997).

NEWSGROUP POSTINGS AND E-MAIL Begin with the author's name (if known) followed by the subject line, the message date (if different from the date of access), and the address of the listserv or newsgroup. (For personal correspondence, include the designation "Personal e-mail" but do not include the personal e-mail address.) Conclude with the date of access.

Catano, Diane. "Transforming Ethics." AAASHRAN@gwuvm

    .gwu.edu (6 Jan. 1997).

Wu, Sheila. "Giacometti's Sculpture." Personal e-mail

    (4 Feb. 1997).

O3-d APA style for electronic sources

The following sample entries reflect Xia Li and Nancy Crane's February 1997 version of *Electronic Sources: APA Style of Citation* (www.uvm.edu/~ncrane/estyles/apa.html). Although Li and Crane's most recent guidelines do not appear in the APA *Publication Manual*, APA has endorsed their system set forth in *Electronic Style: A Guide to Citing Electronic Information* (Westport: Meckler, 1993).

MATERIAL FROM AN INFORMATION SERVICE OR A DATABASE

```
Bersoff, D. N. (1996). The virtue of principle ethics.

    Counseling Psychologist, 24(1), 86-91. (ERIC

    Accession No. EJ 522 601)
```

CD-ROM ABSTRACT

```
Cummings, A. (1995). Test review made easy [CD-ROM].

    Learning, 23(5), 68. Abstract from: ERIC Document

    Reproduction Service: ERIC Item: EJ 509 271
```

WORLD WIDE WEB SITE

```
Boland, P. (No date). Alice Cunningham Fletcher

    [Online]. Available: http://vms.www.uwplatt.edu

    /~nicols/fletcher.html [1997, March 23].
```

ONLINE ARTICLE

```
Caruba, A. (1998, January 1). The plague of boredom.

    The World & I [Online]. 13, p. 318. Available:

    Electric Library (http://www.elibrary.com) [1998,

    March 4].
```

ELECTRONIC DISCUSSION LIST MESSAGE

```
CRCooper. (1997, July 9). Re: Kanzi and ape language.

    Primate Talk. [Online]. Available E-mail:

    primate-talk@primate.wisc.edu [1998, May 1].
```

E-MAIL

```
Castro, Beth (bethcas@aol.com). (1997, May 2). Fast

    food. E-mail to Clare Ma (crm4@tiac.net).
```

C

Composing
and Revising

C

Composing and Revising

Since it's not possible to think about everything all at once, most experienced writers handle a piece of writing in stages. Roughly speaking, those stages are planning, drafting, and revising.

C1

Planning

C1-a Assess the writing situation.

Begin by taking a look at the writing situation in which you find yourself. The following checklist will help you get started.

SUBJECT

— Has a subject (or a range of possible subjects) been given to you, or are you free to choose your own?

— Why is your subject worth writing about?

— How broadly can you cover the subject? Do you need to narrow it to a more specific topic (because of length restrictions, for instance)?

— How detailed should your coverage be?

SOURCES OF INFORMATION

— Where will your information come from: Personal experience? Direct observation? Interviews? Questionnaires? Reading?

— If your information comes from reading, what sort of documentation is required?

PURPOSE

— Why are you writing: To inform readers? To persuade them? To entertain them? To call them to action? Some combination of these?

AUDIENCE

— Who are your readers?

— How well informed are your readers about the subject?

— What do you want them to learn about the subject?

— How interested and attentive are they likely to be?

— Will they resist any of your ideas?
— What is your relationship to them: Employee to supervisor? Citizen to citizen? Expert to novice? Scholar to scholar?
— How much time are they willing to spend reading?
— How sophisticated are they as readers? Do they have large vocabularies? Can they follow long and complex sentences?

LENGTH

— Are you working within any length specifications? If not, what length seems appropriate, given your subject, your purpose, and your audience?

DOCUMENT DESIGN

— Must you use a particular design for your document? If so, do you have guidelines or examples that you can consult? (For academic papers, see D2.)

DEADLINE

— What is your deadline? How much time will you need to allow for the various stages of writing, including typing and proofreading the final draft?

ESL NOTE: What counts as good writing varies from culture to culture and even among groups within cultures. In some situations, you will need to become familiar with the writing styles — such as direct or indirect, personal or impersonal, plain or embellished — that are valued by the culture or discourse community for which you are writing.

C1-b Experiment with techniques for exploring ideas.

Instead of just plunging into a first draft, experiment with one or more techniques for exploring your subject — perhaps listing, clustering, asking questions, or freewriting. Whatever technique you turn to, the goal is the same: to generate a wealth of ideas. At this early stage of the writing process, you should aim for quantity, not necessarily quality, of ideas. If an idea proves to be off the point, trivial, or too farfetched, you can always throw it out later.

Listing

You might begin by simply listing ideas, putting them down in the order in which they occur to you — a technique sometimes known as "brainstorming." Here, for example, is a list one writer jotted down:

> Lifeguarding — an ideal summer job?
>> my love of swimming and lying in the sun
>>
>> hired by Powdermill Village, an apartment complex
>>
>> first, though, there was a test
>>
>> two weeks of training — grueling physical punishment plus book work
>>
>> I passed. The work was over — or so I thought.
>>
>> greeted by manager; handed a broom, hose, disinfectant
>>
>> scrubbing bathrooms, cleaning the pool, clearing the deck of dirt and leaves
>>
>> little kids breaking every pool rule in the book — running on deck, hanging on buoyed ropes, trying to drown each other
>>
>> spent most of my time blowing the whistle
>>
>> working the evening shift no better — adults smuggling in gin and tonics, sexual advances from married men
>>
>> by end of day, a headache and broom-handled hands

The ideas appear here in the order in which they first occurred to the writer. Later she felt free to rearrange them, to cluster them under general categories, to delete some, and to add others. In other words, she treated her initial list as a source of ideas and a springboard to new ideas, not as a formal outline.

Clustering and branching

Unlike listing, the techniques of clustering and branching highlight relationships among ideas. To cluster ideas, write your topic in the center of a sheet of paper, draw a circle around it, and surround that circle with related ideas connected to it with lines. If some of the satellite ideas lead to more specific clusters, write them down as well. The writer of the diagram at the top of page 6 was exploring ideas for an essay on home uses for computers.

To use the branching technique, put the main idea at the top of a page and then list major supporting ideas beneath it, leaving plenty of space between ideas. To the right of each major idea, branch

out to minor ideas, drawing lines to indicate the connections. If minor ideas lead to even more specific ideas, continue branching. Here, for example, is a branching diagram for a newspaper article describing an innovative magnet high school called "School without Walls."

School without Walls — an attractive option

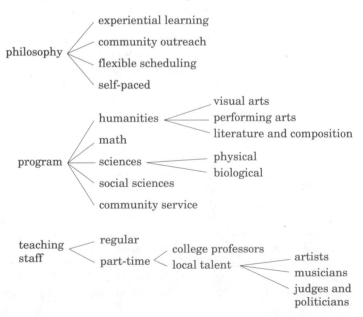

Asking questions

By asking relevant questions, you can generate many ideas — and you can make sure that you have adequately surveyed your subject. When gathering material for a story, journalists routinely ask themselves Who? What? When? Where? Why? and How? In addition to helping journalists get started, these questions ensure that they will not overlook an important fact: the date of a prospective summit meeting, for example, or the exact location of a neighborhood burglary.

Whenever you are writing about events, whether current or historical, the journalist's questions are one way to get started. One student, whose subject was the reaction in 1915 to D. W. Griffith's silent film *The Birth of a Nation,* began exploring her topic with this set of questions:

> *Who* objected to the film?
>
> *What* were the objections?
>
> *When* were the protests first voiced?
>
> *Where* were protests most strongly expressed?
>
> *Why* did protesters object to the film?
>
> *How* did protesters make their views known?

In the academic world, scholars often generate ideas with specific questions related to their discipline: one set of questions for analyzing short stories, another for evaluating experiments in social psychology, still another for reporting field experiences in anthropology. If you are writing in a particular discipline, try to discover the questions that scholars typically explore. These are frequently presented in textbooks as checklists.

Freewriting

In its purest form, freewriting is simply nonstop writing. You set aside ten minutes or so and write whatever comes to you, without pausing to think about word choice, spelling, or even meaning. If you get stuck, you can write about being stuck, but you should keep your pencil moving. The point is to loosen up, relax, and see what happens. Even if nothing much happens, you have lost only ten minutes. It's more likely, though, that something interesting will emerge on paper — perhaps an eloquent sentence, an honest expression of feeling, or a line of thought worth exploring.

C1-c Settle on a tentative focus.

As you explore your subject, you will begin to see possible ways to focus your material. At this point, try to settle on a tentative central idea.

For many types of writing, the central idea can be asserted in one sentence, a generalization preparing readers for the supporting details that will follow. Such a sentence, which often appears in the opening paragraph, is called a *thesis* (see C2-a). A successful thesis — like the following, all taken from articles in *Smithsonian* magazine — points both the writer and the reader in a definite direction:

> Much maligned and the subject of unwarranted fears, most bats are harmless and highly beneficial.

> Geometric forms known as fractals may have a profound effect on how we view the world, not only in art and film but in many branches of science and technology, from astronomy to economics to predicting the weather.

> Aside from his more famous identities as colonel of the Rough Riders and President of the United States, Theodore Roosevelt was a lifelong professional man of letters.

The thesis sentence usually contains a key word or controlling idea that limits its focus. The preceding sentences, for example, prepare for essays that focus on the *beneficial* aspects of bats, the *effect* of fractals on how we view the world, and Roosevelt's identity as a writer, or *man of letters*.

It's a good idea to formulate a thesis early in the writing process, perhaps by jotting it on scratch paper, by putting it at the head of a rough outline, or by attempting to write an introductory paragraph that includes the thesis. Your tentative thesis will probably be less graceful than the thesis you include in the final version of your essay. Here, for example, is one student's early effort:

> Although they both play percussion instruments, drummers and percussionists are very different.

The thesis that appeared in the final draft of the student's paper was more polished.

> Two types of musicians play percussion instruments — drummers and percussionists — and they are as different as Pearl Jam and the New York Philharmonic.

For some types of writing, it may be difficult or impossible to express the central idea in a thesis sentence; or it may be unwise or unnecessary to put a thesis sentence in the paper itself. A personal narrative, for example, may have a focus too subtle to be capsulized in a single sentence, and such a sentence might ruin the story. Strictly informative writing, like that found in many business memos, may be difficult to summarize in a thesis. In such instances, do not try to force the central idea into a thesis sentence. Instead, think in terms of an overriding purpose, which may or may not be stated directly in the paper itself.

C1-d   Sketch a tentative plan.

Once you have generated some ideas and formulated a tentative thesis, you may want to sketch an informal outline. Informal outlines can take many forms. Perhaps the most common is simply the thesis followed by a list of major supporting ideas.

> Hawaii is losing its cultural identity.
>
> — pure-blooded Hawaiians increasingly rare
> — native language diluted
> — natives forced off ancestral lands
> — little emphasis on native culture in schools
> — customs exaggerated and distorted by tourism

Clustering diagrams, often used to generate ideas, can also serve as rough outlines (see page 6). And if you began by jotting down a list of ideas (see page 5), you may be able to turn the list into a rough outline by crossing out some ideas, adding others, and numbering the ideas to create a logical order.

When to use a formal outline

Early in the writing process, rough outlines have certain advantages over their more formal counterparts: They can be produced more quickly, they are more obviously tentative, and they can be revised more easily should the need arise. However, a formal outline may be useful later in the writing process, after you have written a rough draft, especially if your subject matter is complex.

The following formal outline brought order to a difficult subject, methods for limiting and disposing of nuclear waste. Notice that the student's thesis is an important part of the outline. Everything else in the outline supports it, directly or indirectly.

Thesis: Although various methods for limiting or disposing of nuclear waste have been proposed, each has its drawbacks.

  I. Limiting nuclear waste: partitioning and transmutation
      A. The process is complex and costly.
      B. Radiation exposure to nuclear workers would increase.

 II. Antarctic ice sheet disposal
      A. Our understanding of ice sheets is too limited.
      B. An international treaty prohibits disposal in Antarctica.

III. Outer space disposal
      A. The risk of an accident and resulting worldwide disaster is great.
      B. The cost is prohibitive.
      C. The method would be unpopular at home and abroad.

 IV. Seabed disposal
      A. Scientists have not yet solved technical difficulties.
      B. We do not fully understand the impact of such disposal on the ocean's ecology.

  V. Deep underground disposal
      A. There is much pressure against the plan from citizens who do not want their states to become nuclear dumps.
      B. Geologists disagree about the safest disposal sites.

In constructing a formal outline, keep the following guidelines in mind:

1. Put the thesis at the top.
2. Use parallel grammatical structure for ideas at the same level of generality. (See E1.)
3. Use sentences unless phrases are clear.
4. Use the conventional system of numbers and letters for the levels of generality:

    I.
       A.
       B.
          1.
          2.
             a.
             b.
                (1)
                (2)
                    (a)
                    (b)

    II.

5. Always use at least two subdivisions for a category.
6. Limit the number of major sections in the outline; if the list of roman numerals grows too long, find some way of clustering the items into a few major categories with more subcategories.
7. Be flexible. Treat your outline as a tentative plan that may need to be adjusted as your drafts evolve.

C2

Drafting an essay

As you rough out an initial draft, keep your planning materials — lists, diagrams, outlines, and so on — close at hand. In addition to helping you get started, such notes and blueprints will encourage you to keep moving. Writing tends to flow better when it is drafted relatively quickly, without many starts and stops.

For most kinds of writing, an introduction announces a main idea, several body paragraphs develop it, and a conclusion drives it home. You can begin drafting, however, at any point.

C2-a Draft an introduction.

Your introduction will usually be a paragraph of 50 to 150 words. Perhaps the most common strategy is to open the paragraph with a few sentences that engage the reader and to conclude it with a statement of your main point. The sentence stating the main point is called a *thesis* (see C1-c). In the following examples, the thesis has been italicized.

> To the Australian aborigines, the Dreamtime was the time of creation. It was then that the creatures of the earth, including man, came into being. There are many legends about that mystical period, but unfortunately, the koala does not fare too well in any of them. *Slow-witted though it is in life, the koala is generally depicted in myth and folklore as a trickster and a thief.*
> — Roger Caras, "What's a Koala?"

> When I was sixteen, I married and moved to a small town to live. My new husband nervously showed me the house he had rented. It was after dark when we arrived there, and I remember wondering why he seemed so apprehensive about my reaction to the house. I thought the place seemed shabby but potentially cozy

and quite livable inside. The morning sun revealed the reason for his anxiety by exposing the squalor outdoors. Up to that point, my contact with any reality but that of my own middle-class childhood had come from books. *The next four years in a small Iowa town taught me that reading about poverty is a lot different from living with it.* — Julie Reardon, student

Ideally, the sentences leading to the thesis should hook the reader, perhaps with one of the following:

a startling statistic or unusual fact

a vivid example

a description

a paradoxical statement

a quotation or bit of dialogue

a question

an analogy

a joke or an anecdote

Such hooks are particularly important when you cannot assume your reader's interest in the subject. Hooks are less necessary in scholarly essays and other writing aimed at readers with a professional interest in the subject.

Although the thesis frequently appears at the end of the introduction, it can just as easily appear at the beginning. Much work-related writing, in which a straightforward approach is most effective, commonly begins with the thesis.

Flex-time scheduling, which has proved its effectiveness at the Library of Congress, should be introduced on a trial basis at the main branch of the Montgomery County Public Library. By offering flexible work hours, the library can boost employee morale, cut down on absenteeism, and expand its hours of operation.
— David Warren, library employee

In narrative and descriptive writing, it is not always necessary to have an explicitly stated thesis. (See C1-c.) However, an introduction without a thesis should clearly suggest the purpose and direction of the essay to follow.

Characteristics of an effective thesis

An effective thesis should be a generalization, not a fact; it should be limited, not too broad; and it should be sharply focused, not too vague.

Because a thesis must prepare readers for facts and details, it cannot itself be a fact. It must always be a generalization demanding proof or further development.

> **TOO FACTUAL**   The first polygraph was developed by Dr. John A. Larson in 1921.

> **REVISED**   Because the polygraph has not been proved reliable, even under the most controlled conditions, its use by private employers should be banned.

Although a thesis must be a generalization, it must not be *too* general. You will need to narrow the focus of any thesis that you cannot adequately develop in the space allowed. Unless you were writing a book or a very long research paper, the following thesis would be too broad.

> **TOO BROAD**   Many drugs are now being used successfully to treat mental illnesses.

You would need to restrict the thesis, perhaps like this:

> **REVISED**   Despite its risks and side effects, lithium is an effective treatment for depression.

Finally, a thesis should be sharply focused, not too vague. Beware of any thesis containing a fuzzy, hard-to-define word such as *interesting, good,* or *disgusting.*

> **TOO VAGUE**   Many of the songs played on station WXQP are disgusting.

The word *disgusting* is needlessly vague. To sharpen the focus of this thesis, the writer should be more specific.

> **REVISED**   Of the songs played on station WXQP, all too many depict sex crudely, sanction the beating or rape of women, or foster gang violence.

In the process of making a too-vague thesis more precise, you may find yourself outlining the major sections of your paper, as in the preceding example, which prepares readers for a three-part criticism of the songs played on WXQP. This technique, known as *blueprinting,* helps readers know exactly what to expect as they read on. It also helps you, the writer, control the shape of your essay.

ESL NOTE: If you come from a culture that prefers an indirect approach in writing, you may feel that asserting a thesis early in an essay sounds unrefined or even rude. In the United States, however, a direct approach is usually appreciated; when you state your point as directly as possible, you show that you value your reader's time.

C2-b Draft the body.

Before drafting the body of an essay, take a careful look at your introduction, focusing especially on your thesis sentence. What does the thesis promise readers? Try to keep this focus in mind.

It's a good idea to have a plan in mind as well. If you have sketched out a preliminary plan, try to block out your paragraphs accordingly. If you do not have a plan, you would be wise to pause a moment and sketch one (see C1-d). Of course it is also possible to begin without a plan — assuming you are prepared to treat your first attempt as a "discovery draft" that will almost certainly be tossed (or radically rewritten) once you discover what you really want to say.

For detailed advice about paragraphs and paragraphing, see C3.

C2-c Draft a conclusion.

The conclusion should echo your main idea, without dully repeating it. Often the concluding paragraph can be relatively short.

In addition to echoing your main idea, a conclusion might summarize your main point, pose a question for future study, offer advice, or propose a course of action. To end an essay detailing the social skills required of a bartender, one writer concludes with some advice:

> If someone were to approach me one day looking for the secret to running a good bar, I suppose I would offer the following advice: Get your customers to pour out their ideas at a greater rate than you pour out the liquor. You will both win in the end.
> — Kathleen Lewis, student

To make the conclusion memorable, consider including a detail, example, or image from the introduction to bring readers full circle;

a quotation or bit of dialogue; an anecdote; or a humorous, witty, or ironic comment.

Whatever concluding strategy you choose, avoid introducing new ideas at the end of an essay. Also avoid apologies and other limp, indeterminate endings. You should end crisply, preferably on a positive note.

C3

Drafting paragraphs

Except for special-purpose paragraphs, such as introductions and conclusions (see C2-a and C2-c), paragraphs are clusters of information supporting an essay's main point (or advancing a story's action). Aim for paragraphs that are clearly focused, well developed, organized, coherent, and neither too long nor too short for easy reading.

C3-a Focus on a main point.

A paragraph should be unified around a main point. The point should be clear to readers, and all sentences in the paragraph must relate to it.

Stating the main point in a topic sentence

As a rule, state the main point of a paragraph in a topic sentence — a one-sentence summary that tells readers what to expect as they read on. Usually the topic sentence comes first:

> *Nearly all living creatures manage some form of communication.* The dance patterns of bees in their hive help to point the way to distant flower fields or announce successful foraging. Male stickleback fish regularly swim upside-down to indicate outrage in a courtship contest. Male deer and lemurs mark territorial ownership by rubbing their own body secretions on boundary stones or trees. Everyone has seen a frightened dog put his tail between his legs and run in panic. We, too, use gestures, expressions, postures, and movement to give our words point.
> — Olivia Vlahos, *Human Beginnings*

Although the topic sentence usually comes first, sometimes it follows a transitional sentence linking the paragraph to earlier material, and occasionally it is withheld until the end of the paragraph. And at times a topic sentence is not needed: if a paragraph continues developing an idea clearly introduced in an earlier paragraph, if the details of the paragraph unmistakably suggest its main point, or if the paragraph appears in a narrative of events where generalizations might interrupt the flow of the story.

Sticking to the point

Sentences that do not support the topic sentence destroy the unity of a paragraph. If the paragraph is otherwise well focused, such offending sentences can simply be deleted or perhaps moved elsewhere. In the following paragraph describing the inadequate facilities in a high school, the information about the typing instructor (in italics) is clearly off the point.

> As the result of tax cuts, the educational facilities of Lincoln High School have reached an all-time low. Some of the books date back to 1980 and have long since shed their covers. The lack of lab equipment makes it necessary for four to five students to work at one table, with most watching rather than performing experiments. The few typewriters in working order have not been cleaned in so long that most letters come out blotchy and hard to read. There is only one self-correcting typewriter and no prospect of the school's ordering a word processor or computer anytime soon. *Also, the typing instructor left to have a baby at the beginning of the semester, and most of the students don't like the substitute.* As for the furniture, many of the upright chairs have become recliners, and the desk legs are so unbalanced that they play seesaw on the floor.

Sometimes the cure for a disunified paragraph is not as simple as deleting or moving material. Writers often wander into uncharted territory because they cannot think of enough evidence to support a topic sentence. Feeling that it is too soon to break into a new paragraph, they move on to new ideas for which they have not prepared the reader. When this happens, the writer is faced with a choice: Either find more evidence to support the topic sentence or adjust the topic sentence to mesh with the evidence that is available.

C3-b Develop the main point.

Though an occasional short paragraph is fine, particularly if it functions as a transition or emphasizes a point, a series of brief paragraphs suggests inadequate development. How much development is enough? That varies, depending on the writer's purpose and audience.

For example, when she wrote a paragraph attempting to convince readers that it is impossible to lose fat quickly, health columnist Jane Brody knew that she would have to present a great deal of evidence because many dieters want to believe the opposite. She did *not* write:

> When you think about it, it's impossible to lose — as many diets suggest — 10 pounds of *fat* in ten days, even on a total fast. Even a moderately active person cannot lose so much weight so fast. A less active person hasn't a prayer.

This three-sentence paragraph is too skimpy to be convincing. But the paragraph that Brody in fact wrote contains enough evidence to convince even skeptical readers.

> When you think about it, it's impossible to lose — as many diets suggest — 10 pounds of *fat* in ten days, even on a total fast. A pound of body fat represents 3,500 calories. To lose 1 pound of fat, you must expend 3,500 more calories than you consume. Let's say you weigh 170 pounds and, as a moderately active person, you burn 2,500 calories a day. If your diet contains only 1,500 calories, you'd have an energy deficit of 1,000 calories a day. In a week's time that would add up to a 7,000-calorie deficit, or 2 pounds of real fat. In ten days, the accumulated deficit would represent nearly 3 pounds of lost body fat. Even if you ate nothing at all for ten days and maintained your usual level of activity, your caloric deficit would add up to 25,000 calories. . . . At 3,500 calories per pound of fat, that's still only 7 pounds of lost fat.
> — Jane Brody, *Jane Brody's Nutrition Book*

C3-c Choose a suitable pattern of organization.

Although paragraphs may be patterned in an almost infinite number of ways, certain patterns of organization occur frequently, either alone or in combination: examples and illustrations, narration, description, process, comparison and contrast, analogy, cause and effect, classification and division, and definition. There is nothing particularly magical about these patterns (sometimes called "methods of development"). They simply reflect some of the ways in which we think.

Examples and illustrations

Examples, perhaps the most common pattern of organization, are appropriate whenever the reader might be tempted to ask, "For example?"

> Normally my parents abided scrupulously by "The Budget," but several times a year Dad would dip into his battered, black strongbox and splurge on some irrational, totally satisfying luxury. Once he bought over a hundred comic books at a flea market, doled out to us thereafter at the tantalizing rate of two a week. He always got a whole flat of pansies, Mom's favorite flower, for us to give her on Mother's Day. One day a boy stopped at our house selling fifty-cent raffle tickets on a sailboat and Dad bought every ticket the boy had left — three books' worth.
>
>   — Connie Hailey, student

Illustrations are extended examples, frequently presented in story form.

> Part of Harriet Tubman's strategy of conducting was, as in all battle-field operations, the knowledge of how and when to retreat. Numerous allusions have been made to her moves when she suspected that she was in danger. When she feared the party was closely pursued, she would take it for a time on a train southward bound. No one seeing Negroes going in this direction would for an instant suppose them to be fugitives. Once on her return she was at a railway station. She saw some men reading a poster and she heard one of them reading it aloud. It was a description of her, offering a reward for her capture. She took a southbound train to avert suspicion. At another time when Harriet heard men talking about her, she pretended to read a book which she carried. One man remarked, "This cannot be the woman. The one we want can't read or write." Harriet devoutly hoped the book was right side up.   — Earl Conrad, *Harriet Tubman*

Narration

A paragraph of narration tells a story or part of a story. The following paragraph, from Jane Goodall's *In the Shadow of Man,* recounts one of the author's experiences in the African wild.

> One evening when I was wading in the shallows of the lake to pass a rocky outcrop, I suddenly stopped dead as I saw the sinuous black body of a snake in the water. It was all of six feet long, and from the slight hood and the dark stripes at the back of the

neck I knew it to be a Storm's water cobra — a deadly reptile for the bite of which there was, at that time, no serum. As I stared at it an incoming wave gently deposited part of its body on one of my feet. I remained motionless, not even breathing, until the wave rolled back into the lake, drawing the snake with it. Then I leaped out of the water as fast as I could, my heart hammering.
— Jane Goodall, *In the Shadow of Man*

Description

A descriptive paragraph sketches a portrait of a person, place, or thing by using concrete and specific details that appeal to one or more senses — sight, sound, smell, taste, and touch. Consider, for example, the following description of the grasshopper invasions that devastated the midwestern landscape in the late 1860s.

> They came like dive bombers out of the west. They came by the millions with the rustle of their wings roaring overhead. They came in waves, like the rolls of the sea, descending with a terrifying speed, breaking now and again like a mighty surf. They came with the force of a williwaw and they formed a huge, ominous, dark brown cloud that eclipsed the sun. They dipped and touched earth, hitting objects and people like hailstones. But they were not hail. These were live demons. They popped, snapped, crackled, and roared. They were dark brown, an inch or longer in length, plump in the middle and tapered at the ends. They had transparent wings, slender legs, and two black eyes that flashed with a fierce intelligence.   — Eugene Boe, "Pioneers to Eternity"

Process

A process paragraph is structured in chronological order. A writer may choose this pattern either to describe how something is made or done or to explain to readers, step by step, how to do something. This paragraph shows readers how to perform a process — that of opening an oyster.

> An oyster has an irregular shape. The valves are rough and their lips hard to find. Crooked and wrinkled, the hairline crack between the valves can't be widened with the blade of a knife; the point must enter first. Furthermore, a big Chincoteague doesn't fit the left hand. One must hold the animal slanting against the edge of the kitchen sink and poke around, seeking the slot by touch as much as by sight. It takes painful practice. When the knifepoint finds a purchase, push carefully and quickly before the oyster

realizes what's afoot and gets a firmer grip on itself. Push in the wrong place — it's easy to mistake a growth line for the groove — and the knife takes on a life of its own. It can skid and open up your hand. This delicate work requires patient agility to find the groove, push the knife in, then slit the muscle and open the critter without losing too much juice. (Restaurants serve oysters on their flat shell. It's better to throw that one away and lay the delicacies on a bed of crushed ice in the roundest half-shell which holds its delicious liquor. Sprinkle each one with lemon juice — a healthy oyster will wriggle the slightest bit at this point to prove it's alive — lift the dishlike shell to the lips, and drink the oyster down. It's a delicious, addicting experience.)

> — Philip Kopper, "How to Open an Oyster"

Comparison and contrast

To compare two subjects is to draw attention to their similarities, although the word *compare* also has a broader meaning that includes a consideration of differences. To contrast is to focus only on differences.

Whether a paragraph stresses similarities or differences, it may be patterned in one of two ways. The two subjects may be presented one at a time, as in the following paragraph of contrast.

> So Grant and Lee were in complete contrast, representing two diametrically opposed elements in American life. Grant was the modern man emerging; beyond him, ready to come on the stage, was the great age of steel and machinery, of crowded cities and a restless burgeoning vitality. Lee might have ridden down from the old age of chivalry, lance in hand, silken banner fluttering over his head. Each man was the perfect champion of his cause, drawing both his strengths and weaknesses from the people he led.
>
> — Bruce Catton, "Grant and Lee: A Study in Contrasts"

Or a paragraph may proceed point by point, treating two subjects together, one aspect at a time. The following paragraph uses the point-by-point method to contrast the writer's experiences in an American high school and an Irish convent.

> Strangely enough, instead of being academically inferior to my American high school, the Irish convent was superior. In my class at home, *Love Story* was considered pretty heavy reading, so imagine my surprise at finding Irish students who could recite passages from *War and Peace*. In high school we complained about having to study *Romeo and Juliet* in one semester, whereas in Ireland we simultaneously studied *Macbeth* and Dickens's *Hard*

Times, in addition to writing a composition a day in English class. In high school, I didn't even begin algebra until the ninth grade, while at the convent seventh graders (or their Irish equivalent) were doing calculus and trigonometry.

— Margaret Stack, student

Analogy

Analogies draw comparisons between items that appear to have little in common. In the following paragraph, physician Lewis Thomas draws an analogy between the behavior of ants and that of humans.

Ants are so much like human beings as to be an embarrassment. They farm fungi, raise aphids as livestock, launch armies into wars, use chemical sprays to alarm and confuse enemies, capture slaves. The families of weaver ants engage in child labor, holding their larvae like shuttles to spin out the thread that sews the leaves together for their fungus gardens. They exchange information ceaselessly. They do everything but watch television.

— Lewis Thomas, "On Societies as Organisms"

Cause and effect

A paragraph may move from cause to effects or from an effect to its causes. The topic sentence in the following paragraph mentions an effect; the rest of the paragraph lists several causes.

The fantastic water clarity of the Mount Gambier sinkholes results from several factors. The holes are fed from aquifers holding rainwater that fell decades — even centuries — ago, and that has been filtered through miles of limestone. The high level of calcium that limestone adds causes the silty detritus from dead plants and animals to cling together and settle quickly to the bottom. Abundant bottom vegetation in the shallow sinkholes also helps bind the silt. And the rapid turnover of water prohibits stagnation.

— Hillary Hauser, "Exploring a Sunken Realm in Australia"

Classification and division

Classification is the grouping of items into categories according to some consistent principle. The following paragraph classifies species of electric fish.

Scientists sort electric fishes into three categories. The first comprises the strongly electric species like the marine electric rays or the freshwater African electric catfish and South American electric eel. Known since the dawn of history, these deliver a punch strong enough to stun a human. In recent years, biologists have focused on a second category: weakly electric fish in the South American and African rivers that use tiny voltages for communication and navigation. The third group contains sharks, non-electric rays, and catfish, which do not emit a field but possess sensors that enable them to detect the minute amounts of electricity that leak out of other organisms.

> — Anne Rudloe and Jack Rudloe, "Electric Warfare:
> The Fish That Kill with Thunderbolts"

Division takes one item and divides it into parts. As with classification, division should be made according to some consistent principle. The following paragraph describes the parts of a lemon and their uses.

Absolutely every part of a lemon is useful in some way, from its seeds to its outermost peel. Lemon-pip oil, unsaturated and aromatic, is important in the soap industry and in special diets. The pulp left over from squeezed lemons is evaporated and concentrated into "citrus molasses" which is sold as a base for making vinegar and as an ingredient in bland syrups and alcohol. The remains of the "rag" or pulp is also sold as cattle feed. Most of the pectin used to thicken and solidify jams, jellies, and marmalades comes from the white pith of citrus fruits. Among these, lemon and lime pectin has the highest "jelly grade" or capacity to thicken liquids. It is widely used in medicines taken to combat diarrhea. The flavedo, or outer yellow layer of lemon peel, is invaluable for its intense taste and scent. (The word *zest,* which originally meant "skin or peel," then specifically "citrus peel," is now in common use as signifying "lively enjoyment.")

> — Margaret Visser, *Much Depends on Dinner*

Definition

A definition puts a word or concept into a general class and then provides enough details to distinguish it from other members in the same class. In the following paragraph, the writer defines envy as a special kind of desire.

Envy is so integral and so painful a part of what animates human behavior in market societies that many people have forgotten the full meaning of the word, simplifying it into one of the synonyms of desire. It is that, which may be why it flourishes in market societies: democracies of desire, they might be called, with money for ballots, stuffing permitted. But envy is more or less than desire. It begins with the almost frantic sense of emptiness inside oneself, as if the pump of one's heart were sucking on air. One has to be blind to perceive the emptiness, of course, but that's just what envy is, a selective blindness. *Invidia,* Latin for envy, translates as "nonsight," and Dante had the envious plodding along under cloaks of lead, their eyes sewn shut with leaden wire. What they are blind to is what they have, God-given and humanly nurtured, in themselves.   — Nelson W. Aldrich, Jr., *Old Money*

C3-d   Make paragraphs coherent.

When sentences and paragraphs flow from one to another without discernible bumps, gaps, or shifts, they are said to be coherent. Coherence can be improved by strengthening the various ties between old information and new. A number of techniques for strengthening those ties are detailed in this section.

Linking ideas clearly

In the first draft of a paragraph or an essay, writers do not always link their ideas as clearly as possible. To check a draft for clear connections among ideas, try to look at it from the point of view of a reader. Think in terms of the reader's expectations.

WHAT READERS LOOK FOR IN A PARAGRAPH   As you know, readers usually expect to learn a paragraph's main point in a topic sentence early in the paragraph. Then, as they move into the body of the paragraph, they expect to encounter specific details, facts, or examples that support the topic sentence — either directly or indirectly. Consider the following example, in which all of the sentences following the topic sentence directly support it.

A passenger list of the early years of the Orient Express would read like a *Who's Who of the World,* from art to politics. Sarah Bernhardt and her Italian counterpart Eleonora Duse used the train to thrill the stages of Europe. For musicians there were Toscanini and Mahler. Dancers Nijinsky and Pavlova were there, while lesser performers like Harry Houdini and the girls of the Ziegfeld Follies also rode the rails. Violinists were allowed to practice on the train, and occasionally one might see trapeze artists hanging like bats from the baggage racks.
                                        — Barnaby Conrad III, "Train of Kings"

If a sentence does not directly support the topic sentence, readers expect it to support another sentence in the paragraph and therefore to support the topic sentence indirectly. Composition scholar Francis Christensen has invented a useful system for numbering the sentences in a paragraph to depict the hierarchic connections among sentences that readers look for. The topic sentence, being most general, receives the number 1, and any sentences that directly support it receive the number 2. Sentences that support level 2 sentences receive the number 3, and so on. Here, for example, is Christensen's numbering system as applied to a paragraph by columnist Ellen Goodman.

1. In the years since Kitty Genovese's murder, social scientists have learned a great deal about bystander behavior.
    2. They've learned that the willingness to intervene depends on a number of subtle factors beyond fear.
        3. It turns out that people are less likely to help if they are in a crowd of bystanders than if they are the only one.
            4. Their sense of responsibility is diffused.
            4. If the others aren't helping, they begin to reinterpret what they are seeing.
        3. People are also more passive in urban neighborhoods or crowded city spots where they suffer from "excessive overload" or simply turn off.
        3. They rarely get involved if they believe that the victim knows the assailant.
            4. This is especially true if the crime being witnessed is . . . a rape or attempted rape.

Because the sentences in this paragraph are arranged in a clear hierarchy, readers can easily follow the writer's train of thought.

To check one of your own paragraphs for clear connections among ideas, look to see if the hierarchic chain has been broken at any point. The topic sentence should announce the main idea, and the rest of the sentences should support it either directly or indirectly. When a sentence supports the topic sentence indirectly, it must support an earlier sentence that is clearly linked (directly or indirectly) to the topic sentence. If you can't find such a sentence, you'll need to add one or rethink the entire chain of ideas.

WHAT READERS LOOK FOR IN AN ESSAY Like the sentences within paragraphs, the paragraphs within an essay should be arranged in a clear hierarchy. Readers expect to learn the essay's main point in the first paragraph, often in a thesis statement (see C1-c). And by scanning the topic sentence of each paragraph in the body of the essay, readers hope to understand how each paragraph connects with what has come before. As a rule, a topic sentence should tell readers whether the information they are about to read supports the thesis statement directly or supports a key idea in the essay, which in turn supports the thesis.

Consider the following thesis statement and topic sentences, taken from an essay by student Thu Hong Nguyen. Each of Nguyen's topic sentences supports the thesis statement directly.

> **THESIS STATEMENT IN OPENING PARAGRAPH**
> From the moment she is mature enough to understand com-
> mands, to the day she is married off, to the time when she bears
> her own children, a Vietnamese woman tries to establish a good
> name as a diligent daughter, a submissive wife, and an altruistic
> mother.
>
> **TOPIC SENTENCE IN FIRST BODY PARAGRAPH**
> In order to be approved of by everyone, a Vietnamese daughter
> must work diligently to help her parents.
>
> **TOPIC SENTENCE IN SECOND BODY PARAGRAPH**
> Once she enters an arranged marriage, a good Vietnamese woman
> must submit to her husband.
>
> **TOPIC SENTENCE IN THIRD BODY PARAGRAPH**
> Finally, to be recognized favorably, a Vietnamese woman must
> sacrifice herself for the benefit of the children it is her duty to
> bear.

Topic sentences do not always have to interlock with the thesis quite so tightly as in Nguyen's essay. Nevertheless, by scanning the opening sentence or two of each paragraph, readers should have at least a rough sense of the connections among ideas within the whole essay.

Repeating key words

Repetition of key words is an important technique for gaining coherence. To prevent repetitions from becoming dull, you can use variations of the key word (*hike, hiker, hiking*), pronouns referring to the word (*gamblers . . . they*), and synonyms (*run, spring, race, dash*). In the following paragraph describing plots among indentured servants in the seventeenth century, historian Richard Hofstadter binds sentences together by repeating the key word *plots* and echoing it with a variety of synonyms (which are italicized).

Plots hatched by several servants to run away together occurred mostly in the plantation colonies, and the few recorded servant *uprisings* were entirely limited to those colonies. Virginia had been forced from its very earliest years to take stringent steps against *mutinous plots,* and severe punishments for *such behavior* were recorded. Most servant *plots* occurred in the seventeenth century: a contemplated *uprising* was nipped in the bud in York County in 1661; apparently led by some left-wing offshoots of the *Great Rebellion,* servants *plotted* an *insurrection* in Gloucester County in 1663, and four leaders were condemned and executed; some discontented servants apparently joined *Bacon's Rebellion* in the 1670's. In the 1680's, the planters became newly apprehensive of discontent among the servants "owing to their great necessities and want of clothes," and it was feared that they would *rise up* and *plunder* the storehouses and ships; in 1682 there were plant-cutting *riots* in which servants and laborers, as well as some planters, took part. [Italics added.]

— Richard Hofstadter, *America at 1750*

Using parallel structures

Parallel structures are frequently used within sentences to underscore the similarity of ideas (see E1). They may also be used to bind together a series of sentences expressing similar information. In the following passage describing folk beliefs, anthropologist Margaret Mead presents similar information in parallel grammatical form.

Actually, almost every day, even in the most sophisticated home, something is likely to happen that evokes the memory of some old folk belief. The salt spills. A knife falls to the floor. Your nose tickles. Then perhaps, with a slightly embarrassed smile, the person who spilled the salt tosses a pinch over his left shoulder. Or someone recites the old rhyme "Knife falls, gentleman calls." Or as you rub your nose you think, That means a letter. I wonder who's writing?   — Margaret Mead, "New Superstitions for Old"

Maintaining consistency

Coherence suffers whenever a draft shifts confusingly from one point of view to another or from one verb tense to another (see E4).

Providing transitions

Certain words and phrases signal connections between ideas, connections that might otherwise be missed. Frequently used transitions are included in the following list.

TO SHOW ADDITION
and, also, besides, further, furthermore, in addition, moreover, next, too, first, second

TO GIVE EXAMPLES
for example, for instance, to illustrate, in fact, specifically

TO COMPARE
also, in the same manner, similarly, likewise

TO CONTRAST
but, however, on the other hand, in contrast, nevertheless, still, even though, on the contrary, yet, although

TO SUMMARIZE OR CONCLUDE
in other words, in short, in summary, in conclusion, to sum up, that is, therefore

TO SHOW TIME
after, as, before, next, during, later, finally, meanwhile, then, when, while, immediately

TO SHOW PLACE OR DIRECTION
above, below, beyond, farther on, nearby, opposite, close, to the left

TO INDICATE LOGICAL RELATIONSHIP
if, so, therefore, consequently, thus, as a result, for this reason, since

Skilled writers use transitional expressions with care, making sure, for example, not to use a *consequently* when an *also* would be more precise. They are also careful to select transitions with an appropriate tone, perhaps preferring *so* to *thus* in an informal piece, *in summary* to *in short* for a scholarly essay.

In the following paragraph, taken from an argument that dinosaurs had the "'right-sized' brains for reptiles of their body size," biologist Stephen Jay Gould uses transitions (italicized) with skill:

> I don't wish to deny that the flattened, minuscule head of the large bodied "Stegosaurus" houses little brain from our subjective, top-heavy perspective, *but* I do wish to assert that we should not expect more of the beast. *First of all,* large animals have relatively smaller brains than related, small animals. The correlation of brain size with body size among kindred animals (all reptiles, all mammals, *for example*) is remarkably regular. *As* we move from small to large animals, from mice to elephants *or* small lizards to Komodo dragons, brain size increases, *but* not so fast as body size. *In other*

words, bodies grow faster than brains, *and* large animals have low ratios of brain weight to body weight. *In fact,* brains grow only about two-thirds as fast as bodies. *Since* we have no reason to believe that large animals are consistently stupider than their smaller relatives, we must conclude that large animals require relatively less brain to do as well as smaller animals. *If* we do not recognize this relationship, we are likely to underestimate the mental power of very large animals, dinosaurs in particular. [Italics added.]   — Stephen Jay Gould, "Were Dinosaurs Dumb?"

C3-e If necessary, adjust paragraph length.

Most readers feel comfortable reading paragraphs that range between 100 and 200 words. Shorter paragraphs force too much starting and stopping, and longer ones strain the reader's attention span. There are exceptions to this guideline, however. Paragraphs longer than 200 words frequently appear in scholarly writing, where they suggest seriousness and depth. Paragraphs shorter than 100 words occur in newspapers because of narrow columns; in informal essays to quicken the pace; and in business letters, where readers routinely skim for main ideas.

In an essay, the first and last paragraphs will ordinarily be the introduction and conclusion. These special-purpose paragraphs are likely to be shorter than the paragraphs in the body of the essay. Typically, the body paragraphs will follow the essay's outline: one paragraph per point in short essays, a group of paragraphs per point in longer ones. Some ideas require more development than others, however, so it is best to be flexible. If an idea stretches to a length unreasonable for a paragraph, you should divide the paragraph, even if you have presented comparable points in the essay in single paragraphs.

Paragraph breaks are not always made for strictly logical reasons. Writers use them for the following reasons as well.

REASONS FOR BEGINNING A NEW PARAGRAPH

— to mark off the introduction and the conclusion

— to signal a shift to a new idea

— to indicate an important shift in time or place

— to emphasize a point (by placing it at the beginning or the end, not in the middle, of a paragraph)

— to highlight a contrast

— to signal a change of speakers (in dialogue)

— to provide readers with a needed pause

— to break up text that looks too dense

Beware of using too many short, choppy paragraphs, however. Readers want to see how your ideas connect, and they become irritated when you break their momentum by forcing them to pause every few sentences. Here are some reasons you might have for combining some of the paragraphs in a rough draft.

REASONS FOR COMBINING PARAGRAPHS

— to clarify the essay's organization

— to connect closely related ideas

— to bind together text that looks too choppy

C4

Revising

For the experienced writer, revising is rarely a one-step process. The larger elements of writing generally receive attention first — the focus, organization, paragraphing, content, and overall strategy. Improvements in sentence structure, word choice, grammar, punctuation, and mechanics come later.

C4-a Make global revisions.

Global revisions address the larger elements of writing. Usually they affect chunks of text longer than a sentence, and frequently they can be quite dramatic. Whole paragraphs might be dropped, others added. Material once stretched over two or three paragraphs might be condensed into one. Entire sections might be rearranged. Even the content may change dramatically, for the process of revising stimulates thought.

Many of us resist global revisions because we find it difficult to distance ourselves from a draft. We tend to review our work from our own, not from our audience's, perspective.

To distance yourself from a draft, put it aside for a while, preferably overnight or even longer. When you return to it, try to play the role of your audience as you read. If possible, enlist the help of reviewers — persons willing to play the role of audience for you. Ask your reviewers to focus on the larger issues of writing, not on the fine points. The following checklist may help them get started.

Checklist for global revision

PURPOSE AND AUDIENCE

— Does the draft accomplish its purpose — to inform readers, to persuade them, to entertain them, to call them to action (or some combination of these)?

— Is the draft appropriate for its audience? Does it take into consideration the audience's knowledge of the subject, level of interest in the subject, and possible attitudes toward the subject? Is the reading level appropriate?

FOCUS

— Do the introduction and conclusion focus clearly on the main point?

— Are any ideas obviously off the point?

ORGANIZATION AND PARAGRAPHING

— Can readers follow the overall structure?

— Are ideas ordered effectively?

— Does the paragraphing make sense?

— Are any paragraphs too long or too short for easy reading?

CONTENT

— Is the supporting material persuasive?

— Which ideas need further development?

— Are the parts proportioned sensibly? Do major ideas receive enough attention?

— Where might material be deleted?

C4-b Revise and edit sentences.

Most of the rest of this book offers advice on revising sentences for style and clarity and on editing them for grammar, punctuation, and mechanics. The process of revising and editing sentences should ordinarily occur right on the pages of a draft.

> *deciding*
> Finally ~~we decided~~ that perhaps our dream needed
>   ^
> ~~some~~ prompting, ~~and~~ we visited a fertility doctor and

began the expensive, time consuming round of proce-
~~some~~ *our dream's fulfillment. Our*
dures that held out ~~the~~ promise of ~~fulfilling our~~
efforts, however, were *As*
~~dream. All this was~~ to no avail, ~~and as~~ we approached
could no longer
the sixth year of our marriage, we ~~had reached the~~

~~point where we couldn't~~ even discuss our childlessness

without becoming very depressed. We questioned why

this had happened to us. Why had we been singled out
such a
for ~~this~~ major disappointment?

The original paragraph was flawed by wordiness and an excessive reliance on structures connected with *and*. Such problems can be addressed through any number of acceptable revisions. The first sentence, for example, could have been changed like this:

Finally we decided that perhaps our dream needed
After visiting *we*
~~some~~ prompting, ~~and we visited~~ a fertility doctor ~~and~~

began the expensive, time consuming round of proce-
promised hope
dures that ~~held out the promise~~ of fulfilling our

dream.

Though some writers might argue about the effectiveness of these improvements compared with the previous revision, most would agree that both revisions are better than the original.

Some of the paragraph's improvements involve less choice and are less open to debate. For example, the hyphen in *time-consuming* is necessary, and the question mark in the next-to-last sentence must be changed to a period.

As it details the various rules for revising and editing sentences, this reference book suggests when an improvement is simply one among several possibilities and when it is more strictly a matter of right and wrong.

C4-c Proofread the final manuscript.

After revising and editing, you are ready to prepare the final manuscript. (See D2 for guidelines.) At this point, make sure to allow yourself enough time for proofreading — the final and most important step in manuscript preparation.

Proofreading is a special kind of reading: a slow and methodical search for misspellings, typographical mistakes, and omitted words or word endings. Such errors can be difficult to spot in your own work because you may read what you intended to write, not what is actually on the page. To fight this tendency, try proofreading out loud, articulating each word as it is actually written. You might also try proofreading your sentences in reverse order, a strategy that takes your attention away from the meanings you intended and forces you to think about small surface features instead.

Although proofreading may be dull, it is crucial. Errors strewn throughout an essay are distracting and annoying. If the writer doesn't care about this piece of writing, thinks the reader, why should I? A carefully proofread essay, on the other hand, sends a positive message: It shows that you value your writing and respect your readers.

C5

Working on a word processor

A word processor, as you probably know, is a computer equipped with software that allows writers to compose and revise text with ease. Although a word processor cannot think for you, it can be a useful tool at all stages of the writing process: planning, drafting, and revising.

C5-a Planning

You can list or "brainstorm" ideas as easily on a word processor as with pencil and paper, especially if you are a fast typist. Later you can delete ideas, add others, and rearrange the order, all with a few keystrokes. And as you begin to perceive relationships among ideas, you may be able to turn your list into an informal outline.

You can create outlines quite easily on a word processor. Some software packages will generate a formal outline structure for you — not the words, of course, but the conventional system of numbers and letters at appropriate indent levels.

If you like to begin a writing task by asking yourself questions, consider keeping sets of questions on file in your computer. A college student, for example, might use one set of questions for writing about literature, another for science reports, another for case studies in sociology or psychology, and so on. In some disciplines, software is available with sets of questions developed by experts in the field. Check with a professor or with your school's writing center to learn about such computer programs.

Software has also been developed to speed the process of academic research. Instead of taking notes on note cards, you can type notes on the computer, code them to reflect the divisions of your outline, and later print the notes in sorted batches. To rearrange the notes, you simply change their codes.

Although the computer can be a useful tool for planning, its advantages over pencil and paper should not be overstated. Not all planning techniques can be done on a word processor, and a computer will not always be available when an idea strikes. Many writers find that they plan just as easily with pencil and paper; they turn to the computer primarily for drafting and revising.

C5-b Drafting

Whether to write a first draft on a word processor is a matter of personal preference. Some writers prefer the sensation of a pencil or pen moving on paper; others like to get their fingers moving on a keyboard.

One advantage of drafting at a keyboard, if you are a good typist, is speed: Your thoughts are not likely to race ahead of your fingers, as they sometimes do when you are drafting by hand. Another advantage is readability. As you draft, you will find yourself reviewing from time to time what you have already written. Typed copy — whether on a screen or printed out on paper — is easier to read than most handwriting.

A third advantage is flexibility. Because changes are so easy to make, a word processor encourages experimentation. If you get stuck while writing the opening paragraph, for example, you can skip ahead, knowing that it will be easy to insert the introduction later. Or you can switch screens and use an empty screen for brainstorming. Or if you have a creative but unusual idea for the introduction, you can try it out, confident that if you don't like it, you can make it disappear in seconds.

If you decide to type an initial draft on a word processor, it's a good idea to print out hard copy as you go along so that you can easily review what you have written. (Otherwise you will need to scroll from screen to screen.) Be sure to save your draft in the computer's memory periodically as you are working and before turning off the computer.

C5-c Revising

The word processor is an excellent tool for revision. As mentioned earlier, revising is nearly always a two-step process. Global revisions, those that affect blocks of text longer than a sentence, generally should be handled first. They include changes in focus, organization, paragraphing, and content. (See C4-a.) Sentence-level revisions — improvements in sentence structure, word choice, grammar, punctuation, and mechanics — can come later. (See C4-b.)

Global revisions

Let's assume that you have typed and saved your rough draft on a computer equipped with word processing software. You have printed a copy of the draft, reviewed it for global revisions, and marked it up to indicate where you need to add, delete, and move chunks of text.

Once you have called up the text onto the computer's screen, you move the cursor to the place where you want to add, delete, or move text. Most word processing packages allow you to add text simply by typing it in and to delete text by hitting a delete key. Moving blocks of text is a bit more complicated, usually requiring several keystrokes, but with practice it too is relatively simple.

Because the computer saves time, it encourages you to experiment with global revisions. Should you combine two paragraphs? Would your conclusion make a good introduction? Might several paragraphs be rearranged for greater impact? Will boldface headings improve readability? With little risk, you can explore the possibilities. When a revision misfires, it is easy to restore your original draft.

Sentence-level revisions

Some writers handle sentence-level revisions directly at the computer, but most prefer to print out a hard copy of the draft, mark it up, and then return to the computer. Once you've indicated changes on the hard copy, you can enter them into the computer in a matter of minutes.

Software can provide help with sentence-level revisions. Many word-processing programs have spelling checkers that will catch most but not all spelling errors (see S1), and some have thesauruses to help with word choice. Other programs, called *text analyzers* or *style checkers,* will flag a variety of possible problems: wordiness, jargon, weak verbs, long sentences, and so on. Be aware, however, that a text analyzer can only point out *possible* problems. It can tell you that a sentence is long, for example, but you must decide whether your long sentence is effective.

To proofread your final text, either read the words on the screen or, if this is too hard on your eyes, print out a hard copy and proofread it. Enter any necessary corrections into the computer, print a final copy, and you are done. To preserve the final draft, be sure to save it before you turn off the computer.

The term *document* is broad enough to describe anything you might write in an English class, in other classes across the curriculum, in the business world, and in everyday life. How a document is designed (formatted on the page) can affect how it is received.

Instructors have certain expectations about how a college paper should look (see D2). Employers too expect documents such as business letters and memos to be formatted in standard ways (see D3). Although formatting documents is often a matter of following conventions, there is some room for creativity — as current interest in document design attests (see D1).

D1

Principles of document design

Well-designed documents — such as memos, résumés, manuals, and reports — have always been important in the business world, where writers must compete for the attention of readers. By using lists, headings, and a variety of visual cues, business and technical writers make documents accessible to all segments of an audience: readers who want a quick overview, those who are scanning for specific information, those who need in-depth coverage of a topic, and so on.

Document design is becoming increasingly important in the academic world as well. The information explosion has placed unprecedented demands on instructors' and students' time, so professional articles and student essays must be as accessible as possible. Fortunately, today's computers and printers provide academic writers with design strategies that were once prohibitively expensive. With access to software, a student can enhance an essay with boldface headings, formally displayed lists, and even graphs, charts, and other visuals.

Good document design promotes readability, but what this means depends on your purpose and audience and perhaps on other elements of your writing situation, such as your subject and any length restrictions. (See the checklist on pages 3–4.) All of your design choices — word-processing options and use of headings, displayed lists, and other visuals — should be made in light of your specific writing situation.

NOTE: In many writing situations, at least some design choices are dictated by convention. A corporation may require a specific format for all memos, for example. In college, too, certain manuscript formats are standard (see D2). Always check to see which design elements are required and which you are free to create on your own.

D1-a Select appropriate format options.

Most typewriters and word processors present you with several format options. Before you begin typing, you should make sure that your margins, line spacing, and justification are set appropriately. If a number of typeface styles and sizes are available, you should also determine which is most appropriate for your purposes.

Margins, line spacing, and justification

For documents written on 8½″ × 11″ paper, you should leave a margin of between one and one and a half inches on all sides of the page. These margins prevent the text from looking too crowded, and they allow room for annotations, such as an instructor's comments or an editor's suggestions.

Most manuscripts-in-progress are double-spaced to allow room for editing. Final copy is often double-spaced as well, since single-spacing is less inviting to read. But at times the advantages of double-spacing are offset by other considerations. In a business memo, for example, you may single-space to fit the memo on one easily scanned page. And in a technical report, you might single-space to save paper, for both ecological and financial reasons.

Word processors usually give you a choice between a justified and an unjustified (ragged) right margin. When the text is justified, all of the words line up against the right margin, as they do on a typeset page like the one you are now reading. Unfortunately, text that has been justified on a word processor can be hard to read. The problem is that extra space is added between words in some lines, creating "rivers" of white that can be quite distracting. In addition, right-justified margins may create a need for excessive hyphenation at the ends of lines. Unless you have the technology to create the real look of a typeset page, you should turn off the justification feature.

Fonts

If you have a choice of fonts (typeface styles and sizes), you should select a normal size (10 to 12 points) and a style that is not too off-beat. Although unusual styles of type, such as those that look handwritten, may seem attractive, they slow readers down. We all read more efficiently when a text meets our usual expectations.

CAUTION: Never write a college essay or any other document in all capital letters. Research shows that readers experience much frustration when they are forced to read more than a few words in a row printed in all capital letters.

D1-b Consider using headings.

There is little need for headings in short essays, especially if the writer uses paragraphing and clear topic sentences to guide readers. In more complex documents, however, such as research papers, grant proposals, and business reports, headings can be a useful visual cue for readers.

Headings help readers see at a glance the organization of a document. If more than one level of heading is used, the headings also indicate the hierarchy of ideas — as they do throughout this book.

Headings serve a number of functions, depending on the needs of different readers. When readers are simply looking up information, headings will help them find it quickly. When readers are scanning, hoping to pick up the gist of things, headings will guide them. Even when readers are committed enough to read every word, headings can help. Efficient readers preview a document before they begin reading; when previewing and while reading, they are guided by any visual cues the writer provides.

CAUTION: Avoid using more headings (or more levels of headings) than you really need. Excessive use of headings can make a text choppy.

Phrasing headings

Headings should be as brief and as informative as possible. Certain styles of headings — the most common being *-ing* phrases, noun phrases, questions, and imperative sentences — work better for some purposes, audiences, and subjects than others.

Whatever style you choose, use it consistently for headings on the same level of organization. In other words, headings on the same level of organization should be written in parallel structure (see E1).

-ING PHRASES Phrases beginning with verb forms ending in *-ing* suggest actions, so they are a good choice for manuals that show a person how to do something. In a word processing manual, for example, you may have encountered headings such as *Blocking text* and *Moving text.*

Again because they suggest actions, *-ing* verb forms are appropriate in documents that focus on solving problems. The following headings are drawn from a report written for World Resources Institute, an environmental think tank.

Safeguarding the earth's atmosphere

Charting the path to sustainable energy

Conserving global forests

Triggering the technological revolution

Strengthening international institutions

The verb forms *Safeguarding, Charting, Conserving, Triggering,* and *Strengthening* underscore the report's central message: that with forceful action, the world's ecological problems can be solved.

NOUN PHRASES Noun phrases, which are usually concise, work well in a wide range of professional and academic contexts. Business reports frequently use headings such as *Sales projections, Recommendations,* and *Executive summary.* Scientific reports often include headings such as *Materials and methods* and *Results.*

Noun phrases are especially appropriate in essays that survey a variety of persons, places, or things. The following headings have been drawn from a scholarly article surveying methods of teaching a foreign language.

Grammar method

Direct method

Audiolingual method

Communicative method

QUESTIONS Questions used as headings can generate interest in a document. For example, an article on diet and cholesterol might use commonly asked questions to motivate readers. Questions can also be used to help readers scan for information of interest to them, as with the following headings taken from a mutual fund brochure.

How do I buy shares?

How do I redeem shares?

What is the history of the fund's performance?

What are the tax consequences of investing in the fund?

Questions can be useful headings in research essays, since researchers usually pose questions that they hope to answer in their papers. (See pages 317–26 for an example.)

IMPERATIVE SENTENCES Consider using imperative sentences if your purpose is to give advice to readers. An imperative sentence usually begins with a verb because its subject is an understood *You* (see B2-a). The following imperative sentences appear as headings in a garden designer's newsletter.

Fertilize roses in the fall.

Feed them again in the spring.

Prune roses when dormant and after flowering.

Spray roses during their growing season.

Placing and highlighting headings

Headings on the same level of organization should be placed and highlighted in a consistent way. For example, you might center your first-level headings and print them in boldface; then you might place the second-level headings flush left (against the left margin) and underline them, like this:

First-level heading

Second-level heading

Headings are usually centered or placed flush left, but at times you might decide to indent them five spaces from the left margin, like a paragraph indent. Or in a business document, you might choose to place headings in a column to the left of the text.

To highlight headings, consider using boldface, italics, all capital letters, color, larger or smaller typeface than the text, or some combination of these:

boldface

italics

underlining

ALL CAPITAL LETTERS

color

larger typeface

smaller typeface

On the whole, it is best to use restraint. Excessive highlighting results in a page that looks too busy, and it defeats its own purpose, since readers need to see which headings are more important than others.

Important headings can be highlighted by using a fair amount of white space around them. Less important headings can be downplayed by using less white space or even by running them in with the text (as with the small all-capitals headings on page 42 of this section).

D1-c Consider using displayed lists.

Lists are easy to read or scan when they are displayed, rather than run into your text. You might reasonably choose to display the following kinds of lists:

— steps in a process
— materials needed for a project
— parts of an object
— advice or recommendations
— items to be discussed
— criteria for evaluation (as in checklists)

Displayed lists should usually be introduced with an independent clause followed by a colon (see P4-a and the above list). Periods are not used after items in a list unless the items are sentences.

Lists are most readable when they are presented in parallel grammatical form (see E1). In the sample list, for instance, the items are all noun phrases. As with headings, some kinds of lists might be more appropriately presented as *-ing* phrases, as imperative sentences, or as questions.

To draw the reader's eye to a list, consider using bullets (circles or squares) or dashes if there is no need to number the items. If there is some reason to number the items, use an arabic number followed by a period for each item.

Although displayed lists can be a useful visual cue, they should not be overdone. Too many of them will give a document a choppy, cluttered look. And lists that are very long (sometimes called "laundry lists") should be avoided as well. Readers can hold only so many ideas in their short-term memory, so if a list grows too long, you should find some way of making it more concise or clustering similar items.

D1-d Consider adding visuals.

Visuals such as charts, graphs, tables, diagrams, maps, and photographs convey information concisely and vividly. In a student essay not intended for publication, you can use another person's visuals as long as you credit the borrowing (see R2-a and R2-b). And with access to computer graphics, you can create your own visuals to enhance an essay or a report.

This section suggests when charts, graphs, tables, and diagrams might be appropriate for your purposes. It also discusses where you might place such visuals.

Using charts, graphs, tables, and diagrams

In documents that help readers follow a process or make a decision, flow charts can be useful; for an example, see page 159 of this book. Pie charts are appropriate for indicating ratios or apportionment, as in the following example.

PIE CHART

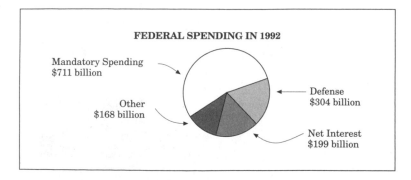

Line graphs and bar graphs illustrate disparities in numerical data. Line graphs are appropriate when you want to illuminate trends over a period of time, such as trends in sales, in unemployment, or in population growth. Bar graphs can be used for the same purpose. In addition, bar graphs are useful for highlighting comparisons, such as vote totals for rival political candidates or the number of refugees entering the United States during different time periods.

LINE GRAPH

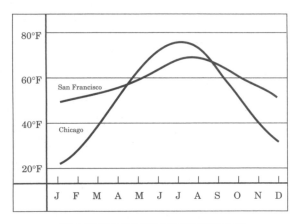

**MONTHLY MEAN TEMPERATURE IN
SAN FRANCISCO AND CHICAGO**

BAR GRAPH

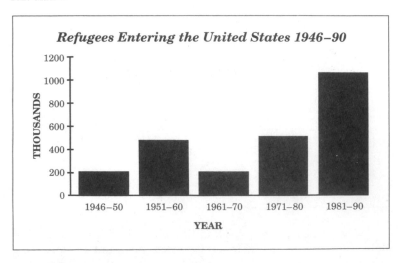

Tables are not as visually interesting as line graphs or charts, but they allow for inclusion of specific numerical data, such as exact percentages. The following table presents the responses of students and faculty to one question on a campus-wide questionnaire.

TABLE

Is American education based too much on European history and values?

	PERCENT		
	NO	UNDECIDED	YES
Nonwhite students	21	25	54
White students	55	29	16
Nonwhite faculty	15	19	65
White faculty	57	27	16

Diagrams are useful — and sometimes indispensable — in scientific and technical writing. It is more concise, for example, to use the following diagram than it would be to explain the chemical formula in words.

DIAGRAM

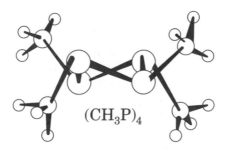

$(CH_3P)_4$

Placing visuals

A visual may be placed in the text of a document, near a discussion to which it relates, or it can be put in an appendix, labeled, and referred to in the text. In much college writing, the convention is to place visuals in an appendix; when in doubt, check with your professor.

Placing visuals in the text of a document can be tricky. Usually you will want the visual to appear close to the sentences that relate to it, but page breaks won't always allow this placement. At times you may need to insert the visual at a later point and tell readers where it can be found or, with the help of software, you may be able to make the text flow around the visual.

In newsletters and in business and technical documents, page layout is both an art and a science. The best way to learn how to lay out pages is to work with colleagues who have had experience solving the many problems that can arise.

D2

Academic manuscript formats

If your instructor provides formal guidelines for formatting an essay — or a more specialized document such as a lab report, a case study, or a research paper — you should of course follow them. Otherwise, use the manuscript format that is standard for the discipline in which you are writing.

This section describes two manuscript formats: MLA, used in English and the humanities, and APA, used in the social sciences. For manuscript formats used in other disciplines, consult a specialized style manual; a list of such style manuals appears in A3.

NOTE: The guidelines in this section apply to academic manuscripts both with and without documentation. If you are writing a paper that uses sources, you should also consult the documentation guidelines in the appropriate tabbed section: M for MLA documentation style or A for alternative styles such as APA.

D2-a MLA manuscript guidelines (English and the humanities)

In most English and humanities classes, you will be asked to use the MLA (Modern Language Association) manuscript format. The following guidelines are based on the *MLA Handbook for Writers of Research Papers,* 4th ed. (New York: MLA, 1995).

To see how an MLA essay is formatted, take a look at these models:

— An MLA essay based on personal experience (pages 50–51)

— An MLA research paper (pages 292–303)

Materials

Use 8½″×11″, 20-pound white paper. If the paper emerges from the printer in a continuous sheet, separate the pages, remove the feeder strips from the sides of the paper, and assemble the pages in order. Secure the pages with a paper clip. Unless your instructor suggests otherwise, do not staple the pages together or use any sort of binder.

Title and identification

Essays written for English and humanities classes do not require a title page unless your instructor requests one. Unless you are told otherwise, against the left margin about one inch from the top of the page, place your name, the instructor's name, the course name and number, and the date on separate lines; double-space between lines. Double-space again and center the title of the paper in the width of the page. Capitalize the first and last words of the title and all other words except articles, prepositions, and coordinating conjunctions (see S3-c). Double-space after the title and begin typing the text of the paper. (See the essay on pages 50–51.)

If you use a title page, follow the model on page 292.

Margins, spacing, and indentation

Leave margins of at least one inch but no more than an inch and a half on all sides of the page. Do not justify the right margin.

Double-space between lines and indent the first line of each paragraph five spaces from the left margin.

For quotations longer than four typed lines of prose or three lines of verse, indent each line ten spaces from the left margin. Double-space between the body of the paper and the quotation, and double-space the lines of the quotation. Quotation marks are not needed when a quotation is indented. See page 266 for an example; see also P6-b.

Pagination

Number all pages at the upper right corner, one-half inch below the top edge. (If you have a separate title page, the title page is uncounted and unnumbered.) Use arabic numerals (1, 2, 3, and so on). Do not put a period after the number and do not enclose the number in parentheses.

Weitzel 1

Tom Weitzel

Dr. Fry

English 101

15 October 1994

Double-
spacing
throughout

Title,
centered

Who Goes to the Races?

5-space
indent

A favorite pastime of mine is observing people,
and my favorite place to observe is at the horse
races. After many encounters with the racing crowd,
I have discovered that there are four distinct
groups at the track: the once-a-year bunch, the
professionals, the clubhouse set, and the unemployed.

The largest group at the track consists of
those who show up once a year. They know little
about horses or betting and rely strictly on racetrack gimmick sheets and newspaper predictions for
selecting possible winners. If that doesn't work,
they use intuition, lucky numbers, favorite colors,
or appealing names. They bet larger amounts as the
day goes along, gambling on every race, including
long-shot bets on exactas and daily doubles. The
vast majority go home broke and frustrated.

A more subtle and quiet group is the
professionals. They follow the horses from track to
track and live in campers and motor homes. Many are
married couples, some are retired, and all are
easily spotted with their lunch sacks, water jugs,
and binoculars. Since most know one another, they
section themselves off in a particular area of the
stadium. All rely on the racing form and on

personal knowledge of each horse, jockey, and track
in making the proper bet. They bet only on the
smart races, rarely on the favorites. Never do
they bet on exactas or daily doubles. More often
than not they either break even or go home winners.

Isolated from the others is the clubhouse set.
Found either at the cocktail lounge or in the restaurant, usually involved in business transactions,
these racing fans rarely see a race in person and do
their betting via the waiter. It's difficult to
tell whether they go home sad, happy, or in between.
They keep their emotions to themselves.

The most interesting members of the racetrack
population are the unemployed. They won't be found
in the clubhouse, but right down at the rail next
to the finish line. Here one can discover the
real emotion of the racetrack--the screaming, the
cursing, and the pushing. The unemployed are not in
it for the sport. Betting is not a game for them,
but a battle for survival. If they lose, they must
borrow enough money to carry them until the next
check comes in, and then, of course, they head right
back to the track. This particular group arrives at
the track beaten and leaves beaten.

I have probably lost more money than I have won
at the track, but observing these four interesting
groups of people makes it all worthwhile.

Punctuation and typing

In typing the text of the paper, leave one space after words, commas, colons, and semicolons and between the dots in ellipses. Leave two spaces after periods, question marks, and exclamation points. To form a dash, type two hyphens with no space between them; do not put a space on either side of the dash.

Headings

The Modern Language Association neither encourages nor discourages use of headings and currently provides no guidelines for their use. If you would like to use headings in a long essay or research paper, check first with your instructor. Although headings are not used as frequently in English and the humanities as in other disciplines, the trend seems to be changing.

Visuals

The Modern Language Association classifies visuals as tables and figures (figures include graphs, charts, maps, photographs, and drawings). Label each table with an arabic numeral (Table 1, Table 2, etc.) and provide a clear caption that identifies the subject; the label and caption should appear on separate lines above the table. For figures, a label and a caption are usually placed below the figure, and they need not appear on separate lines. The word "Figure" may be abbreviated to "Fig."

In professional articles, visuals should be placed in the text, as close as possible to the sentences that relate to them. For student essays, some instructors may prefer that you put visuals at the end of your essay.

Documentation

If your essay draws on secondary sources, consult the MLA documentation guidelines and the sample research paper in the tabbed section marked M.

Sample student essay without documentation

The student essay on pages 50–51 illustrates MLA manuscript format. Because the essay is based on personal experience rather than written sources, it does not illustrate MLA documentation style. For a sample research paper that uses MLA documentation, see M4.

D2-b APA manuscript guidelines (the social sciences)

In most social science classes, such as psychology, sociology, anthropology, and business, you will be asked to use the APA (American Psychological Association) manuscript format. The following guidelines are based on the *Publication Manual of the American Psychological Association,* 4th ed. (Washington, D.C.: APA, 1994).

To see how an APA paper is formatted, take a look at the research paper on pages 315–24.

Materials and typeface

Use 8½″ × 11″ white paper of at least 20-pound weight. For a paper typed on a word processor, make sure that the print quality meets your instructor's standards. Avoid a typeface that is unusual or hard to read.

Title and identification

Begin your paper with a title page. Type the page number, flush right (against the right margin), about one-half inch from the top of the page. Before the page number type a short title of your paper, separated from the page number by five spaces.

The APA manual does not provide guidelines for the placement of certain information necessary for college papers, but most instructors will want you to supply a title page similar to the one on page 315.

Margins, spacing, and indentation

Use margins of at least one inch on all sides of the page. If you are working on a word processor, do not justify the right margin.

Double-space throughout the paper, and indent the first line of each paragraph five spaces from the left margin.

For quotations longer than forty words, indent each line five spaces from the left margin. Double-space between the body of the paper and the quotation, and double-space between lines in the quotation. Quotation marks are not needed when a quotation is indented. (See P6-b.)

Page numbers and short title

In the upper right-hand corner of each page, about one-half inch from the top of the page, type the page number, preceded by the short title that you typed on the title page. Number all pages, including the title page.

Punctuation and typing

Although the APA guidelines call for one space after all punctuation, most college professors prefer two spaces at the end of a sentence. Use one space after all other punctuation.

To form a dash, type two hyphens with no space between them. Do not put a space on either side of a dash.

Abstract

If your instructor requires one, include an abstract right after the title page. An abstract is a 75-to-100-word paragraph that provides readers with a quick overview of your essay. It should express your thesis (or central idea) and your key points; it should also briefly suggest any implications or applications of the research you discuss in the paper.

Headings

Although headings are not necessary, their use is encouraged in the social sciences. For most undergraduate papers, use no more than one or two levels of headings. Major headings should be centered, with the first letter of important words capitalized; minor words — articles, short prepositions, and coordinating conjunctions — are not capitalized unless they are the first word. Subheadings should be typed flush left (against the left margin) and underlined; the rules on capitalization are the same as for major headings. (For an example of an APA paper that uses major headings, see pages 317–26.)

Visuals

The American Psychological Association classifies visuals as tables and figures (figures include graphs, charts, drawings, and photographs). Use visuals for important, directly relevant information that would be needlessly hard to follow if presented wholly in written form.

Keep visuals as simple as possible and label them clearly: Table 1, Figure 3, and so on. Each visual should include a caption that concisely describes its subject; in the bar graph on page 46, for example, the caption "Refugees Entering the United States

1946–90" describes the data included in the graph. Always discuss a visual in the text of your paper, drawing the reader's attention to its most significant features.

According to the APA manual, tables and figures in student manuscripts are often placed in the text of the paper. It is a good idea, however, to ask your instructor for guidelines.

Documentation

If your essay draws on secondary sources, consult the APA documentation guidelines and the sample paper in A1.

D3

Business documents

This section provides guidelines for preparing business letters, résumés, and memos. For a more detailed discussion of these and other business documents — proposals, reports, executive summaries, and so on — consult a business writing textbook or take a look at examples currently being written at the organization for which you are writing.

D3-a Business letters

In writing a business letter, be direct, clear, and courteous, but do not hesitate to be firm if necessary. State your purpose or request at the beginning of the letter and include only pertinent information in the body. By being as direct and concise as possible, you show that you value your reader's time.

A sample business letter appears on page 56. This letter is typed in what is known as "block" style. The return address at the top and the close and signature at the bottom are lined up just to the right of the center of the width of the page. The inside address, the salutation, and the body of the letter are flush left (against the left margin). The paragraphs are not indented.

If you choose to indent your paragraphs, you are using "semiblock" style, which is considered less formal. If you choose to move all elements of the letter flush left, you are using the most formal

BUSINESS LETTER IN BLOCK FORM

Return address —
121 Knox Road, #6
College Park, MD 20740
March 4, 1995

Linda Hennessee, Managing Editor
World Discovery
1650 K Street, NW
Washington, DC 20036

— Inside address

Dear Ms. Hennessee: —— Salutation

I am applying for the summer editorial internship you listed with the Career Development Center at the University of Maryland. I am currently a junior at the University of Maryland, with a double major in English and Latin American Studies.

Over the past three years I have gained considerable experience in newspaper and magazine journalism, as you will see on my enclosed résumé. I am familiar with the basic procedures of editing and photographic development, but my primary interests lie in feature writing and landscape photography. My professional goal is to work as a photojournalist with an international focus, preferably for a major magazine. I cannot imagine a better introduction to that career than a summer at World Discovery.

— Body

I am available for an interview almost any time and can be reached at 301-555-2651. I will be in Virginia from April 4 to April 12; if you want to contact me there, the number is 703-555-2006.

I look forward to hearing from you.

Close —— Sincerely,

Signature —— *Jeffrey Richardson*
Jeffrey Richardson

Enc.

style, "full block." This style is usually preferred when the letter is typed on letterhead stationery that gives the return address of the writer or the writer's company.

In the salutation, use *Ms.* if you are writing to a woman whose title or marital status is unknown or if the woman prefers this form of address. If you are not writing to a particular person, you can use the salutation *Dear Sir or Madam* or you can address the company itself — *Dear Solar Technology.*

Below the signature, flush left, you may include the abbreviation *Enc.* to indicate that something is being enclosed with the letter or the abbreviation *cc* followed by a colon and the name of someone who is receiving a copy of the letter.

D3-b Résumés

An effective résumé presents relevant information in a clear and concise form. The trick is to present yourself in the best possible light without going on at length and wasting your reader's time.

A sample résumé appears on page 58. Notice that the writer has used headings and bullets to make his résumé easy to scan and to draw attention to important information. Notice too that he presents his work experience and his educational history in reverse chronological order — to highlight his most recent accomplishments.

When you send your résumé, you should include a letter that tells what position you seek and where you learned about it. The letter should also summarize your education and past experience, relating them to the job you are applying for. End the letter with a suggestion for a meeting, and tell your prospective employer when you will be available.

D3-c Memos

Business memos (short for *memorandums*) are a form of communication used within a company or an organization. Usually brief and to the point, a memo reports information, makes a request, or recommends an action. The format of a memo, which varies from company to company, is designed for easy distribution, quick reading, and efficient filing.

Most memos display the name of the recipient, the name of the sender, the date, and the subject on separate lines at the top of the

RÉSUMÉ

Jeffrey Richardson
121 Knox Road, #6
College Park, MD 20740
301-555-2651

OBJECTIVE: To obtain an editorial internship with a magazine.

SKILLS

- Ability to write analytical stories, features, and interviews on deadline and under pressure.
- Strong background in photography: use of various types of cameras; darkroom procedures; landscape photography.
- Knowledge of copyediting and proofreading procedures.
- Languages: Spanish, French (reading).

WORK EXPERIENCE

The Diamondback (circulation 20,000), University of Maryland, College Park, Maryland, January 1992-present.
Edit photos for daily student newspaper.

Globe (circulation 80,000), Fairfax, Virginia, summers 1991-93.
Worked as intern on assignments from staff editors of this suburban Washington, DC, weekly paper: wrote stories about local issues and personalities; interviewed political candidates; performed editorial tasks (editing, proofreading, caption writing); coedited and took photographs for special supplement "The Landscapes of Northern Virginia: A Photoessay" (1993).

ADDITIONAL EXPERIENCE

Fairfax County Adult Education Program, summer 1993.
Tutored Latino students in English as a Second Language.

EDUCATION

University of Maryland, College Park, Maryland.
Bachelor of Arts expected June 1995, English and Latin American Studies.

Activities: Photographers' Workshop, Spanish Club.

References available on request.

BUSINESS MEMO

Commonwealth Press

MEMORANDUM

To: Production, Promotion, and Editorial Assistants

cc: Stephen Chapman

From: Helen Brown

Date: February 28, 1994

Subject: New computers for staff

We will receive the new personal computers next week for the assistants in production, promotion, and editorial. In preparation, I would like you to take part in a training program and to rearrange your work areas to accommodate the new equipment.

Training Program

A computer consultant will teach in-house workshops on how to use our spreadsheet program. If you have already tried the program, be prepared to discuss any problems you have encountered.

Workshops for our three departments will be held in the training room at the following times:

- Production: Monday, March 14, 10:00 a.m. to 2:00 p.m.
- Promotion: Wednesday, March 16, 10:00 a.m. to 2:00 p.m.
- Editorial: Friday, March 18, 10:00 a.m. to 2:00 p.m.

Lunch will be provided in the cafeteria. If you cannot attend, please let me know by March 4.

Allocation and Setup

To give everyone access to a computer, we will set up the new computers as follows: two in the assistants' work space in production; two in the area outside the conference room for the promotion assistants; and two in the library for the editorial assistants.

Assistants in all three departments should see me before the end of the week to discuss preparation of the spaces to accommodate the new equipment.

page. Many companies have preprinted forms for memos, and some word processors allow you to call up a memo "template" that prints standard memo lines — "To," "From," "Date," and "Subject" — at the top of the page.

Because readers of memos are busy people, you cannot assume that they will read your memo word for word. Therefore the subject line should describe the subject as clearly and concisely as possible, and the introductory paragraph should get right to the point. In addition, the body of the memo should be well organized and easy to scan. To promote scanning, use headings where possible and display any items that deserve special attention by setting them off from the text. A sample memo with headings and a displayed list appears on page 59.

Effective
Sentences

E

Effective Sentences

E1

If two or more ideas are parallel, they should be expressed in parallel grammatical form. Single words should be balanced with single words, phrases with phrases, clauses with clauses.

A kiss can be a comma, a question mark, or an exclamation point.
— Mistinguett

This novel is not to be tossed lightly aside, but to be hurled with great force.
— Dorothy Parker

In matters of principle, stand like a rock; in matters of taste, swim with the current.
— Thomas Jefferson

E1-a Balance parallel ideas in a series.

Readers expect items in a series to appear in parallel grammatical form. When one or more of the items violates readers' expectations, a sentence will be needlessly awkward.

▶ Abused children commonly exhibit one or more of the

following symptoms: withdrawal, rebelliousness,
depression.
restlessness, and ~~they are depressed~~.
  ^

The revision presents all of the items as nouns.

▶ Esperanza is responsible for stocking merchandise, writing
selling
orders for delivery, and ~~sales of~~ computers.
  ^

The revision uses *-ing* forms for all items in the series.

63

▶ After assuring us that he was sober, Sam drove down the

went through

middle of the road, ran one red light, and ~~two stop signs.~~
^

The revision adds a verb to make the three items parallel: *drove . . . ,
ran . . . , went through. . . .*

NOTE: In headings and lists, aim for as much parallelism as the content allows. See D1-b and D1-c.

E1-b Balance parallel ideas presented as pairs.

When pairing ideas, underscore their connection by expressing them in similar grammatical form. Paired ideas are usually connected in one of three ways: (1) with a coordinating conjunction such as *and, but,* or *or*; (2) with a pair of correlative conjunctions such as *either . . . or* or *not only . . . but also*; or (3) with a word introducing a comparison, usually *than* or *as*.

Parallel ideas linked with coordinating conjunctions

Coordinating conjunctions (*and, but, or, nor, for, so,* and *yet*) link ideas of equal importance. When those ideas are closely parallel in content, they should be expressed in parallel grammatical form.

▶ At Lincoln High School, vandalism can result in suspension

expulsion

or even ~~being expelled~~ from school.
^

The revision balances the nouns *suspension* and *expulsion.*

▶ Many states are reducing property taxes for homeowners and

extending

~~extend~~ financial aid in the form of tax credits to renters.
^

The revision balances the *-ing* verb forms *reducing* and *extending.*

Parallel ideas linked with correlative conjunctions

Correlative conjunctions come in pairs: *either . . . or, neither . . . nor, not only . . . but also, both . . . and, whether . . . or.* Make sure that the grammatical structure following the second half of the pair is the same as that following the first half.

▶ The shutters were not only too long but also ~~were~~ too wide.

The words *too long* follow *not only,* so *too wide* should follow *but also.* Repeating *were* creates an unbalanced effect.

▶ I was advised either to change my flight or ^to^ take the train.

To change my flight, which follows *either,* should be balanced with *to take the train,* which follows *or.*

Comparisons linked with than *or* as

In comparisons linked with *than* or *as,* the elements being compared should be expressed in parallel grammatical structure.

▶ It is easier to speak in abstractions than ^to ground^ ~~grounding~~ one's

thoughts in reality.

▶ Mother could not persuade me that giving is as much a joy as *receiving.* ~~to receive.~~
^

To speak in abstractions is balanced with *to ground one's thoughts in reality. Giving* is balanced with *receiving.*

NOTE: Comparisons should also be logical and complete. See E2-c.

E2

Needed words

Do not omit words necessary for grammatical or logical completeness. Readers need to see at a glance how the parts of a sentence are connected.

ESL NOTE: Languages sometimes differ in the need for certain words. In particular, be alert for missing articles, verbs, subjects, or expletives. See T1, T2-e, and T3-a.

E2-a Add words needed to complete compound structures.

In compound structures, words are often omitted for economy: *Tom is a man who means what he says and [who] says what he means.* Such omissions are perfectly acceptable as long as the omitted word is common to both parts of the compound structure.

If the shorter version defies grammar or idiom because an omitted word is not common to both parts of the compound structure, the word must be put back in.

> Some of the regulars are acquaintances whom we see at work or ^{who}ʌ
>
> live in our community.
>
> The word *who* must be included because *whom live in our community* is not grammatically correct.

> SETI (the Search for Extraterrestrial Intelligence) has and will ^{excited}ʌ
>
> continue to excite interest among space buffs.
>
> *Has . . . excite* is not grammatically correct.

> Many of these tribes in the South Pacific still believe and live by ⁱⁿʌ
>
> ancient laws.
>
> *Believe . . . by* is not idiomatic English.

E2-b Add the word *that* if there is any danger of misreading without it.

If there is no danger of misreading, the word *that* may sometimes be omitted when it introduces a subordinate clause: *The value of a principle is the number of things [that] it will explain.* Occasionally, however, a sentence might be misread without *that*.

> From the family room Sarah saw her favorite tree, which she had ^{that}ʌ
>
> climbed so often as a child, was gone.
>
> Sarah didn't see the tree; she saw that the tree was gone.

E2-c Add words needed to make comparisons logical and complete.

Comparisons should be made between like items. To compare unlike items is illogical and distracting.

> Henry preferred the restaurants in Pittsburgh to *those in* Philadelphia.

Restaurants must be compared with restaurants.

> Some say that Ella Fitzgerald's renditions of Cole Porter's songs are better than any other ~~singer.~~ *singer's.*

Ella Fitzgerald's renditions cannot be logically compared to a singer. The revision uses the possessive form *singer's,* with the word *renditions* being implied.

Sometimes the word *other* must be inserted to make a comparison logical.

> Jupiter is larger than any *other* planet in our solar system.

Jupiter cannot be larger than itself.

Sometimes the word *as* must be inserted to make a comparison grammatically correct.

> Our nursing graduates are as skilled, *as* if not more skilled than, those of any other state college.

The construction *as skilled . . . than* is not grammatical.

Comparisons should be complete enough so that readers will understand what is being compared.

INCOMPLETE Brand X is a lighter beer.

COMPLETE Brand X is a lighter beer than Brand Y.

Also, you should leave no ambiguity about meaning. In the following sentence, two interpretations are possible.

AMBIGUOUS	Mr. Kelly helped me more than Sam.
CLEAR	Mr. Kelly helped me more than he helped Sam.
CLEAR	Mr. Kelly helped me more than Sam did.

E3

Problems with modifiers

Modifiers, whether they are single words, phrases, or clauses, should point clearly to the words they modify. As a rule, related words should be kept together.

E3-a Put limiting modifiers in front of the words they modify.

Limiting modifiers such as *only, even, almost, nearly,* and *just* should appear in front of a verb only if they modify the verb: *At first I couldn't even touch my toes.* If they limit the meaning of some other word in the sentence, they should be placed in front of that word.

▶ Lasers ~~only~~ destroy *only* the target, leaving the surrounding healthy tissue intact.

▶ Our team didn't ~~even~~ score *even* once.

The limiting modifier *not* is frequently misplaced, suggesting a meaning the writer did not intend.

▶ ~~All~~ *Not all* wicker is **not** antique.

The original version means that no wicker is antique. The revision makes the writer's real meaning clear.

E3-b Place phrases and clauses so that readers can see at a glance what they modify.

Although phrases and clauses can appear at some distance from the words they modify, make sure that your meaning is clear. When phrases or clauses are oddly placed, absurd misreadings can result.

> MISPLACED   The king returned to the clinic where he underwent heart surgery in 1992 in a limousine sent by the White House.

> REVISED   Traveling in a limousine sent by the White House, the king returned to the clinic where he underwent heart surgery in 1992.

The king did not undergo heart surgery in a limousine. The revision corrects this false impression.

> ► ~~There~~ are many pictures of comedians who have performed at
> *On the walls*
>
> Gavin's, ~~on the walls~~.

The comedians weren't performing on the walls; the pictures were on the walls.

> ► The robber was described as a six-foot-tall man with a mustache,
> *150-pound,*
> ~~weighing 150 pounds~~.

The robber, not the mustache, weighed 150 pounds.

Occasionally the placement of a modifier leads to an ambiguity, in which case two revisions will be possible, depending on the writer's intended meaning.

> AMBIGUOUS   The exchange students we met for coffee occasionally questioned us about our latest slang.

> CLEAR   The exchange students we occasionally met for coffee questioned us about our latest slang.

> CLEAR   The exchange students we met for coffee questioned us occasionally about our latest slang.

In the original version, it was not clear whether the meeting or the questioning happened occasionally. The revisions eliminate the ambiguity.

E3-c Move awkwardly placed modifiers.

As a rule, a sentence should flow from subject to verb to object, without lengthy detours along the way. When a long adverbial element separates a subject from its verb, a verb from its object, or a helping verb from its main verb, the result is usually awkward.

> A   *my brother*
> ▶ ~~My brother,~~ after doctors told him that he would never walk again,
>
> initiated an intensive program of rehabilitation.

There is no reason to separate the subject *brother* from the verb *initiated* with a long adverb clause.

E3-d Do not split infinitives needlessly.

An infinitive consists of *to* plus a verb: *to think, to breathe, to dance.* When a modifier appears between its two parts, an infinitive is said to be "split": *to carefully balance.* If a split infinitive is obviously awkward, it should be revised.

> *If possible, patients*
> ▶ ~~Patients~~ should try to ~~if possible~~ avoid going up and down stairs.

Usage varies when a split infinitive is less awkward than the preceding one. To be on the safe side, however, you should not split infinitives, especially in formal writing.

> *formally.*
> ▶ The candidate decided to ~~formally~~ launch her campaign.

When a split infinitive is more natural and less awkward than alternative phrasing, most readers find it acceptable. *We decided to actually enforce the law* is a perfectly natural construction in English. *We decided actually to enforce the law* is not.

E3-e Repair dangling modifiers.

A dangling modifier fails to refer logically to any word in the sentence. Dangling modifiers are usually word groups (such as verbal phrases) that suggest but do not name an actor. When a sentence opens with such a modifier, readers expect the subject of the next clause to name the actor. If it doesn't, the modifier dangles.

DANGLING   Deciding to join the navy, the recruiter enthusiastically pumped Joe's hand. [*Participial phrase*]

DANGLING   Upon seeing the barricade, our car screeched to a halt. [*Preposition followed by a gerund phrase*]

DANGLING   To please the children, some fireworks were set off a day early. [*Infinitive phrase*]

DANGLING   Though only sixteen, UCLA accepted Martha's application. [*Elliptical clause with an understood subject and verb*]

Identifying dangling modifiers

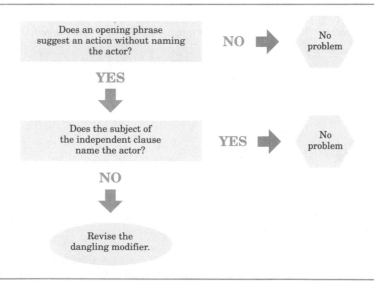

Does an opening phrase suggest an action without naming the actor?   NO → No problem

YES

Does the subject of the independent clause name the actor?   YES → No problem

NO

Revise the dangling modifier.

These dangling modifiers falsely suggest that the recruiter decided to join the navy, that the car saw the barricade, that the fireworks intended to please the children, and that UCLA is sixteen years old.

To repair a dangling modifier, you can revise the sentence in one of two ways:

1. Name the actor immediately following the introductory modifier; or
2. turn the modifier into a word group that includes the actor.

I noticed
▶ Upon entering the doctor's office, a skeleton, ~~caught my attention.~~

As I entered
▶ ~~Upon entering~~ the doctor's office, a skeleton caught my attention.

A dangling modifier cannot be repaired simply by moving it: *A skeleton caught my attention upon entering the doctor's office.* The sentence still suggests — absurdly, of course — that the skeleton was entering the doctor's office. The only way to avoid this suggestion is to put the word *I* into the sentence.

When the driver opened
▶ ~~Opening~~ the window to let out a huge bumblebee, the car

accidentally swerved into an oncoming car.

The car didn't open the window; the driver did.

women have often been denied
▶ After completing seminary training, ~~women's~~ access to the pulpit,

~~has often been denied.~~

The women (not their access to the pulpit) complete the training.

To check for dangling modifiers, use the flow chart on page 71.

E4

Shifts

E4-a Make the point of view consistent.

The point of view of a piece of writing is the perspective from which it is written: first person (*I* or *we*), second person (*you*), or third person (*he/she/it/one* or *they*). The *I* (or *we*) point of view, which emphasizes the writer, is a good choice for informal letters and writing based primarily on personal experience. The *you* point of view, which emphasizes the reader, works well for giving advice or explaining how to do something. The third-person point of view, which emphasizes the subject, is appropriate in formal academic and professional writing.

Writers who are having difficulty settling on an appropriate point of view sometimes shift confusingly from one to another. The solution is to choose a suitable perspective and then stay with it.

> One week our class met in a junkyard to practice rescuing a
>
> victim trapped in a wrecked car. We learned to dismantle the car
>
>   *We*   *our*   *our*
> with the essential tools. ~~You~~ were graded on ~~your~~ speed and ~~your~~
>   ^   ^   ^
> skill in extricating the victim.

The writer should have stayed with the *we* point of view. *You* is inappropriate because the writer is not addressing the reader directly. *You* should not be used in a vague sense meaning *anyone*. (See G3-b.)

>   *You*
> ~~Everyone~~ should purchase a lift ticket unless you plan to spend
>   ^
> most of your time walking or crawling up a steep hill.

Here *you* is an appropriate choice, since the writer is giving advice directly to readers.

Shifts from the third-person singular to the third-person plural are especially common.

>   *Police officers are*
> ~~A police officer is~~ often criticized for always being there when they
>   ^
> aren't needed and never being there when they are.

The writer shifted from the third-person singular (*police officer*) to the third-person plural (*they*). (See also G3-a.)

E4-b Maintain consistent verb tenses.

Consistent verb tenses clearly establish the time of the actions being described. When a passage begins in one tense and then shifts without warning and for no reason to another, readers are distracted and confused.

▶ There was no way I could fight the current and win. Just as I was losing

　　　　　　　　　　　jumped　　　　　　　　　　*swam*
hope, a stranger ~~jumps~~ off a passing boat and ~~swims~~ toward me.
　　　　　　　　　　　∧　　　　　　　　　　　　　　∧

Writers often shift verb tenses when writing about literature. The literary convention is to describe fictional events consistently in the present tense. (See G2-f.)

▶ The scarlet letter is a punishment sternly placed on Hester's

　　　　　　　　　　　　　　　　　　　　　is
breast by the community, and yet it ~~was~~ an extremely fanciful and
　　　　　　　　　　　　　　　　　　∧

imaginative product of Hester's own needlework.

E4-c Make verbs consistent in mood and voice.

Unnecessary shifts in the mood of a verb can be as distracting as needless shifts in tense. There are three moods in English: the indicative, used for facts, opinions, and questions; the imperative, used for orders or advice; and the subjunctive, used for wishes or conditions contrary to fact (see G2-g).

The following passage shifts confusingly from the indicative to the imperative mood.

▶ The officers advised against allowing access to our homes without

　　　　　　　　　　　　They also suggested that we
proper identification. ~~Also,~~ alert neighbors to vacation schedules.
　　　　　　　　　　　∧

Since the writer's purpose was to report the officers' advice, the revision puts both sentences in the indicative.

The voice of a verb may be either active (with the subject doing the action) or passive (with the subject receiving the action). (See G2-h.) If a writer shifts without warning from one to the other, readers may be left wondering why.

▶ When the tickets are ready, the travel agent notifies the client*,* *lists*

　e　　　　　　　　　　　　　　　　　*files*　　∧
~~F~~ach ticket ~~is then listed~~ on a daily register form, and a copy of
　　　　　　　　　　　　　　　　　　　　　∧

the itinerary *is filed.*
　　　　　∧

The original version began in the active voice (*agent notifies*) and then switched to the passive (*ticket is listed . . . copy is filed*). Because the active voice is clearer and more direct, the writer put all the verbs in the active voice.

E4-d Avoid sudden shifts from indirect to direct questions or quotations.

An indirect question reports a question without asking it: *We asked whether we could take a swim.* A direct question asks directly: *Can we take a swim?* Sudden shifts from indirect to direct questions are awkward.

> ▶ I wonder whether the sister knew of the murder, and if so,
>   *whether she reported*
>   ~~did she report~~ it to the police.
>   ^
>
> The revision poses both questions indirectly. The writer could also ask both questions directly: *Did the sister know of the murder, and if so, did she report it to the police?*

An indirect quotation reports someone's words without quoting word for word: *Anna said that she is a Virgo.* A direct quotation presents someone's exact words, set off with quotation marks: *Anna said, "I am a Virgo."* Unannounced shifts from indirect to direct quotations are distracting and confusing.

>   *asked me not to*
> ▶ Mother said that she would be late for dinner and ~~please do not~~
>   ^
>   *came*
>   leave for choir practice until Dad ~~comes~~ home.
>   ^
>
> The revision reports all of the mother's words. The writer could also quote directly: *Mother said, "I will be late for dinner. Please do not leave for choir practice until Dad comes home."*

E5

Mixed constructions

A mixed construction contains elements that do not sensibly fit together. The mismatch may be a matter of grammar or of logic.

E5-a Untangle the grammatical structure.

Once you head into a sentence, your choices are limited by the range of grammatical patterns in English. (See B2 and B3.) You cannot begin with one grammatical plan and switch without warning to another.

> **MIXED** For most drivers who have a blood alcohol level of .05 percent double their risk of causing an accident.

> **REVISED** For most drivers who have a blood alcohol level of .05 percent, the risk of causing an accident is doubled.

> **REVISED** Most drivers who have a blood alcohol level of .05 percent double their risk of causing an accident.

The writer began with a long prepositional phrase that was destined to be a modifier but then tried to press it into service as the subject of the sentence. This cannot be done. If the sentence is to begin with the prepositional phrase, the writer must finish the sentence with a subject and verb (*risk . . . is doubled*). The writer who wishes to stay with the original verb (*double*) must head into the sentence another way: *Most drivers. . . .*

▶ Although I feel that Mr. Dawe is an excellent counselor, ~~but~~ a few

changes in his approach would benefit both him and his clients.

The *Although* clause is subordinate, so it cannot be linked to an independent clause with the coordinating conjunction *but*.

Occasionally a mixed construction is so tangled that it defies grammatical analysis. When this happens, back away from the sentence, rethink what you want to say, and then say it again as clearly as you can.

> **MIXED** In the whole-word method children learn to recognize entire words rather than by the phonics method in which they learn to sound out letters and groups of letters.

> **REVISED** The whole-word method teaches children to recognize entire words; the phonics method teaches them to sound out letters and groups of letters.

ESL NOTE: English does not allow double subjects; nor does it allow an object or adverb to be repeated in an adjective clause. See T3-b and T3-c.

▶ The squirrel that came down our chimney ~~it~~ did much damage.

▶ Hearing screams, Serena ran over to the pool that her daughter

was swimming in ~~it~~.

E5-b Straighten out the logical connections.

The subject and the predicate should make sense together. When they don't, the error is known as *faulty predication*.

▶ Reluctantly we decided that ~~Tiffany's welfare~~ *Tiffany* would not be safe living

with her mother.

Tiffany, not her welfare, would not be safe.

▶ Under the revised plan, the elderly, ~~who now receive a double~~ *double personal exemption for the*

~~personal exemption,~~ will be abolished.

The exemption, not the elderly, will be abolished.

An appositive and the noun to which it refers should be logically equivalent. When they are not, the error is known as *faulty apposition*.

▶ ~~The tax accountant,~~ *Tax accounting,* a very lucrative field, requires intelligence,

patience, and attention to detail.

The tax accountant is a person, not a field.

E5-c Avoid *is when, is where,* and *reason . . . is because* constructions.

In formal English many readers object to *is when, is where,* and *reason . . . is because* constructions on either logical or grammatical grounds.

▶ Anorexia nervosa is ~~where people~~ *a disorder suffered by people who* diet to the point of starvation

because they believe they are too fat.

Anorexia nervosa is a disorder, not a place.

▶ ~~The reason~~ I missed the party ~~is~~ because my motorcycle broke down.

The writer might have replaced the word *because* with *that,* but the revision above is more concise.

E6

Coordination and subordination

When combining ideas in one sentence, use coordination to create equal emphasis and use subordination to create unequal emphasis.

Coordination

Coordination draws equal attention to two or more ideas. To coordinate words or phrases, join them with a coordinating conjunction (*and, but, or, nor, for, so, yet*). To coordinate independent clauses (word groups that can stand alone as sentences), join them with a comma and a coordinating conjunction or with a semicolon. The semicolon is often accompanied by a conjunctive adverb such as *therefore, moreover,* or *however*.

> Grandmother lost her sight, but her hearing sharpened.

> Grandmother lost her sight; however, her hearing sharpened.

Subordination

To give unequal emphasis to two or more ideas, express the major idea in an independent clause and place any minor ideas in subordinate clauses or phrases. (See B3.) Subordinate clauses, which cannot stand alone, typically begin with one of the following words.

after	before	though	where	who
although	if	unless	whether	whom
as	since	until	which	whose
because	that	when	while	

Deciding which idea to emphasize is not simply a matter of right and wrong. Consider the two ideas about Grandmother's sight and hearing.

> Grandmother lost her sight. Her hearing sharpened.

If your purpose is to stress your grandmother's acute hearing rather than her blindness, subordinate the idea concerning her blindness.

> *As Grandmother lost her sight,* her hearing sharpened.

To focus on your grandmother's blindness, subordinate the idea concerning her hearing.

> *Though her hearing sharpened,* Grandmother gradually lost her sight.

E6-a Combine choppy sentences.

Short sentences demand attention, so they should be used primarily for emphasis. Too many short sentences, one after the other, create a choppy style.

If an idea is not important enough to deserve its own sentence, try combining it with a sentence close by. Put any minor ideas in subordinate structures such as phrases or subordinate clauses.

CHOPPY The huts vary in height. They measure from ten to fifteen feet in diameter. They contain no modern conveniences.

IMPROVED The huts, which vary in height and measure from ten to fifteen feet in diameter, contain no modern conveniences.

Three sentences have become one, with minor ideas expressed in a subordinate clause beginning with *which.*

▶ Agnes, ~~was~~ another student I worked with/, ~~She~~ was a hyperactive child.

A minor idea is now expressed in an appositive phrase describing Agnes.

▶ ~~Sister Consilio was~~ *E*nveloped in a black robe with only her face and *Sister Consilio* hands visible/, ~~She~~ was an imposing figure.

A minor idea is now expressed in a participial phrase beginning with *Enveloped.*

▶ My sister owes much of her recovery to a bodybuilding program/ *that she* ~~She~~ began ~~the program~~ three years ago.

A minor idea is now expressed in an adjective clause beginning with *that.*

▶ *When my*
   M̶y̶ son asked his great-grandmother if she had been a slave̷, *she* S̶h̶e̶

became very angry.

A minor idea is now expressed in an adverb clause beginning with
When.

Although subordination is ordinarily the most effective technique for combining short, choppy sentences, coordination is appropriate when the ideas are equal in importance.

▶ The hospital decides when patients will sleep and wake̷, I̶t̶
                                           and
   dictates what and when they will eat̷, I̶t̶ tells them when they

   may be with family and friends.

Three sentences have become one, with equivalent ideas expressed in a
coordinate series.

ESL NOTE: When combining or restructuring sentences, do not
repeat the subject of the sentence; also do not repeat an object
or an adverb in an adjective clause. See T3-b and T3-c.

▶ The apartment that we moved into i̶t̶ needed many repairs.

▶ Kim climbed into the tree house that the boys were playing in̷, i̶t̶.

E6-b Avoid ineffective coordination.

Coordinate structures are appropriate only when you intend to draw
the reader's attention equally to two or more ideas: *Gregory praises
loudly, and he criticizes softly.* If one idea is more important than
another — or if a coordinating conjunction does not clearly signal the
relation between the ideas — you should subordinate the lesser idea.

▶ We keep our use of insecticides, herbicides, and fungicides to a
            because
   minimum̷ a̶n̶d̶ we are concerned about the environment.

The revision puts the less important idea in an adverb clause beginning
with *because.* Notice that the subordinating conjunction *because* signals
the connection between the ideas more clearly than the coordinating
conjunction *and.*

> *noticing*
> ▶ My uncle, ~~noticed~~ the frightened look on my face, ~~and~~ told me
>   ^   ^
>
> that the dentures in the glass were not real teeth.

The less important idea has become a participial phrase modifying the noun *uncle*.

> *After four hours,*
> ▶ ~~Four hours went by, and~~ a rescue truck finally arrived, but by
>   ^
>
> that time we had been evacuated in a helicopter.

Three independent clauses were excessive. The least important idea has become a prepositional phrase.

E6-c Do not subordinate major ideas.

If a sentence buries its major idea in a subordinate construction, readers are not likely to give it enough attention. Express the major idea in an independent clause and subordinate any minor ideas.

> *As*
> ▶ I was driving home from my new job, heading down New York
>   ^
>
> Avenue, ~~when~~ my car suddenly overheated.

The revision puts the major idea — that the car overheated — in the independent clause and subordinates the other information.

E6-d Do not subordinate excessively.

In attempting to avoid short, choppy sentences, writers sometimes move to the opposite extreme, putting more subordinate ideas into a sentence than its structure can bear. If a sentence collapses of its own weight, occasionally it can be restructured. More often, however, such sentences must be divided.

> ▶ Our job is to stay between the stacker and the tie machine
>   *If they do,*
>   watching to see if the newspapers jam /. ~~in which case~~ we pull the
>   ^
>   bundles off and stack them on a skid, because otherwise they
>
>   would back up in the stacker.

E7

Sentence variety

When a rough draft is filled with too many same-sounding sentences, try to inject some variety — as long as you can do so without sacrificing clarity or ease of reading.

E7-a Use a variety of sentence structures.

A writer should not rely too heavily on simple sentences and compound sentences, for the effect tends to be both monotonous and choppy. (See E6-a and E6-b.) Too many complex sentences, however, can be equally monotonous. If your style tends to one or the other extreme, try to achieve a better mix of sentence types.

For a discussion of sentence types, see B4-a.

E7-b Use a variety of sentence openings.

Most sentences in English begin with the subject, move to the verb, and continue to an object, with modifiers tucked in along the way or put at the end. For the most part, such sentences are fine. Put too many of them in a row, however, and they become monotonous.

Adverbial modifiers, being easily movable, can often be inserted ahead of the subject. Such modifiers might be single words, phrases, or clauses.

> *Eventually a*
> ▶ A few drops of sap ~~eventually~~ began to trickle into the pail.

> *Just as the sun was coming up, a*
> ▶ A pair of black ducks flew over the lake. ~~just as the sun was coming up.~~

Adjectives and participial phrases can frequently be moved to the beginning of a sentence without loss of clarity.

> *Dejected and withdrawn,*
> ▶ Edward, ~~dejected and withdrawn,~~ nearly gave up his search for a job.

▶ ~~John and I~~, *A* anticipating a peaceful evening, sat *John and I* down at the

campfire to brew a cup of coffee.

CAUTION: When beginning a sentence with an adjective or a participial phrase, make sure that the subject of the sentence names the person or thing described in the introductory phrase. If it doesn't, the phrase will dangle. (See E3-e.)

E7-c Try inverting sentences occasionally.

A sentence is inverted if it does not follow the normal subject-verb-object pattern. Many inversions sound artificial and should be avoided except in the most formal contexts. But if an inversion sounds natural, it can provide a welcome touch of variety.

▶ *Opposite the produce section is a*
A refrigerated case of mouth-watering cheeses ~~is opposite the~~

~~produce section.~~

▶ *Set at the top two corners of the stage were huge*
Huge lavender hearts outlined in bright white lights ~~were set at~~

~~the top two corners of the stage.~~

W

Word Choice

W

Word Choice

W1

Glossary of usage

This glossary includes words commonly confused (such as *accept* and *except*), words commonly misused (such as *hopefully*), and words that are nonstandard (such as *hisself*). It also lists colloquialisms and jargon. Colloquialisms are expressions that may be appropriate in informal speech but are inappropriate in formal writing. Jargon is needlessly technical or pretentious language that is inappropriate in most contexts.

a, an   Use *an* before a vowel sound, *a* before a consonant sound; *an apple, a peach.* Problems sometimes arise with words beginning with *h*. If the *h* is silent, the word begins with a vowel sound, so use *an: an hour, an heir, an honest senator, an honorable deed.* If the *h* is pronounced, the word begins with a consonant sound, so use *a: a hospital, a hymn, a historian, a hotel.*

accept, except   *Accept* is a verb meaning "to receive." *Except* is usually a preposition meaning "excluding." *I will accept all the packages except that one. Except* is also a verb meaning "to exclude." *Please except that item from the list.*

adapt, adopt   *Adapt* means "to adjust or become accustomed"; it is usually followed by *to*. *Adopt* means "to take as one's own." *Our family adopted a Vietnamese orphan, who quickly adapted to his new surroundings.*

adverse, averse   *Adverse* means "unfavorable." *Averse* means "opposed" or "reluctant"; it is usually followed by "to." *I am averse to your proposal because it could have an adverse impact on the economy.*

advice, advise   *Advice* is a noun, *advise* is a verb: *We advise you to follow John's advice.*

affect, effect   *Affect* is usually a verb meaning "to influence." *Effect* is usually a noun meaning "result." *The drug did not affect the disease, and it had several adverse side effects. Effect* can also be a verb meaning "to bring about." *Only the president can effect such a dramatic change.*

aggravate   *Aggravate* means "to make worse or more troublesome": *Overgrazing aggravated the soil erosion.* In formal writing, avoid the colloquial use of *aggravate* meaning "to annoy or irritate." *Her babbling annoyed* [not *aggravated*] *me.*

agree to, agree with   *Agree to* means "to give consent to." *Agree with* means "to be in accord with" or "to come to an understanding with." *He agrees with me about the need for change, but he won't agree to my plan.*

ain't *Ain't* is nonstandard. Use *am not, are not (aren't),* or *is not (isn't).*
I am not [not *ain't*] *going home for spring break.*

all ready, already *All ready* means "completely prepared." *Already*
means "previously." *Susan was all ready for the concert, but her friends
had already left.*

all right *All right* is written as two words. *Alright* is nonstandard.

all together, altogether *All together* means "everyone gathered."
Altogether means "entirely." *We were not altogether certain that we
could bring the family all together for the reunion.*

allude To *allude* to something is to make an indirect reference to it. Do
not use *allude* to mean "to refer directly." *In his lecture the economist
referred* [not *alluded*] *to several pre-Keynesian theories.*

allusion, illusion An *allusion* is an indirect reference. An *illusion* is
a misconception or false impression. *Did you catch my allusion to
Shakespeare? Mirrors give the room an illusion of depth.*

a lot *A lot* is two words. Do not write *alot. We have had a lot of rain
this spring.* See also *lots, lots of.*

A.M., P.M., a.m., p.m. Use these abbreviations with numerals: *6 P.M., 11
a.m.* Do not use them as substitutes for the words *morning* and *evening.*
I worked until late in the evening [not *p.m.*] *yesterday.*

among, between See *between, among.*

amoral, immoral *Amoral* means "neither moral nor immoral"; it also
means "not caring about moral judgments." *Immoral* means "morally
wrong." *Until recently, most business courses were taught from an
amoral perspective. Murder is immoral.*

amount, number Use *amount* with quantities that cannot be counted;
use *number* with those that can. *This recipe calls for a large amount of
sugar. We have a large number of toads in our garden.*

an, a See *a, an.*

and etc. *Et cetera (etc.)* means "and so forth"; therefore, *and etc.* is
redundant. See also *etc.*

and/or Avoid the awkward construction *and/or* except in technical or
legal documents.

angry at, angry with To write that one is *angry at* another person is
nonstandard. Use *angry with* instead.

ante-, anti- The prefix *ante-* means "earlier" or "in front of"; the prefix
anti- means "against" or "opposed to." *William Lloyd Garrison was one
of the leaders of the antislavery movement during the antebellum period.*
Anti- should be used with a hyphen when it is followed by a capital letter or a word beginning with *i.*

anxious   *Anxious* means "worried" or "apprehensive." In formal writing, avoid using *anxious* to mean "eager." *We are eager* [not *anxious*] *to see your new house.*

anybody   *Anybody* is singular. (See G1-d and G3-a.)

anymore   Reserve the adverb *anymore* for negative contexts, where it means "any longer." *Moviegoers are rarely shocked anymore by profanity.* Do not use *anymore* in positive contexts. Use *now* or *nowadays* instead. *Homes are so expensive nowadays* [not *anymore*] *that few young people can afford to buy them.*

anyone   *Anyone* is singular. (See G1-d and G3-a.)

anyone, any one   *Anyone,* an indefinite pronoun, means "any person at all." *Any one,* the pronoun *one* preceded by the adjective *any,* refers to a particular person or thing in a group. *Anyone from Chicago may choose any one of the games on display.*

anyplace   *Anyplace* is informal for *anywhere.* Avoid *anyplace* in formal writing.

anyways, anywheres   *Anyways* and *anywheres* are nonstandard. Use *anyway* and *anywhere.*

as   *As* is sometimes used to mean "because." But do not use it if there is any chance of ambiguity. *We canceled the picnic because* [not *as*] *it began raining. As* here could mean "because" or "when."

as, like   See *like, as.*

averse, adverse   See *adverse, averse.*

awful   The adjective *awful* means "awe-inspiring." Colloquially it is used to mean "terrible" or "bad." The adverb *awfully* is sometimes used in conversation as an intensifier meaning "very." In formal writing, avoid these colloquial uses. *I was very* [not *awfully*] *upset last night. Susan had a terrible* [not *an awful*] *time calming her nerves.*

awhile, a while   *Awhile* is an adverb; it can modify a verb, but it cannot be the object of a preposition such as *for.* The two-word form *a while* is a noun preceded by an article and therefore can be the object of a preposition. *Stay awhile. Stay for a while.*

bad, badly   *Bad* is an adjective, *badly* an adverb. (See G4.) *They felt bad about being early and ruining the surprise. Her arm hurt badly after she slid headfirst into second base.*

being as, being that   *Being as* and *being that* are nonstandard expressions. Write *because* or *since* instead. *Because* [not *Being as*] *I slept late, I had to skip breakfast.*

beside, besides   *Beside* is a preposition meaning "at the side of" or "next to." *Annie Oakley slept with her gun beside her bed. Besides* is a preposition meaning "except" or "in addition to." *No one besides Terrie can have that ice cream. Besides* is also an adverb meaning "in addition." *I'm not hungry; besides, I don't like ice cream.*

between, among　Ordinarily, use *among* with three or more entities, *between* with two. *The prize was divided among several contestants. You have a choice between carrots and beans.*

bring, take　Use *bring* when an object is being transported toward you, *take* when it is being moved away. *Please bring me a glass of water. Please take these flowers to Mr. Scott.*

burst, bursted; bust, busted　*Burst* is an irregular verb meaning "to come open or fly apart suddenly or violently." Its principal parts are *burst, burst, burst.* The past-tense form *bursted* is nonstandard. *Bust* and *busted* are slang for *burst* and, along with *bursted,* should not be used in formal writing.

can, may　The distinction between *can* and *may* is fading, but many careful writers still observe it in formal writing. *Can* is traditionally reserved for ability, *may* for permission. *Can you ski down the advanced slope without falling? May I help you?*

capital, capitol　*Capital* refers to a city, *capitol* to a building where lawmakers meet. *Capital* also refers to wealth or resources. *The capitol has undergone extensive renovations. The residents of the state capital protested the development plans.*

censor, censure　*Censor* means "to remove or suppress material considered objectionable." *Censure* means "to criticize severely." *The library's new policy of censoring controversial books has been censured by the media.*

cite, site　*Cite* means "to quote as an authority or example." *Site* is usually a noun meaning "a particular place." *He cited the zoning law in his argument against the proposed site of the gas station.*

climactic, climatic　*Climactic* is derived from *climax,* the point of greatest intensity in a series or progression of events. *Climatic* is derived from *climate*; it refers to meteorological conditions. *The climactic period in the dinosaurs' reign was reached just before severe climatic conditions brought on an ice age.*

coarse, course　*Coarse* means "crude" or "rough in texture." *The coarse weave of the wall hanging gave it a three-dimensional quality. Course* usually refers to a path, a playing field, or a unit of study; the expression *of course* means "certainly." *I plan to take a course in car repair this summer. Of course, you are welcome to join me.*

compare to, compare with　*Compare to* means "to represent as similar." *She compared him to a wild stallion. Compare with* means "to examine the ways in which two things are similar." *The study compared the language ability of apes with that of dolphins.*

complement, compliment *Complement* is a verb meaning "to go with or complete" or a noun meaning "something that completes." *Compliment* as a verb means "to flatter"; as a noun it means "flattering remark." *Her skill at rushing the net complements his skill at volleying. Mother's flower arrangements receive many compliments.*

conscience, conscious *Conscience* is a noun meaning "moral principles." *Conscious* is an adjective meaning "aware or alert." *Let your conscience be your guide. Were you conscious of his love for you?*

contact Although the use of *contact* meaning "to get in touch with" is common in speech, it is not appropriate in formal writing. If possible, use a precise verb such as *write* or *telephone*. *We will telephone* [not *contact*] *you soon.*

continual, continuous *Continual* means "repeated regularly and frequently." *She grew weary of the continual telephone calls. Continuous* means "extended or prolonged without interruption." *The broken siren made a continuous wail.*

could care less *Could care less* is a nonstandard expression. Write *couldn't care less* instead. *He couldn't* [not *could*] *care less about the rips in his jeans.*

could of *Could of* is nonstandard for *could have. We could have* [not *could of*] *had steak for dinner if we had been hungry.*

council, counsel A *council* is a deliberative body, and a *councilor* is a member of such a body. *Counsel* usually means "advice" and can also mean "lawyer"; *counselor* is one who gives advice or guidance. *The councilors met to draft the council's position paper. The pastor offered wise counsel to the troubled teenager.*

criteria *Criteria* is the plural of *criterion,* which means "a standard, rule, or test on which a judgment or decision can be based." *The only criterion for the job is a willingness to work overtime.*

data *Data* is a plural noun technically meaning "facts or propositions." But *data* is increasingly being accepted as a singular noun. *The new data suggest* [or *suggests*] *that our theory is correct.* (The singular *datum* is rarely used.)

different from, different than Ordinarily, write *different from. Your sense of style is different from Jim's.* However, *different than* is acceptable to avoid an awkward construction. *Please let me know if your plans are different than* [to avoid *from what*] *they were six weeks ago.*

differ from, differ with *Differ from* means "to be unlike"; *differ with* means "to disagree." *She differed with me about the wording of the agreement. My approach to the problem differed from hers.*

disinterested, uninterested *Disinterested* means "impartial, objective"; *uninterested* means "not interested." *We sought the advice of a disinter-*

ested counselor to help us solve our problem. He was uninterested in any-one's opinion but his own.

don't   *Don't* is the contraction for *do not. I don't want any. Don't* should not be used as the contraction for *does not,* which is *doesn't. He doesn't* [not *don't*] *want any.*

due to   *Due to* is an adjective phrase and should not be used as a preposition meaning "because of." *The trip was canceled because of* [not *due to*] *lack of interest. Due to* is acceptable as a subject complement and usually follows a form of the verb *be. His success was due to hard work.*

each   *Each* is singular. (See G1-d and G3-a.)

effect, affect   See *affect, effect.*

e.g.   In formal writing, replace the Latin abbreviation *e.g.* with its English equivalent: *for example* or *for instance.*

either   *Either* is singular. (See G1-d and G3-a.) For *either . . . or* constructions, see G1-c.

elicit, illicit   *Elicit* is a verb meaning "to bring out" or "to evoke." *Illicit* is an adjective meaning "unlawful." *The reporter was unable to elicit any information from the police about illicit drug traffic.*

emigrate from, immigrate to   *Emigrate* means "to leave one country or region to settle in another." *In 1900, my grandfather emigrated from Russia to escape the religious pogroms. Immigrate* means "to enter another country and reside there." *Many Mexicans immigrate to the United States to find work.*

eminent, imminent   *Eminent* means "outstanding" or "distinguished." *We met an eminent archaeologist. Imminent* means "about to happen." *The announcement is imminent.*

enthused   Many people object to the use of *enthused* as an adjective. Use *enthusiastic* instead. *The children were enthusiastic* [not *enthused*] *about going to the circus.*

-ess   Many people find the *-ess* suffix demeaning. Write *poet,* not *poet-ess; Jew,* not *Jewess; author,* not *authoress.*

etc.   Avoid ending a list with *etc.* It is more emphatic to end with an example, and in most contexts readers will understand that the list is not exhaustive. When you don't wish to end with an example, *and so on* is more graceful than *etc.* See also *and etc.*

eventually, ultimately   Although these words are often used inter-changeably, *eventually* is the better choice to mean "at an unspecified time in the future," and *ultimately* is better to mean "the furthest possible extent or greatest extreme." *He knew that eventually he would solve the mystery. The existentialist considered suicide the ultimately rational act.*

everybody, everyone *Everybody* and *everyone* are singular. (See G1-d and G3-a.)

everyone, every one *Everyone* is an indefinite pronoun. *Every one,* the pronoun *one* preceded by the adjective *every,* means "each individual or thing in a particular group." *Every one* is usually followed by *of. Everyone wanted to go. Every one of the missing books was found.*

except, accept See *accept, except.*

expect Avoid the colloquial use of *expect* meaning "to believe, think, or suppose." *I think* [not *expect*] *it will rain tonight.*

explicit, implicit *Explicit* means "expressed directly" or "clearly defined"; *implicit* means "implied, unstated." *I gave him explicit instructions not to go swimming. My mother's silence indicated her implicit approval.*

farther, further *Farther* describes distances. *Miami is farther from Chicago than I thought. Further* suggests quantity or degree. *You extended the curfew further than you should have.*

female, male The terms *female* and *male* are jargon for "woman" and "man." *Two women* [not *females*] *and one man* [not *male*] *applied for the position.*

fewer, less *Fewer* refers to items that can be counted; *less* refers to general amounts. *Fewer people are living in the city. Please put less sugar in my tea.*

finalize *Finalize* is jargon meaning "to make final or complete." Use ordinary English instead. *The architect prepared final drawings* [not *finalized the drawings*].

firstly *Firstly* sounds pretentious, and it leads to the ungainly series *firstly, secondly, thirdly, fourthly,* and so on. Write *first, second, third* instead.

folks *Folks* is an informal expression for "parents" or "relatives" or "people" in general. Use a more formal expression instead.

further, farther See *farther, further.*

get *Get* has many colloquial uses. In formal writing, avoid using *get* to mean the following: "to evoke an emotional response" (*That music always gets to me*); "to annoy" (*After a while his sulking got to me*); "to take revenge on" (*I got back at her by leaving the room*); "to become" (*He got sick*); "to start or begin" (*Let's get going*). Avoid using *have got to* in place of *must. I must* [not *have got to*] *clean the kitchen tonight before the guests arrive.*

good, well *Good* is an adjective, *well* an adverb. (See G4.) *He hasn't felt good about his game since he sprained his wrist last season. She performed well on the uneven parallel bars.*

hanged, hung   *Hanged* is the past-tense and past-participle form of the verb *hang* meaning "to execute." *The prisoner was hanged. Hung* is the past-tense and past-participle form of the verb *hang* meaning "to fasten or suspend." *The stockings were hung by the chimney with care.*

hardly   Avoid expressions such as *can't hardly* and *not hardly,* which are considered double negatives. (See G4-d.) *I can* [not *can't*] *hardly describe my elation at getting the job.*

has got, have got   *Got* is unnecessary and awkward in such constructions. It should be dropped. *We have* [not *have got*] *three days to prepare for the opening.*

he   At one time *he* was used to mean "he or she." Today such usage is inappropriate. See G3-a and W3-e for alternative constructions.

he/she, his/her   In formal writing, use *he or she* or *his or her.* For alternatives to these wordy constructions, see G3-a and W3-e.

hisself   *Hisself* is nonstandard. Use *himself.*

hopefully   *Hopefully* means "in a hopeful manner." *Esperanza looked hopefully to the future.* Do not use *hopefully* in constructions such as the following: *Hopefully, your daughter will recover soon.* Indicate who is doing the hoping: *I hope that your daughter will recover soon.*

hung, hanged   See *hanged, hung.*

i.e.   In formal writing, replace the Latin abbreviation *i.e.* with its English equivalent: *that is.*

if, whether   Use *if* to express a condition and *whether* to express alternatives. *If you go on a trip, whether it be to Nebraska or New Jersey, remember to bring traveler's checks.*

illusion, allusion   See *allusion, illusion.*

imminent, eminent   See *eminent, imminent.*

immoral, amoral   See *amoral, immoral.*

implement   *Implement* is a pretentious way of saying "do," "carry out," or "accomplish." Use ordinary language instead. *We carried out* [not *implemented*] *the director's orders with some reluctance.*

imply, infer   *Imply* means "to suggest or state indirectly"; *infer* means "to draw a conclusion." *John implied that he knew all about computers, but the interviewer inferred that John was inexperienced.*

in, into   *In* indicates location or condition; *into* indicates movement or a change in condition. *They found the lost letters in a box after moving into the house.*

individual   *Individual* is a pretentious substitute for *person. We invited several persons* [not *individuals*] *from the audience to participate in the experiment.*

infer, imply   See *imply, infer.*

ingenious, ingenuous   *Ingenious* means "clever." *Sarah's solution to the problem was ingenious. Ingenuous* means "naive" or "frank." *For a successful manager, Ed is surprisingly ingenuous.*

in regards to   *In regards to* confuses two different phrases: *in regard to* and *as regards.* Use one or the other. *In regard to* [or *As regards*] *the contract, ignore the first clause.*

into, in   See *in, into.*

irregardless   *Irregardless* is nonstandard. Use *regardless.*

is when, is where   These mixed constructions are often incorrectly used in definitions. *A run-off election is a second election held to break a tie* [not *is when a second election is held to break a tie*]. (See E5-c.)

it is   *It is* is nonstandard when used to mean "there is." *There is* [not *It is*] *a fly in my soup.*

its, it's   *Its* is a possessive pronoun; *it's* is a contraction for *it is.* (See P5-c.) *The dog licked its wound whenever its owner walked into the room. It's a perfect day to walk the twenty-mile trail.*

kind(s)   *Kind* is singular and should be treated as such. Don't write *These kind of chairs are rare.* Write instead *This kind of chair is rare. Kinds* is plural and should be used only when you mean more than one kind. *These kinds of chairs are rare.*

kind of, sort of   Avoid using *kind of* or *sort of* to mean "somewhat." *The movie was a little* [not *kind of*] *boring.* Do not put *a* after either phrase. *That kind of* [not *kind of a*] *salesclerk annoys me.*

lead, led   *Lead* is a noun referring to a metal. *Led* is the past tense of the verb *lead. He led me to the treasure.*

learn, teach   *Learn* means "to gain knowledge"; *teach* means "to impart knowledge." *I must teach* [not *learn*] *my sister to read.*

leave, let   *Leave* means "to exit." Avoid using it with the nonstandard meaning "to permit." *Let* [not *leave*] *me help you with the dishes.*

less, fewer   See *fewer, less.*

liable   *Liable* means "obligated" or "responsible." Do not use it to mean "likely." *You're likely* [not *liable*] *to trip if you don't tie your shoelaces.*

lie, lay   *Lie* is an intransitive verb meaning "to recline or rest on a surface." Its principal parts are *lie, lay, lain. Lay* is a transitive verb meaning "to put or place." Its principal parts are *lay, laid, laid.* (See G2-b.)

like, as   *Like* is a preposition, not a subordinating conjunction. It should be followed only by a noun or a noun phrase. *As* is a subordinating conjunction that introduces a subordinate clause. In casual speech you may say *She looks like she hasn't slept* or *You don't know her like I do.* But in formal writing, use *as. She looks as if she hasn't slept. You don't know her as I do.* (See B3-a and B3-e.)

loose, lose   *Loose* is an adjective meaning "not securely fastened." *Lose* is a verb meaning "to misplace" or "to not win." *Did you lose your only loose pair of work pants?*

lots, lots of   *Lots* and *lots of* are colloquial substitutes for *many, much,* or *a lot.* Avoid using them in formal writing.

male, female   See *female, male.*

mankind   Avoid *mankind* whenever possible. It offends many readers because it excludes women. Use *humanity, humans, the human race,* or *humankind* instead.

may, can   See *can, may.*

maybe, may be   *Maybe* is an adverb meaning "possibly." *May be* is a verb phrase. *Maybe the sun will shine tomorrow. Tomorrow may be a brighter day.*

may of, might of   *May of* and *might of* are nonstandard for *may have* and *might have. We may have* [not *may of*] *had too many cookies.*

media, medium   *Media* is the plural of *medium. Of all the media that cover the Olympics, television is the medium that best captures the spectacle of the events.*

most   *Most* is colloquial when used to mean "almost" and should be avoided. *Almost* [not *Most*] *everyone went to the parade.*

must of   See *may of, might of.*

myself   *Myself* is a reflexive or intensive pronoun. Reflexive: *I cut myself.* Intensive: *I will drive you myself.* Do not use *myself* in place of *I* or *me. He gave the flowers to Melinda and me* [not *myself*]. (See also G3-c.)

neither   *Neither* is singular. (See G1-d and G3-a.) For *neither . . . nor* constructions, see G1-c.

none   *None* is usually singular. (See G1-d and G3-a.)

nowheres   *Nowheres* is nonstandard for *nowhere.*

number, amount   See *amount, number.*

of   Use the verb *have,* not the preposition *of,* after the verbs *could, should, would, may, might,* and *must. They must have* [not *of*] *left early.*

off of   *Off* is sufficient. Omit *of. The ball rolled off* [not *off of*] *the table.*

OK, O.K., okay   All three spellings are acceptable, but in formal speech and writing avoid these colloquial expressions for consent or approval.

parameters   *Parameter* is a mathematical term that has become jargon for "fixed limit," "boundary," or "guideline." Use ordinary English instead. *The task force was asked to work within certain guidelines* [not *parameters*].

passed, past   *Passed* is the past tense of the verb *pass. Mother passed me another slice of cake. Past* usually means "belonging to a former time" or "beyond a time or place." *Our past president spoke until past midnight. The hotel is just past the next intersection.*

percent, per cent, percentage   *Percent* (also spelled *per cent*) is always used with a specific number. *Percentage* is used with a descriptive term such as *large* or *small,* not with a specific number. *The candidate won 80 percent of the primary vote. Only a small percentage of registered voters turned out for the election.*

phenomena   *Phenomena* is the plural of *phenomenon,* which means "an observable occurrence or fact." *Strange phenomena occur at all hours of the night in that house, but last night's phenomenon was the strangest of all.*

plus   *Plus* should not be used to join independent clauses. *This raincoat is dirty; moreover* [not *plus*], *it has a hole in it.*

precede, proceed   *Precede* means "to come before." *Proceed* means "to go forward." *As we proceeded up the mountain, we noticed fresh tracks in the mud, evidence that a group of hikers had preceded us.*

principal, principle   *Principal* is a noun meaning "the head of a school or an organization" or "a sum of money." It is also an adjective meaning "most important." *Principle* is a noun meaning "a basic truth or law." *The principal expelled her for three principal reasons. We believe in the principle of equal justice for all.*

proceed, precede   See *precede, proceed.*

quote, quotation   *Quote* is a verb; *quotation* is a noun. Avoid using *quote* as a shortened form of the noun. *Her quotations* [not *quotes*] *from Shakespeare intrigued us.*

raise, rise   *Raise* is a transitive verb meaning "to move or cause to move upward." It takes a direct object. *I raised the shades. Rise* is an intransitive verb meaning "to go up." It does not take a direct object. *Heat rises.*

real, really   *Real* is an adjective; *really* is an adverb. *Real* is sometimes used informally as an adverb, but avoid this use in formal writing. *She was really* [not *real*] *angry.* (See G4.)

reason is because   Use *that* instead of *because. The reason I'm late is that* [not *because*] my car broke down. (See E5-c.)

reason why The expression *reason why* is redundant. *The reason* [not *The reason why*] *Jones lost the election is clear.*

relation, relationship *Relation* describes a connection between things. *She studied the relation between poverty and infant mortality. Relationship* describes a connection between people. *Our business relationship has cooled over the years.*

respectfully, respectively *Respectfully* means "showing or marked by respect." *He respectfully submitted his opinion to the judge. Respectively* means "each in the order given." *John, Tom, and Larry were a butcher, a baker, and a lawyer, respectively.*

rise, raise See *raise, rise.*

sensual, sensuous *Sensual* means "gratifying the physical senses," especially those associated with sexual pleasure. *Sensuous* means "pleasing to the senses," especially those involved in the experience of art, music, and nature. *The sensuous music and balmy air led the dancers to more sensual movements.*

set, sit *Set* is a transitive verb meaning "to put" or "to place." Its principal parts are *set, set, set. Sit* is an intransitive verb meaning "to be seated." Its principal parts are *sit, sat, sat. She set the dough in a warm corner of the kitchen. The cat sat in the warmest part of the room.*

shall, will *Shall* was once used as the helping verb with *I* or *we: I shall, we shall, you will, he/she/it will, they will.* Today, however, *will* is generally accepted even when the subject is *I* or *we.* The word *shall* occurs primarily in polite questions. (*Shall I find you a pillow?*) and in legalistic sentences suggesting duty or obligation. (*The applicant shall file form 1080 by December 31*).

should of *Should of* is nonstandard for *should have. They should have* [not *should of*] *been home an hour ago.*

since Do not use *since* to mean "because" if there is any chance of ambiguity. *Since we won the game, we have been celebrating with a pitcher of beer. Since* here could mean "because" or "from the time that."

sit, set See *set, sit.*

site, cite See *cite, site.*

somebody, someone *Somebody* and *someone* are singular. (See G1-d and G3-a.)

something *Something* is singular. (See G1-d and G3-a.)

sometime, some time, sometimes *Sometime* is an adverb meaning "at an indefinite or unstated time." *Some time* is the adjective *some* modifying the noun *time* and is spelled as two words to mean "a period of time." *Sometimes* is an adverb meaning "at times, now and then." *I'll see you sometime soon. I haven't lived there for some time. I call him sometimes.*

suppose to, use to See *use to, suppose to.*

sure and *Sure and* is nonstandard for *sure to. We were all taught to be sure to* [not *sure and*] *look both ways before crossing a street.*

take, bring See *bring, take.*

than, then *Than* is a conjunction used in comparisons; *then* is an adverb denoting time. *That pizza is more than I can eat. Tom laughed, and then we recognized him.*

that See *who, which, that.*

that, which Many writers reserve *that* for restrictive clauses, *which* for nonrestrictive clauses. (See P1-e.)

theirselves *Theirselves* is nonstandard for *themselves. The two people were able to push the Audi out of the way themselves* [not *theirselves*].

them The use of *them* in place of *those* is nonstandard. *Please send those* [not *them*] *flowers to the patient in room 220.*

then, than See *than, then.*

there, their, they're *There* is an adverb specifying place; it is also an expletive. Adverb: *Sylvia is lying there unconscious.* Expletive: *There are two plums left. Their* is a possessive pronoun. *They're* is a contraction of *they are. Fred and Jane finally washed their car. They're later than usual today.*

they The use of *they* to indicate possession is nonstandard. Use *their* instead. *Cindy and Sam decided to sell their* [not *they*] *1975 Corvette.*

this kind See *kind(s).*

to, too, two *To* is a preposition; *too* is an adverb; *two* is a number. *Too many of your shots slice to the left, but the last two were right on the mark.*

toward, towards *Toward* and *towards* are generally interchangeable, although *toward* is preferred in American English.

try and *Try and* is nonstandard for *try to. The teacher asked us all to try to* [not *try and*] *write an original haiku.*

ultimately, eventually See *eventually, ultimately.*

unique Avoid expressions such as *more unique* and *most unique.* Something either is unique or it isn't. It is illogical to suggest degrees of uniqueness. (See G4-c.)

usage The noun *usage* should not be substituted for *use* when the meaning is "employment of." *The use* [not *usage*] *of computers dramatically increased the company's profits.*

use to, suppose to *Use to* and *suppose to* are nonstandard for *used to* and *supposed to.*

utilize *Utilize* means "to make use of." It often sounds pretentious; in most cases, *use* is sufficient. *I used* [not *utilized*] *the best workers to get the job done fast.*

wait for, wait on *Wait for* means "to be in readiness for" or "await." *Wait on* means "to serve." *We're waiting for* [not *waiting on*] *Ruth to take us to the game.*

ways *Ways* is colloquial when used to mean "distance." *The city is a long way* [not *ways*] *from here.*

weather, whether The noun *weather* refers to the state of the atmosphere. *Whether* is a conjunction referring to a choice between alternatives. *We wondered whether the weather would clear up in time for our picnic.*

well, good See *good, well.*

where Do not use *where* in place of *that*. *I heard that* [not *where*] *the crime rate is increasing.*

which See *that, which* and *who, which, that.*

while Avoid using *while* to mean "although" or "whereas" if there is any chance of ambiguity. *Although* [not *While*] *Gloria lost money in the slot machine, Tom won it at roulette.* Here *While* could mean either "although" or "at the same time that."

who, which, that Do not use *which* to refer to persons. Use *who* instead. *That*, though generally used to refer to things, may be used to refer to a group or class of people. *Fans wondered how an old man who* [not *that* or *which*] *walked with a limp could play football. The team that scores the most points in this game will win the tournament.*

who, whom *Who* is used for subjects and subject complements; *whom* is used for objects. (See G3-d.)

who's, whose *Who's* is a contraction of *who is; whose* is a possessive pronoun. *Who's ready for more popcorn? Whose coat is this?*

will, shall See *shall, will.*

would of *Would of* is nonstandard for *would have*. *She would have* [not *would of*] *had a chance to play if she had arrived on time.*

you In formal writing, avoid *you* in an indefinite sentence meaning "anyone." (See G3-b.) *Any spectator* [not *You*] *could tell by the way John caught the ball that his throw would be too late.*

your, you're *Your* is a possessive pronoun; *you're* is a contraction of *you are*. *Is that your new motorcycle? You're on the list of finalists.*

W2

Wordy sentences

Long sentences are not necessarily wordy, nor are short sentences always concise. A sentence is wordy if its meaning can be conveyed in fewer words.

W2-a Eliminate redundancies.

Redundancies such as *cooperate together, close proximity, basic essentials,* and *true fact* are a common source of wordiness. There is no need to say the same thing twice.

▶ Black slaves were ~~portrayed or~~ stereotyped as lazy even though

they were the main labor force of the South.

▶ Daniel ~~is now employed~~ at a private rehabilitation center ~~working~~
    ^works
as a registered physical therapist.

Although modifiers ordinarily add meaning to the words they modify, occasionally they are redundant.

▶ Sylvia ~~very hurriedly~~ scribbled her name, address, and phone

number on the back of a greasy napkin.

▶ Joel was determined ~~in his mind~~ to lose weight.

W2-b Avoid unnecessary repetition of words.

Although words may be repeated deliberately, for effect, repetitions will seem awkward if they are clearly unnecessary. When a more concise version is possible, choose it.

▶ Our fifth patient, in room six, is a mentally ill~~, patient~~.

                                          grow

▶ The best teachers help each student to ~~become a better student~~

both academically and emotionally.

W2-c Cut empty or inflated phrases.

An empty phrase can be cut with little or no loss of meaning. Common examples are introductory word groups that apologize or hedge: *in my opinion, I think that, it seems that, one must admit that,* and so on.

           Our

▶ ~~In my opinion, our~~ current policy in Central America is misguided

on several counts.

Inflated phrases can be reduced to a word or two without loss of meaning.

INFLATED	CONCISE
along the lines of	like
as a matter of fact	in fact
at all times	always
at the present time	now, currently
at this point in time	now, currently
because of the fact that	because
by means of	by
due to the fact that	because
for the purpose of	for
for the reason that	because
have the ability to	be able to
in the nature of	like
in order to	to
in spite of the fact that	although, though
in the event that	if
in the final analysis	finally
in the neighborhood of	about
until such time as	until

                                                if

▶ We will file the appropriate papers ~~in the event that~~ we are

unable to meet the deadline.

W2-d Simplify the structure.

If the structure of a sentence is needlessly indirect, try simplifying it. Look for opportunities to strengthen the verb.

▶ The financial analyst claimed that because of volatile market conditions

she could not ~~make an~~ estimate ~~of~~ the company's future profits.

The verb *estimate* is more vigorous and more concise than *make an esti- mate of.*

The colorless verbs *is, are, was,* and *were* frequently generate excess words.

▶ The administrative secretary ~~is responsible for monitoring and~~ *monitors and balances*

~~balancing~~ the budgets for travel, contract services, and personnel.

The expletive constructions *there is* and *there are* (or *there was* and *there were*) can also generate excess words. The same is true of expletive constructions beginning with *it.*

▶ ~~There is~~ ^A^nother videotape ~~that~~ tells the story of Charles Darwin

and introduces the theory of evolution.

▶ ~~It is important that~~ ^H^ikers *must* remain inside the park boundaries.

Finally, verbs in the passive voice may be needlessly indirect. When the active voice expresses your meaning as well, use it. (See G2-h.)

▶ All too often, athletes with marginal academic skills ~~have been~~ *our coaches have recruited*

~~recruited by our coaches.~~

W2-e Reduce clauses to phrases, phrases to single words.

Word groups functioning as modifiers can often be made more com- pact. Look for any opportunities to reduce clauses to phrases or phrases to single words.

▶ We took a side trip to Monticello, ~~which was~~ the home of Thomas Jefferson.

leather
▶ Susan's stylish pants, ~~made of leather~~, were too warm for our
   ^
climate.

W3

Appropriate language

Language is appropriate when it suits your subject, conforms to the needs of your audience, and blends naturally with your own voice.

W3-a Stay away from jargon.

Jargon is specialized language used among members of a trade, profession, or group. Use jargon only when readers will be familiar with it; even then, use it only when plain English will not do as well.

> JARGON For years the indigenous body politic of South Africa attempted to negotiate legal enfranchisement without result.

> REVISED For years the native population of South Africa negotiated in vain for the right to vote.

Broadly defined, jargon includes puffed-up language designed more to impress readers than to inform them. Common examples in business, government, higher education, and the military are given in the following list, with plain English translations in parentheses.

ameliorate (improve)	impact on (affect)
commence (begin)	indicator (sign)
components (parts)	optimal (best, most favorable)
endeavor (try)	parameters (boundaries, limits)
exit (leave)	peruse (read, look over)
facilitate (help)	prior to (before)
factor (consideration, cause)	utilize (use)
finalize (finish)	viable (workable)

Sentences filled with jargon are hard to read, and they are often wordy as well.

▶ All ~~employees functioning in the capacity of~~ work-study students *must prove that they are currently enrolled.* ~~are required to give evidence of current enrollment.~~
     ^

▶ Mayor Summers will ~~commence~~ *begin* his term of office by ~~ameliorating~~ *improving*
     ^ *poor neighborhoods.* ^
living conditions in ~~economically deprived zones~~.
     ^

W3-b Avoid pretentious language and most euphemisms.

Hoping to sound profound or poetic, some writers embroider their thoughts with large words and flowery phrases, language that in fact sounds pretentious. Pretentious language is so ornate and often so wordy that it obscures the thought that lies beneath.

▶ When our ~~progenitors reach their silver-haired and golden years,~~ *parents become old,*
    ^ *bury*   *old-age*
we frequently ~~ensepulcher~~ them in homes ~~for senescent beings~~ as
    ^   *dead.*   ^
if they were already ~~among the deceased.~~
     ^

Euphemisms, nice-sounding words or phrases substituted for words thought to sound harsh or ugly, are sometimes appropriate. It is customary, for example, to say that a couple is "sleeping together" or that someone has "passed away." Most euphemisms, however, are needlessly evasive or even deceitful. Like pretentious language, they obscure the intended meaning.

EUPHEMISM	PLAIN ENGLISH
adult entertainment	pornography
preowned automobile	used car
economically deprived	poor
selected out	fired
negative savings	debts
strategic withdrawal	retreat or defeat
revenue enhancers	taxes
chemical dependency	drug addiction
incendiary device	bomb
the Peacekeeper	a nuclear missile
correctional facility	prison

W3-c In most contexts, avoid slang, regional expressions, and nonstandard English.

Slang is an informal and sometimes private vocabulary that expresses the solidarity of a group such as teenagers, rock musicians, or football fans; it is subject to more rapid change than standard English. For example, the slang teenagers use to express approval changes every few years; *cool, groovy, neat, wicked, awesome,* and *fresh* have replaced one another within the last three decades. Sometimes slang becomes so widespread that it is accepted as standard vocabulary. *Jazz,* for example, started as slang but is now generally accepted to describe a style of music.

Although slang has a certain vitality, it is a code that not everyone understands, and it is very informal. Therefore, it is inappropriate in most written work.

▶ If we don't begin studying for the final, a whole semester's work ~~is~~
  will be wasted.
  ~~going down the tubes.~~
  ^

                                              disgust you.
▶ The government's "filth" guidelines for food will ~~gross you out.~~
                                              ^

Regional expressions are common to a group in a geographical area. *Let's talk with the bark off* (for *Let's speak frankly*) is an expression in the southern United States, for example. Regional expressions have the same limitations as slang and are therefore inappropriate in most writing.

                                              turn on
▶ John was four blocks from the house before he remembered to ~~cut~~
                                                              ^

  the headlights ₌ ~~on.~~
              ^

▶ I'm not ~~for~~ sure, but I think the dance has been postponed.

Standard English is the language used in all academic, business, and professional fields. Nonstandard English is spoken by people with a common regional or social heritage. Although nonstandard English may be appropriate when spoken within a close group, it is out of place in most formal and informal writing.

          has
▶ The counselor ~~have~~ so many problems in her own life that she
  doesn't   ^
  ~~don't~~ know how to advise anyone else.
  ^

If you speak a nonstandard dialect, try to identify the ways in which your dialect differs from standard English. Look especially for the following features of nonstandard English, which commonly cause problems in writing:

Misuse of verb forms such as *began* and *begun* (See G2-a.)

Omission of *-s* endings on verbs (See G1 and G2-c.)

Omission of *-ed* endings on verbs (See G2-d.)

Omission of necessary verbs (See G2-e.)

Double negatives (See G4-d.)

You might also scan the Glossary of Usage (W1), which alerts you to nonstandard words and expressions such as *ain't, could of, hisself, theirselves, them* (meaning "those"), *they* (meaning "their"), *it is* (meaning "there is"), and so on.

W3-d Choose an appropriate level of formality.

In deciding on a level of formality, consider both your subject and your audience. Does the subject demand a dignified treatment, or is a relaxed tone more suitable? Will the audience be put off if you assume too close a relationship with them, or might you alienate them by seeming too distant?

For most college and professional writing, some degree of formality is appropriate. In a letter applying for a job, for example, it is a mistake to sound too breezy and informal.

TOO INFORMAL I'd like to get that receptionist's job you've got in the paper.

MORE FORMAL I would like to apply for the receptionist's position listed in the *Peoria Journal Star*.

Informal writing is appropriate for private letters, business correspondence between close associates, articles in popular magazines, and personal narratives. In such writing, formal language can seem out of place.

▶ Once a pitcher for the Cincinnati Reds, Bob shared with me the
began
secrets of his trade. His lesson ~~commenced~~ with his famous curve
which he threw   ^
ball, ~~implemented~~ by tucking the little finger behind the ball
^
revealed
instead of holding it straight out. Next he ~~elucidated~~ the mysteries
^
of the sucker pitch, a slow ball coming behind a fast windup.

W3-e Avoid sexist language.

Sexist language is language that stereotypes or demeans men or women, usually women. Some sexist language reflects genuine contempt for women: referring to a woman as a "broad," for example, or calling a lawyer a "lady lawyer," or saying in an advertisement, "If our new sports car were a lady, it would get its bottom pinched."

Other forms of sexist language, while they may not suggest conscious sexism, reflect stereotypical thinking: referring to nurses as women and doctors as men, using different conventions when naming or identifying women and men, or assuming that all of one's readers are men.

▶ After the nursing student graduates, *he or* she must face a difficult state

board examination.

▶ Running for city council are Jake Stein, an attorney, and ~~Mrs.~~

Cynthia Jones, a professor of English, ~~and mother of three.~~

▶ If you are a senior government official, your *spouse* ~~wife~~ is required to

he or
report any gifts she receives that are valued at more than $100.

Still other forms of sexist language result from outmoded traditions. The pronouns *he, him,* and *his,* for instance, were traditionally used to refer indefinitely to persons of either sex.

TRADITIONAL   A journalist is stimulated by *his* deadline.

Today, however, such usage is widely viewed as sexist because it excludes women and encourages sex-role stereotyping — the view that men are somehow more suited than women to be journalists, doctors, and so on.

One option, of course, is to substitute a pair of pronouns: *A journalist is stimulated by his or her deadline.* This strategy is fine in small doses, but it generates extra words that become awkward when repeated throughout an essay. A better strategy, many writers have discovered, is simply to write in the plural.

REVISED   *Journalists* are stimulated by *their* deadlines.

Yet another strategy is to revise the sentence so that the problem does not arise.

REVISED   A journalist is stimulated by *a* deadline.

Like the pronouns *he, him,* and *his,* the nouns *man* and *men* were once used indefinitely to refer to persons of either sex. Current usage demands gender-neutral terms instead.

INAPPROPRIATE	APPROPRIATE
chairman	chairperson, moderator, chair, head
clergyman	member of the clergy, minister, pastor
congressman	member of Congress, representative, legislator
fireman	firefighter
foreman	supervisor
mailman	mail carrier, postal worker, letter carrier
mankind	people, humans
manpower	personnel
policeman	police officer
salesman	salesperson, sales associate, salesclerk
to man	to operate, to staff
weatherman	weather forecaster, meteorologist
workman	worker, laborer

W4

Exact language

Two reference works will help you find words to express your meaning exactly: a good dictionary and a book of synonyms and antonyms such as *Roget's International Thesaurus* (see W5).

W4-a Select words with appropriate connotations.

In addition to their strict dictionary meanings (or *denotations*), words have *connotations,* emotional colorings that affect how readers respond to them. The word *steel* denotes "made of or resembling commercial iron that contains carbon," but it also calls up a cluster of images associated with steel, such as the sensation of touching it. These associations give the word its connotations — cold, smooth, unbending.

If the connotation of a word does not seem appropriate for your purpose, your audience, or your subject matter, the word should be changed. When a more appropriate word does not come quickly to mind, consult a dictionary or a thesaurus.

▶ The model was ~~skinny~~ *slender* and fashionable.

The connotation of the word *skinny* is too negative.

▶ As I covered the boats with marsh grass, the ~~perspiration~~ *sweat* I had worked up evaporated in the wind, making the cold morning air even colder.

The term *perspiration* is too dainty for the context, which suggests vigorous exercise.

W4-b Prefer specific, concrete nouns.

Unlike general nouns, which refer to broad classes of things, specific nouns point to definite and particular items. *Film,* for example, names a general class, *science fiction film* names a narrower class, and *Jurassic Park* is more specific still.

Unlike abstract nouns, which refer to qualities and ideas (*justice, beauty, realism, dignity*), concrete nouns point to immediate, often sensate experience and to physical objects (*steeple, asphalt, lilac, stone, garlic*).

Specific, concrete nouns express meaning more vividly than general or abstract ones. Although general and abstract language is sometimes necessary to convey your meaning, ordinarily prefer specific, concrete alternatives.

▶ The senator spoke about the challenges of the future: problems *of famine, pollution, dwindling resources, and arms control.* ~~concerning the environment and world peace.~~

Nouns such as *thing, area, factor,* and *individual* are especially dull and imprecise.

▶ A career in transportation management offers many ~~things.~~ *challenges.*

▶ Try pairing a trainee with an ~~individual with technical experience.~~ *experienced technician.*

W4-c Prefer active verbs.

Active verbs express meaning more emphatically and vigorously than their weaker counterparts — forms of the verb *be* or verbs in the passive voice. Forms of the verb *be* (*be, am, is, are, was, were, being, been*) lack vigor because they convey no action. Verbs in the passive voice lack strength because their subjects receive the action instead of doing it (see B2-b and G2-h).

Although the forms of *be* and passive verbs have legitimate uses, if an active verb can carry your meaning, use it.

> **BE VERB** A surge of power *was* responsible for the destruction of the coolant pumps.

> **PASSIVE** The coolant pumps *were destroyed* by a surge of power.

> **ACTIVE** A surge of power *destroyed* the coolant pumps.

Even among active verbs, some are more active — and therefore more vigorous and colorful — than others. Carefully selected verbs can energize a piece of writing.

> ▶ The goalie crouched low, ~~reached~~ *swept* out his stick, and ~~sent~~ *hooked* the
>
> rebound away from the mouth of the net.

When to replace be *verbs*

Not every *be* verb needs replacing. The forms of *be* (*be, am, is, are, was, were, being, been*) work well when you want to link a subject to a noun that clearly renames it or to an adjective that describes it: *History is a bucket of ashes. Scoundrels are always sociable.* (See B2-b.) And when used as helping verbs before present participles (*is flying, are disappearing*) to express ongoing action, *be* verbs are fine: *Derrick was plowing the field when his wife went into labor.* (See G2-f.)

If using a *be* verb makes a sentence needlessly wordy, however, consider replacing it. Often a phrase following the verb will contain a word (such as *destruction*) that suggests a more vigorous, active alternative (*destroyed*).

> ▶ Burying nuclear waste in Antarctica would ~~be in violation of~~ *violate*
>
> an international treaty.

> *Violate* is less wordy and more vigorous than *be in violation of.*

> *rebelled against*
> ▶ Escaping into the world of drugs, I ~~was rebellious about~~ every
>   ∧
>
> rule set down by my parents.

Rebelled against is more active than *was rebellious about*.

When to replace passive verbs

In the active voice, the subject of the sentence does the action; in the passive, the subject receives the action.

  ACTIVE   Hernando *caught* the fly ball.

  PASSIVE   The fly ball *was caught* by Hernando.

In passive sentences, the actor (in this case *Hernando*) frequently disappears from the sentence: *The fly ball was caught.*

  In most cases, you will want to emphasize the actor, so you should use the active voice. To replace a passive verb with an active alternative, make the actor the subject of the sentence.

> *Lightning struck the transformer,*
> ▶ ~~The transformer was struck by lightning,~~ plunging us into darkness.
>   ∧

The active verb (*struck*) makes the point more forcefully than the passive verb (*was struck*).

  The passive voice is appropriate when you wish to emphasize the receiver of the action or to minimize the importance of the actor. For example, in the sentence about the fly ball, you would choose the active voice if you wanted to emphasize the actor, Hernando: *Hernando caught the fly ball.* But you would choose the passive voice if you wanted to emphasize the fly ball's being caught: *The fly ball was caught by Hernando.* (See also G2-h.)

ESL NOTE: Some speakers of English as a second language avoid the passive voice even when it is appropriate. For advice on transforming an active-voice sentence to the passive, see B2-b.

W4-d Do not misuse words.

If a word is not in your active vocabulary, you may find yourself misusing it, sometimes with embarrassing consequences. When in doubt, check the dictionary.

> *climbing*
> ▶ The fans were ~~migrating~~ up the bleachers in search of good seats.
> ⌃

> ▶ Liu Kwan began his career as a lawyer, but now he is a real estate
> *mogul.*
> ~~mongrel.~~
> ⌃

> *permeated*
> ▶ Drugs have so ~~diffused~~ our culture that they touch all segments of
> ⌃
>
> our society.

Be especially alert for misused word forms — using a noun such as *absence, significance,* or *persistence,* for example, when your meaning requires the adjective *absent, significant,* or *persistent.*

> *persistent*
> ▶ Most dieters are not ~~persistence~~ enough to make a permanent change
> ⌃
>
> in their eating habits.

W4-e Use standard idioms.

Idioms are speech forms that follow no easily specified rules. The British say "Maria went *to hospital,*" an idiom strange to American ears, which are accustomed to hearing *the* in front of *hospital.* Native speakers of a language seldom have problems with idioms, but prepositions sometimes cause trouble, especially when they follow certain verbs and adjectives. When in doubt, consult a good desk dictionary: Look up the word preceding the troublesome preposition.

UNIDIOMATIC	IDIOMATIC
abide with (a decision)	abide by (a decision)
according with	according to
angry at (a person)	angry with (a person)
capable to	capable of
comply to	comply with
desirous to	desirous of
different than	different from
intend on doing	intend to do
off of	off
plan on doing	plan to do
preferable than	preferable to
prior than	prior to
superior than	superior to
sure and	sure to
try and	try to
type of a	type of

ESL NOTE: Because idioms follow no particular rules, you must learn them individually. You may find it helpful to keep a list of idioms that you frequently encounter in conversation and in reading.

W4-f Avoid clichés.

The pioneer who first announced that he had "slept like a log" no doubt amused his companions with a fresh and unlikely comparison. Today, however, that comparison is a cliché, a saying that has lost its dazzle from overuse. No longer can it surprise.

To see just how predictable clichés are, put your hand over the right-hand column below and then finish the phrases on the left.

cool as a	cucumber
beat around	the bush
blind as a	bat
busy as a	bee
crystal	clear
dead as a	doornail
out of the frying pan	into the fire
light as a	feather
like a bull	in a china shop
playing with	fire
nutty as a	fruitcake
selling like	hotcakes
starting out at the bottom	of the ladder
water over the	dam
white as a	sheet, ghost
avoid clichés like the	plague

The cure for clichés is frequently simple: Just delete them. When this won't work, try adding some element of surprise. One woman, for example, who had written that she had butterflies in her stomach, revised her cliché like this:

If all of the action in my stomach is caused by butterflies, there must be a horde of them, with horseshoes on.

The image of butterflies wearing horseshoes is fresh and unlikely, not dully predictable like the original cliché.

W4-g Use figures of speech with care.

A figure of speech is an expression that uses words imaginatively (rather than literally) to make abstract ideas concrete. Most often, figures of speech compare two seemingly unlike things to reveal surprising similarities.

In a *simile,* the writer makes the comparison explicitly, usually by introducing it with *like* or *as:* "By the time cotton had to be picked, grandfather's neck was as red as the clay he plowed." In a *metaphor,* the *like* or *as* is omitted, and the comparison is implied. For example, in the Old Testament Song of Solomon, a young woman compares the man she loves to a fruit tree: "With great delight I sat in his shadow, and his fruit was sweet to my taste."

Writers sometimes use figures of speech without thinking carefully about the images they evoke. This can result in a *mixed metaphor,* the combination of two or more images that don't make sense together.

▶ Crossing Utah's salt flats in his new Corvette, my father flew
   at jet speed.
   ~~under a full head of steam.~~
   ^

▶ Our office had decided to put all controversial issues on a back

   burner, ~~in a holding pattern.~~
   ^

W5

The dictionary and thesaurus

W5-a The dictionary

A good desk dictionary — such as *The American Heritage Dictionary of the English Language, The Random House College Dictionary,* or *Merriam-Webster's Collegiate* or *New World Dictionary of the American Language* — is an indispensable writer's aid.

A sample dictionary entry, taken from *The American Heritage Dictionary,* appears on page 116. Labels show where various kinds of information about a word can be found in that dictionary.

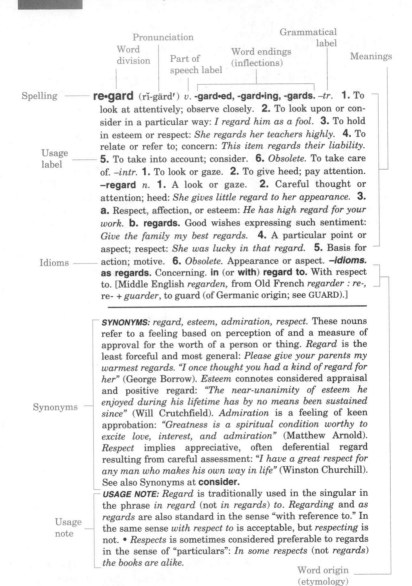

Pronunciation

Word division

Part of speech label

Word endings (inflections)

Grammatical label

Meanings

Spelling

re·gard (rĭ-gärd′) *v.* **-gard·ed, -gard·ing, -gards.** *–tr.* **1.** To look at attentively; observe closely. **2.** To look upon or consider in a particular way: *I regard him as a fool.* **3.** To hold in esteem or respect: *She regards her teachers highly.* **4.** To relate or refer to; concern: *This item regards their liability.* **5.** To take into account; consider. **6.** *Obsolete.* To take care of. *–intr.* **1.** To look or gaze. **2.** To give heed; pay attention. **–regard** *n.* **1.** A look or gaze. **2.** Careful thought or attention; heed: *She gives little regard to her appearance.* **3.** **a.** Respect, affection, or esteem: *He has high regard for your work.* **b. regards.** Good wishes expressing such sentiment: *Give the family my best regards.* **4.** A particular point or aspect; respect: *She was lucky in that regard.* **5.** Basis for action; motive. **6.** *Obsolete.* Appearance or aspect. *–idioms.* **as regards.** Concerning. **in** (or **with**) **regard to.** With respect to. [Middle English *regarden,* from Old French *regarder : re-,* re- + *guarder,* to guard (of Germanic origin; see GUARD).]

Usage label

Idioms

SYNONYMS: *regard, esteem, admiration, respect.* These nouns refer to a feeling based on perception of and a measure of approval for the worth of a person or thing. *Regard* is the least forceful and most general: *Please give your parents my warmest regards.* "*I once thought you had a kind of regard for her*" (George Borrow). *Esteem* connotes considered appraisal and positive regard: "*The near-unanimity of esteem he enjoyed during his lifetime has by no means been sustained since*" (Will Crutchfield). *Admiration* is a feeling of keen approbation: "*Greatness is a spiritual condition worthy to excite love, interest, and admiration*" (Matthew Arnold). *Respect* implies appreciative, often deferential regard resulting from careful assessment: "*I have a great respect for any man who makes his own way in life*" (Winston Churchill). See also Synonyms at **consider.**

Synonyms

USAGE NOTE: *Regard* is traditionally used in the singular in the phrase *in regard* (not *in regards*) *to. Regarding* and *as regards* are also standard in the sense "with reference to." In the same sense *with respect to* is acceptable, but *respecting* is not. • *Respects* is sometimes considered preferable to *regards* in the sense of "particulars": *In some respects* (not *regards*) *the books are alike.*

Usage note

Word origin (etymology)

Spelling, word division, pronunciation

The main entry (*re·gard* in the sample entry) shows the correct spelling of the word. When there are two correct spellings of a word (as in *collectible, collectable,* for example), both are given, with the preferred spelling usually appearing first.

The main entry also shows how the word is divided into syllables. The dot between *re* and *gard* separates the word's two syllables. When a word is compound, the main entry shows how to write it: as one word (*crossroad*), as a hyphenated word (*cross-stitch*), or as two words (*cross section*).

The word's pronunciation is given just after the main entry. The accents indicate which syllables are stressed; the other marks are explained in the dictionary's pronunciation key. In some dictionaries this key appears at the bottom of every page or every other page.

Word endings and grammatical labels

When a word takes endings to indicate grammatical functions (called *inflections*), the endings are listed in boldface, as with *-garded, -garding,* and *-gards* in the sample entry.

Labels for the parts of speech and for other grammatical terms are abbreviated. The most commonly used abbreviations are these:

n.	noun	adj.	adjective
pl.	plural	adv.	adverb
sing.	singular	pron.	pronoun
v.	verb	prep.	preposition
tr.	transitive verb	conj.	conjunction
int.	intransitive verb	interj.	interjection

Meanings, word origin, synonyms, and antonyms

Each meaning for the word is given a number. Occasionally a word's use is illustrated in a quoted sentence.

Sometimes a word can be used as more than one part of speech (*regard,* for instance, can be used as either a verb or a noun). In such a case, all the meanings for one part of speech are given before all the meanings for another, as in the sample entry. The entry also gives idiomatic uses of the word.

The origin of the word, called its *etymology,* appears in brackets after all the meanings (in some dictionaries it appears before the meanings).

Synonyms, words similar in meaning to the main entry, are frequently listed. In the sample entry, the dictionary draws distinctions in meaning among the various synonyms. Antonyms, which do not appear in the sample entry, are words having a meaning opposite from that of the main entry.

Usage

Usage labels indicate when, where, or under what conditions a particular meaning for a word is appropriately used. Common labels are *informal* (or *colloquial*), *slang, nonstandard, dialect, obsolete, archaic, poetic,* and *British.* In the sample entry, two meanings of *regard* are labeled *obsolete* because they are no longer in use.

Dictionaries sometimes include usage notes as well. In the sample entry, the dictionary offers advice on several uses of *regard* not specifically covered by the meanings. Such advice is based on the opinions of many experts and on actual usage in current magazines, newspapers, and books.

W5-b The thesaurus

When you are looking for just the right word, you may want to consult a book of synonyms and antonyms such as *Roget's International Thesaurus* (or its software equivalent). In the back of *Roget's* is an index to the groups of synonyms that make up the bulk of the book. Look up the adjective *still,* for example, and you will find references to lists containing the words *dead, motionless, silent,* and *tranquil.* If *tranquil* is close to the word you have in mind, turn to its section in the front of the book. There you will find a long list of synonyms, including such words as *quiet, quiescent, reposeful, calm, pacific, halcyon, placid,* and *unruffled.* Unless your vocabulary is better than average, the list will contain words you've never heard of or with which you are only vaguely familiar. Whenever you are tempted to use one of these words, look it up in the dictionary first to avoid misusing it.

On discovering the thesaurus, many writers use it for the wrong reasons, so a word of caution is in order. Do not turn to a thesaurus in search of exotic, fancy words — such as *halcyon* — with which to embellish your essays. Look instead for words that express your meaning exactly. Most of the time these words will be familiar to both you and your readers. *Tranquil* was probably the word you were looking for all along.

G

Grammatical
Sentences

G

Grammatical Sentences

G1

Subject-verb agreement

In the present tense, verbs agree with their subjects in number (singular or plural) and in person (first, second, or third). If the subject is third-person singular, use the *-s* form of the verb, such as *gives, has,* or *does.* For all other subjects use the base form of the verb, such as *give, have,* or *do.*

PRESENT-TENSE FORMS OF *GIVE* (A TYPICAL VERB)

	SINGULAR	PLURAL
FIRST PERSON	I give	we give
SECOND PERSON	you give	you give
THIRD PERSON	he/she/it gives	they give
	Alison gives	parents give

PRESENT-TENSE FORMS OF *HAVE*		PRESENT-TENSE FORMS OF *DO*	
I have	we have	I do	we do
you have	you have	you do	you do
he/she/it has	they have	he/she/it does	they do

The verb *be* varies from this pattern, and unlike any other verb, it has special forms in both the present and the past tense.

PRESENT-TENSE FORMS OF *BE*		PAST-TENSE FORMS OF *BE*	
I am	we are	I was	we were
you are	you are	you were	you were
he/she/it is	they are	he/she/it was	they were

Speakers of standard English know by ear that *he gives, she has,* and *it doesn't* (not *he give, she have,* and *it don't*) are the standard forms. For such speakers, problems with subject-verb agreement arise only in certain tricky situations, which are detailed in this section. If you don't trust your ear, consult the models on this page when in doubt as to the correct form. (See also G2-c.)

G1-a Make the verb agree with its subject, not with a word that comes between.

Word groups often come between the subject and the verb. Such word groups, usually modifying the subject, may contain a noun that at first appears to be the subject. By mentally stripping away such modifiers, you can isolate the noun that is in fact the subject.

The *tulips* in the pot on the balcony *need* watering.

▶ High levels of air pollution causes damage to the respiratory tract.

The subject is *levels,* not *pollution.* Strip away the phrase *of air pollution* to hear the correct verb: *levels cause.*

costs
▶ A good set of golf clubs cost about eight hundred dollars.

The subject is *set,* not *clubs.* Strip away the phrase *of golf clubs* to hear the correct verb: *set costs.*

NOTE: Phrases beginning with the prepositions *as well as, in addition to, accompanied by, together with,* and *along with* do not make a singular subject plural.

was
▶ The governor, as well as his press secretary, were shot.

To emphasize that two people were shot, the writer could use *and* instead: *The governor and his press secretary were shot.*

G1-b Treat most compound subjects connected by *and* as plural.

A subject with two or more parts is said to be compound. If the parts are connected by *and,* the subject is nearly always plural.

Leon and *Jan* often *jog* together.

have
▶ Jill's natural ability and her desire to help others has led to a

career in the ministry.

EXCEPTIONS: When the parts of the subject form a single unit or when they refer to the same person or thing, treat the subject as singular.

Strawberries and cream was a last-minute addition to the menu.

Sue's friend and adviser was surprised by her decision.

When a compound subject is preceded by *each* or *every,* treat the subject as singular.

> Each tree, shrub, and vine needs to be sprayed.

G1-c With compound subjects connected by *or* or *nor,* make the verb agree with the part of the subject nearer to the verb.

> A driver's *license* or credit *card is* required.

> A driver's *license* or two credit *cards are* required.

> ▸ If a relative or neighbor ~~are~~ abusing a child, notify the police.
>   *is*

> ▸ Neither the professor nor his assistants ~~was~~ able to solve the
>   *were*
>   mystery of the eerie glow in the laboratory.

G1-d Treat most indefinite pronouns as singular.

Indefinite pronouns refer to nonspecific persons or things. Even though the following indefinite pronouns may seem to have plural meanings, treat them as singular in formal English: *anybody, anyone, each, either, everybody, everyone, everything, neither, none, no one, someone, something.*

> *Everyone* on the team *supports* the coach.

> ▸ Each of the furrows ~~have~~ been seeded.
>   *has*

> ▸ Everybody who signed up for the ski trip ~~were~~ taking lessons.
>   *was*

The indefinite pronouns *none* and *neither* are considered singular when used alone.

> Three rooms are available; *none has* a private bath.

> *Neither is* able to attend.

When these pronouns are followed by prepositional phrases with a plural meaning, however, usage varies. Some experts insist on treating the pronouns as singular, but many writers disagree. It is safer to treat them as singular.

> *None* of these trades *requires* a college education.

> *Neither* of those pejoratives *fits* Professor Brady.

A few indefinite pronouns (*all, any, some*) may be singular or plural depending on the noun or pronoun they refer to.

> *Some* of the *lemonade has* disappeared.

> *Some* of the *rocks were* slippery.

G1-e Treat collective nouns as singular unless the meaning is clearly plural.

Collective nouns such as *jury, committee, audience, crowd, class, troop, family,* and *couple* name a class or a group. In American English collective nouns are usually treated as singular: They emphasize the group as a unit. Occasionally, when there is some reason to draw attention to the individual members of the group, a collective noun may be treated as plural. (See also G3-a.)

> SINGULAR   The *class respects* the teacher.

> PLURAL   The *class are* debating among themselves.

To underscore the notion of individuality in the second sentence, many writers would add a clearly plural noun such as *members: The members of the class are debating among themselves.*

> *meets*
> ► The scout troop ~~meet~~ in our basement on Tuesdays.

> The troop as a whole meets in the basement; there is no reason to draw attention to its individual members.

> *were*
> ► A young couple ~~was~~ arguing about politics while holding hands.

> The meaning is clearly plural. Only individuals can argue and hold hands.

NOTE: The phrase *the number* is treated as singular, *a number* as plural.

SINGULAR *The number* of school-age children *is* declining.

PLURAL *A number* of children *are* attending the wedding.

NOTE: When units of measurement are used collectively, treat them as singular; when they refer to individual persons or things, treat them as plural.

SINGULAR *Three-fourths* of the pie *has* been eaten.

PLURAL *One-fourth* of the drivers *were* drunk.

G1-f Make the verb agree with its subject even when the subject follows the verb.

Verbs ordinarily follow subjects. When this normal order is reversed, it is easy to become confused. Sentences beginning with *there is* or *there are* (or *there was* or *there were*) are inverted; the subject follows the verb.

There *are* surprisingly few *children* in our neighborhood.

Occasionally you may decide to invert a sentence for variety or effect. When you do so, check to make sure that your subject and verb agree.

▶ At the back of the room ~~is~~ *are* a small aquarium and an enormous

terrarium.

The subject *aquarium and terrarium* is plural, so the verb must be *are*.

G1-g Make the verb agree with its subject, not with a subject complement.

One sentence pattern in English consists of a subject, a linking verb, and a subject complement: *Jack is an attorney.* (See B2-b.) Because the subject complement names or describes the subject, it is sometimes mistaken for the subject.

▶ A tent and a sleeping bag ~~is~~ *are* the required equipment.

Tent and bag is the subject, not *equipment.*

▶ A major force in today's economy ~~are~~ *is* women — as earners,

consumers, and investors.

Force is the subject, not *women.* If the correct sentence seems awkward,
you can make *women* the subject: *Women are a major force.* . . .

G1-h *Who, which,* and *that* take verbs that agree with their antecedents.

Like most pronouns, the relative pronouns *who, which,* and *that*
have antecedents, nouns or pronouns to which they refer. Relative
pronouns used as subjects of subordinate clauses take verbs that
agree with their antecedents. (See B3-e.)

Take a *suit that travels* well.

Problems arise with the constructions *one of the* and *only one of
the.* As a rule, treat *one of the* constructions as plural, *only one of the*
constructions as singular.

▶ Our ability to use language is one of the things that sets us apart

from animals.

The antecedent of *that* is *things,* not *one.* Several things set us apart
from animals.

▶ Carmen is the only one of the applicants who ~~have~~ *has* the ability to

step into this position.

The antecedent of *who* is *one,* not *applicants.* Only one applicant has
the ability to step into the position.

G1-i Words such as *athletics, economics, mathematics, physics, statistics, measles,* and *news* are usually singular, despite their plural form.

▶ Statistics ~~are~~ *is* among the most difficult courses in our program.

EXCEPTION: When they describe separate items rather than a collective body of knowledge, words such as *athletics, mathematics, physics,* and *statistics* are plural: *The statistics on school retention rates are impressive.*

G1-j Titles of works and words mentioned as words are singular.

> *describes*
> ▶ *Lost Cities* ~~describe~~ the discoveries of many ancient civilizations.
>   ^

> *is*
> ▶ *Controlled substances* ~~are~~ a euphemism for illegal drugs.
>   ^

G2

Other problems with verbs

The verb is the heart of the sentence, so it is important to get it right. Section G1 deals with the problem of subject-verb agreement. This section describes a number of other potential problems with verbs:

a. irregular verb forms (such as *drive, drove, driven*)
b. *lie* and *lay*
c. *-s* (or *-es*) endings on verbs
d. *-ed* endings on verbs
e. omitted verbs
f. tense
g. subjunctive mood
h. active versus passive voice

ESL NOTE: If English is not your native language, see also T2, Special Problems with Verbs.

G2-a Choose standard English forms of irregular verbs.

Except for the verb *be,* all verbs in English have five forms. The following list gives the five forms and provides a sample sentence in which each might appear.

BASE FORM	Usually I (*walk, ride*).
PAST TENSE	Yesterday I (*walked, rode*).
PAST PARTICIPLE	I have (*walked, ridden*) many times before.
PRESENT PARTICIPLE	I am (*walking, riding*) right now.
-S FORM	He/she/it usually (*walks, rides*).

For regular verbs, such as *walk,* the past-tense and past-participle forms are the same (ending in *-ed* or *-d*), so there is no danger of confusion. This is not true, however, for irregular verbs such as *ride.* Writers sometimes confuse the past-tense and past-participle forms of irregular verbs, producing nonstandard sentences.

NONSTANDARD	Have you rode on the new subway?
STANDARD	Have you ridden on the new subway?

Choosing standard English forms

The past-tense form, which expresses action that occurred entirely in the past, never has a helping verb. (For a complete list of helping verbs, see B1-c.) The past participle is used with a helping verb — either with *has, have,* or *had* to form one of the perfect tenses or with *be, am, is, are, was, were, being,* or *been* to form the passive voice.

PAST TENSE	Last July, we *went* to Paris.
PAST PARTICIPLE	We have *gone* to Paris twice.

When you aren't sure which verb form to choose (*went* or *gone, began* or *begun,* and so on), consult the list of common irregular verbs that starts on page 129. Choose the past-tense form if the verb in your sentence doesn't have a helping verb; use the past-participle form if it does.

▶ Yesterday we ~~seen~~ *saw* an unidentified flying object.

▶ The reality of the situation ~~sunk~~ *sank* in.

The past-tense forms *saw* and *sank* are required.

▶ The truck was apparently ~~stole~~ *stolen* while the driver ate lunch.

▶ The teacher asked Dwain if he had d̶i̶d̶ his homework.
<small>done</small>
<small>^</small>

Because of the helping verbs *was* and *had,* the past-participle forms *stolen* and *done* are required.

Common irregular verbs

When in doubt about the standard English forms of irregular verbs, consult the following list or look up the base form of the verb in the dictionary, which also lists any irregular forms. (If no additional forms are listed in the dictionary, the verb is regular, not irregular.)

BASE FORM	PAST TENSE	PAST PARTICIPLE
arise	arose	arisen
awake	awoke, awaked	awaked, awoke
be	was, were	been
beat	beat	beaten, beat
become	became	become
begin	began	begun
bend	bent	bent
bite	bit	bitten, bit
blow	blew	blown
break	broke	broken
bring	brought	brought
build	built	built
burst	burst	burst
buy	bought	bought
catch	caught	caught
choose	chose	chosen
cling	clung	clung
come	came	come
cost	cost	cost
deal	dealt	dealt
dig	dug	dug
dive	dived, dove	dived
do	did	done
drag	dragged	dragged
draw	drew	drawn
dream	dreamed, dreamt	dreamed, dreamt
drink	drank	drunk
drive	drove	driven
eat	ate	eaten
fall	fell	fallen
fight	fought	fought
find	found	found

BASE FORM	PAST TENSE	PAST PARTICIPLE
fly	flew	flown
forget	forgot	forgotten, forgot
freeze	froze	frozen
get	got	gotten, got
give	gave	given
go	went	gone
grow	grew	grown
hang (suspend)	hung	hung
hang (execute)	hanged	hanged
have	had	had
hear	heard	heard
hide	hid	hidden
hurt	hurt	hurt
keep	kept	kept
know	knew	known
lay (put)	laid	laid
lead	led	led
lend	lent	lent
let (allow)	let	let
lie (recline)	lay	lain
lose	lost	lost
make	made	made
prove	proved	proved, proven
read	read	read
ride	rode	ridden
ring	rang	rung
rise (get up)	rose	risen
run	ran	run
say	said	said
see	saw	seen
send	sent	sent
set (place)	set	set
shake	shook	shaken
shoot	shot	shot
shrink	shrank	shrunk, shrunken
sing	sang	sung
sink	sank	sunk
sit (be seated)	sat	sat
slay	slew	slain
sleep	slept	slept
speak	spoke	spoken
spin	spun	spun
spring	sprang	sprung
stand	stood	stood
steal	stole	stolen

BASE FORM	PAST TENSE	PAST PARTICIPLE
sting	stung	stung
strike	struck	struck, stricken
swear	swore	sworn
swim	swam	swum
swing	swung	swung
take	took	taken
teach	taught	taught
throw	threw	thrown
wake	woke, waked	waked, woken
wear	wore	worn
wring	wrung	wrung
write	wrote	written

G2-b Distinguish among the forms of *lie* and *lay*.

Writers and speakers frequently confuse the various forms of *lie* (meaning "to recline or rest on a surface") and *lay* (meaning "to put or place something"). *Lie* is an intransitive verb; it does not take a direct object: *The tax forms lie on the table.* The verb *lay* is transitive; it takes a direct object: *Please lay the tax forms on the table.* (See B2-b.)

In addition to confusing the meaning of *lie* and *lay,* writers and speakers are often unfamiliar with the standard English forms of these verbs.

BASE FORM	PAST TENSE	PAST PARTICIPLE	PRESENT PARTICIPLE
lie	lay	lain	lying
lay	laid	laid	laying

▶ Sue was so exhausted that she l̶a̶i̶d̶ *lay* down for a nap.

The past-tense form of *lie* ("to recline") is *lay.*

▶ Mary l̶a̶y̶ *laid* the baby on my lap.

The past-tense form of *lay* ("to place") is *laid.*

▶ My grandmother's letters were l̶a̶y̶i̶n̶g̶ *lying* in the corner of the chest.

The present participle of *lie* ("to rest on a surface") is *lying.*

G2-c Use *-s* (or *-es*) endings on present-tense verbs that have third-person singular subjects.

When the subject of a sentence is third-person singular, its verb takes an *-s* or *-es* ending in the present tense. (See also G1.)

	SINGULAR		PLURAL	
FIRST PERSON	I	know	we	know
SECOND PERSON	you	know	you	know
THIRD PERSON	he/she/it	knows	they	know
	child	knows	parents	know
	everyone	knows		

All singular nouns (such as *child*) and the pronouns *he, she,* and *it* are third-person singular; indefinite pronouns (such as *everyone*) are also third-person singular.

In nonstandard speech, the *-s* ending required by standard English is sometimes omitted.

> ▶ Sulfur dioxide ~~turn~~ leaves yellow, ~~dissolve~~ marble, and ~~eat~~ away
>
> iron and steel.

(turns) *(dissolves)* *(eats)*

The subject *sulfur dioxide* is third-person singular, so the verbs must end in *-s*.

CAUTION: Do not add the *-s* ending to the verb if the subject is not third-person singular.

> ▶ I prepares program specifications and logic diagrams.

> ▶ The dirt floors requires continual sweeping.

The subject *I* is first-person singular. The subject *floors* is third-person plural.

In nonstandard speech, the *-s* verb form *has, does,* or *doesn't* is sometimes replaced with *have, do,* or *don't*. In standard English, use *has, does,* or *doesn't* with a third-person singular subject. (See also G1.)

> *has*
> ▶ This respected musician always ~~have~~ a message to convey in his
>   ⌃
>
> work.

> *Does*
> ▶ ~~Do~~ she know the correct procedure for the experiment?
>   ⌃

> *doesn't*
> ▶ My uncle ~~don't~~ want to change jobs right now.
>   ⌃

G2-d Do not omit *-ed* endings on verbs.

Speakers who do not fully pronounce *-ed* endings sometimes omit them unintentionally in writing. Failure to pronounce *-ed* endings is common in many dialects and in informal speech even in standard English. In the following frequently used words and phrases, for example, the *-ed* ending is not always fully pronounced.

advised	developed	prejudiced	stereotyped
asked	fixed	pronounced	used to
concerned	frightened	supposed to	

When a verb is regular, both the past tense and the past participle are formed by adding *-ed* to the base form of the verb.

Past tense

Use an *-ed* or *-d* ending to express the past tense of regular verbs. The past tense is used when the action occurred entirely in the past.

> *fixed*
> ▶ Over the weekend, Ed ~~fix~~ his brother's skateboard and tuned up
>   ⌃
>
> his mother's 1955 Thunderbird.

> *advised*
> ▶ Last summer my counselor ~~advise~~ me to ask my family for help.
>   ⌃

Past participles

Past participles are used in three ways: (1) following *have, has,* or *had* to form one of the perfect tenses; (2) following *be, am, is, are, was, were, being,* or *been* to form the passive voice; and (3) as adjectives modifying nouns or pronouns. The perfect tenses are listed on page 136, and the passive voice is discussed in G2-h. For a discussion of participles functioning as adjectives, see B3-b.

▶ Robin has ~~ask~~ *asked* me to go to California with her.

Has asked is present perfect tense (*have* or *has* followed by a past participle).

▶ Though it is not a new phenomenon, wife battery is ~~publicize~~ *publicized*
more frequently than before.

Is publicized is in the passive voice (a form of *be* followed by a past participle).

▶ It took all of Daryl's strength to control the ~~frighten~~ *frightened* horse.

The past participle *frightened* functions as an adjective modifying the noun *horse*.

G2-e Do not omit needed verbs.

Although standard English allows some linking verbs and helping verbs to be contracted, at least in informal contexts, it does not allow them to be omitted.

Linking verbs, used to link subjects to subject complements, are frequently a form of *be: be, am, is, are, was, were, being, been.* (See B2-b.) Some of these forms may be contracted (*I'm, she's, we're*), but they should not be omitted altogether.

▶ Although he has been in two serious accidents this year, David
isn't a bad driver. He *is* just unlucky.

Helping verbs, used with main verbs, include forms of *be, do,* and *have* or the words *can, will, shall, could, would, should, may, might,* and *must.* (See B1-c.) Some helping verbs may be contracted (*he's leaving, we'll celebrate, they've been told*), but they should not be omitted altogether.

▶ Do you know someone who *would* be good for the job?

ESL NOTE: Speakers of English as a second language sometimes have problems with omitted verbs. See T2-e.

G2-f Choose the appropriate verb tense.

Tenses indicate the time of an action in relation to the time of the speaking or writing about that action.

The most common problem with tenses — shifting from one tense to another — is discussed in E4-b. Other problems with tenses are detailed in this section, after the following survey of tenses.

Survey of tenses

Tenses are classified as present, past, and future, with simple, perfect, and progressive forms for each.

The simple tenses indicate relatively simple time relations. The simple present tense is used primarily for actions occurring at the time of the speaking or for actions occurring regularly. The simple past tense is used for actions completed in the past. The simple future tense is used for actions that will occur in the future. In the following table, the simple tenses are given for the regular verb *walk,* the irregular verb *ride,* and the highly irregular verb *be.*

SIMPLE PRESENT

SINGULAR		PLURAL	
I	walk, ride, am	we	walk, ride, are
you	walk, ride, are	you	walk, ride, are
he/she/it	walks, rides, is	they	walk, ride, are

SIMPLE PAST

SINGULAR		PLURAL	
I	walked, rode, was	we	walked, rode, were
you	walked, rode, were	you	walked, rode, were
he/she/it	walked, rode, was	they	walked, rode, were

SIMPLE FUTURE
I, you, he/she/it, we, they   will walk, ride, be

More complex time relations are indicated by the perfect tenses. A verb in one of the perfect tenses (a form of *have* plus the past participle) expresses an action that was or will be completed at the time of another action.

PRESENT PERFECT
I, you, we, they   have walked, ridden, been
he/she/it   has walked, ridden, been

PAST PERFECT
I, you, he/she/it, we, they   had walked, ridden, been

FUTURE PERFECT
I, you, he/she/it, we, they   will have walked, ridden, been

The simple and perfect tenses just discussed have progressive forms that describe actions in progress. A progressive verb consists of a form of *be* followed by a present participle.

PRESENT PROGRESSIVE
I   am walking, riding, being
he/she/it   is walking, riding, being
you, we, they   are walking, riding, being

PAST PROGRESSIVE
I, he/she/it   was walking, riding, being
you, we, they   were walking, riding, being

FUTURE PROGRESSIVE
I, you, he/she/it, we, they   will be walking, riding, being

PRESENT PERFECT PROGRESSIVE
I, you, we, they   have been walking, riding, being
he/she/it   has been walking, riding, being

PAST PERFECT PROGRESSIVE
I, you, we, they   had been walking, riding, being

FUTURE PERFECT PROGRESSIVE
I, you, he/she/it, we, they   will have been walking, riding, being

---

ESL NOTE: The progressive forms are not normally used with mental activity verbs such as *believe*. See T2-a.

Special uses of the present tense

Use the present tense when expressing general truths, when writing about literature, and when quoting, summarizing, or paraphrasing an author's views.

General truths or scientific principles should appear in the present tense, unless such principles have been disproved.

> ▶ Galileo taught that the earth ~~revolved~~ around the sun.
>   *revolves*

Since Galileo's teaching has not been discredited, the verb should be in the present tense. The following sentence, however, is acceptable: *Ptolemy taught that the sun revolved around the earth.*

When writing about a work of literature, you may be tempted to use the past tense. The convention, however, is to describe fictional events in the present tense.

> ▶ In Masuji Ibuse's *Black Rain,* a child ~~reached~~ for a pomegranate
>   *reaches*
> in his mother's garden, and a moment later he ~~was~~ dead, killed by
>   *is*
> the blast of the atomic bomb.

When you are quoting, summarizing, or paraphrasing the author of a nonliterary work, use present-tense verbs such as *writes, reports, asserts,* and so on. (See page 265 for a more complete list.) This convention is followed even when the author is dead.

> ▶ Baron Bowan of Colwood ~~wrote~~ that a metaphysician is "one who goes
>   *writes*
> into a dark cellar at midnight without a light, looking for a black cat
> that is not there."

EXCEPTION: When you are documenting a paper with the APA (American Psychological Association) style of in-text citations, which include a date after the author's name, use past-tense verbs such as *reported* or *demonstrated* or present perfect verbs such as *has reported* or *has demonstrated.*

E. Wilson (1994) reported that positive reinforcement alone was a less effective teaching technique than a mixture of positive reinforcement and constructive criticism.

The past perfect tense

The past perfect tense consists of a past participle preceded by *had* (*had worked, had gone*). This tense is used for an action already completed by the time of another past action or for an action already completed at some specific past time.

> Everyone *had spoken* by the time I arrived.

> Everyone *had spoken* by 10:00 A.M.

Writers sometimes use the simple past tense when they should use the past perfect.

▶ We built our cabin high on a pine knoll, forty feet above an
  had been
  abandoned quarry that .was flooded in 1920 to create a lake.
                       ^

The building of the cabin and the flooding of the quarry both occurred in the past, but the flooding was completed before the time of building.

                                                    had
▶ By the time we arrived at the party, the guest of honor left.
                                                         ^

The past perfect tense is needed because the action of leaving was completed at a specific past time (by the time we arrived).

Some writers tend to overuse the past perfect tense. Do not use the past perfect if two past actions occurred at the same time.

▶ When we arrived in Paris, Pauline h̶a̶d̶ met us at the train station.

Sequence of tenses with infinitives and participles

An infinitive is the base form of a verb preceded by *to*. (See B3-b.) Use the present infinitive to show action at the same time as or later than the action of the verb in the sentence.

              raise
▶ The club had hoped to h̶a̶v̶e̶ ̶r̶a̶i̶s̶e̶d̶ a thousand dollars by April 1.
                      ^

The action expressed in the infinitive (*to raise*) occurred later than the action of the sentence's verb (*had hoped*).

Use the perfect form of an infinitive (*to have* followed by the past participle) for an action occurring earlier than that of the verb in the sentence.

             have joined
▶ Dan would like to j̶o̶i̶n̶ the navy, but he did not pass the physical.
                   ^

The liking occurs in the present; the joining would have occurred in the past.

Like the tense of an infinitive, the tense of a participle is also governed by the tense of the sentence's verb. Use the present participle (ending in *-ing*) for an action occurring at the same time as that of the sentence's verb.

Hiking the Appalachian Trail in early spring, we spotted many wildflowers.

Use the past participle (such as *given* or *helped*) or the present perfect participle (*having* plus the past participle) for an action occurring before that of the verb.

Discovered off the coast of Florida, the ship yielded many treasures.

Having worked her way through college, Lee graduated debt-free.

G2-g Use the subjunctive mood in the few contexts that require it.

There are three moods in English: the *indicative,* used for facts, opinions, and questions; the *imperative,* used for orders or advice; and the *subjunctive,* used in certain contexts to express wishes, requests, or conditions contrary to fact. Of these moods, the subjunctive is most likely to cause problems for writers.

Forms of the subjunctive

In the subjunctive mood, present-tense verbs do not change form to indicate the number and person of the subject (see G1). Instead, the subjunctive uses the base form of the verb (*be, drive, employ*) with all subjects.

It is important that you *be* [not *are*] prepared for the interview.

We asked that she *drive* [not *drives*] more slowly.

Also, in the subjunctive mood, there is only one past-tense form of *be: were* (never *was*).

If I *were* [not *was*] you, I'd proceed more cautiously.

Uses of the subjunctive

The subjunctive mood appears in only a few contexts: in contrary-to-fact clauses beginning with *if* or expressing a wish; in *that* clauses following verbs such as *ask, insist, recommend, request,* and *suggest;* and in certain set expressions.

IN CONTRARY-TO-FACT CLAUSES BEGINNING WITH *IF*   When a subordinate clause beginning with *if* expresses a condition contrary to fact, use the subjunctive mood.

> *were*
> ▶ If I ~~was~~ a member of Congress, I would vote for that bill.
>   ^

>   *were*
> ▶ We could be less cautious if Jake ~~was~~ more trustworthy.
>   ^

The verbs in these sentences express conditions that do not exist: The writer is not a member of Congress, and Jake is not trustworthy.

Do not use the subjunctive mood in *if* clauses expressing conditions that exist or may exist.

If Marjorie *wins* the contest, she will leave for Barcelona in June.

IN CONTRARY-TO-FACT CLAUSES EXPRESSING A WISH   In formal English the subjunctive is used in clauses expressing a wish or desire; in informal speech, however, the indicative is more commonly used.

FORMAL   I wish that Dr. Kurtinitis *were* my professor.

INFORMAL   I wish that Dr. Kurtinitis *was* my professor.

IN *THAT* CLAUSES FOLLOWING VERBS SUCH AS *ASK, INSIST, RECOMMEND, REQUEST,* AND *SUGGEST*   Because requests have not yet become reality, they are expressed in the subjunctive mood.

>   *be*
> ▶ Professor Moore insists that her students ~~are~~ on time.
>   ^

>   *file*
> ▶ We recommend that Lambert ~~files~~ form 1050 soon.
>   ^

IN CERTAIN SET EXPRESSIONS   The subjunctive mood, once more widely used in English, remains in certain set expressions: *Be that as it may, as it were, come rain or shine, far be it from me,* and so on.

G2-h Use the active voice unless you have a good reason for choosing the passive.

Transitive verbs (verbs that take a direct object) appear in either the active or the passive voice. (See B2-b.) In the active voice, the subject of the sentence does the action; in the passive, the subject receives the action. Although both voices are grammatically correct, the active voice is usually more effective because it is simpler and more direct. (See also W4-c.)

ACTIVE The committee *reached* a decision.

PASSIVE A decision *was reached* by the committee.

To transform a sentence from the passive voice to the active voice, make the actor the subject of the sentence.

▶ For the opening number, ~~a dance was choreographed by~~
    choreographed a dance
Mr. Martins to the song "America the Beautiful."
    ^

The passive voice is appropriate if you wish to emphasize the receiver of the action or to minimize the importance of the actor.

APPROPRIATE Many native Hawaiians *are forced* to leave their
PASSIVE   beautiful beaches to make room for hotels and
             condominiums.

APPROPRIATE As the time for harvest approaches, the tobacco
PASSIVE   plants *are sprayed* with a chemical to retard the
             growth of suckers.

The writer of the first sentence wished to emphasize the receivers of the action, Hawaiians. The writer of the second sentence wished to focus on the tobacco plants, not on the people spraying them.

ESL NOTE: Some speakers of English as a second language tend to avoid the passive voice even when it is appropriate. For advice on transforming an active-voice sentence to the passive, see B2-b.

G3

Problems with pronouns

Pronouns are words that substitute for nouns (see B1-b). Four frequently encountered problems with pronouns are discussed in this section:

a. pronoun-antecedent agreement (singular vs. plural)
b. pronoun reference (clarity)
c. pronoun case (personal pronouns such as *I* vs. *me, she* vs. *her*)
d. pronoun case (*who* vs. *whom*)

For other problems with pronouns, consult the Glossary of Usage (W1).

G3-a Make pronouns and antecedents agree.

The antecedent of a pronoun is the word the pronoun refers to. A pronoun and its antecedent agree when they are both singular or both plural.

SINGULAR   The *doctor* finished *her* rounds.

PLURAL   The *doctors* finished *their* rounds.

ESL NOTE: The pronouns *he, his, she, her, it,* and *its* must agree in gender (masculine, feminine, or neuter) with their antecedents, not with the words they modify.

▶ *Jane* visited *her* [not *his*] brother in Denver.

Indefinite pronouns

Indefinite pronouns refer to nonspecific persons or things. Even though the following indefinite pronouns may seem to have plural meanings, treat them as singular in formal English: *anybody, anyone, anything, each, either, everybody, everyone, everything, neither, nobody, none, no one, somebody, someone, something.*

In this class *everyone* performs at *his or her* [not *their*] fitness level.

When a plural pronoun refers mistakenly to a singular indefinite pronoun, you will usually have three options for revision:

1. Replace the plural pronoun with *he or she* (or *his or her*);
2. make the antecedent plural; or
3. rewrite the sentence so that no problem of agreement arises.

▶ When someone has been drinking, ~~they are~~ more likely to speed.
he or she is

▶ When ~~someone has~~ been drinking, they are more likely to speed.
drivers have

▶ ~~When someone~~ has been drinking, ~~they are~~ more likely to speed.
Someone who ... *is*

Because the *he or she* construction is wordy, often the second or third revision strategy is more effective.

NOTE: The traditional use of *he* (or *his*) to refer to persons of either sex is now widely considered sexist (see W3-e).

Generic nouns

A generic noun represents a typical member of a group, such as a typical student, or any member of a group, such as any lawyer. Although generic nouns may seem to have plural meanings, they are singular.

Every *runner* must train vigorously if *he or she* wants [not *they want*] to excel.

When a plural noun refers mistakenly to a generic noun, you will usually have the same three revision options as just mentioned for indefinite pronouns.

▶ A medical student must study hard if ~~they want~~ to succeed.
he or she wants

▶ ~~A medical student~~ must study hard if they want to succeed.
Medical students

▶ A medical student must study hard ~~if they want~~ to succeed.

Collective nouns

Collective nouns such as *jury, committee, audience, crowd, class, troop, family, team,* and *couple* name a class or group. If the group functions as a unit, treat the noun as singular; if the members of the group function individually, treat the noun as plural.

> AS A UNIT   The planning *committee* granted *its* permission to build.

> AS INDIVIDUALS   The *committee* put *their* signatures on the document.

When treating a collective noun as plural, many writers prefer to add a clearly plural antecedent such as *members* to the sentence: *The members of the committee put their signatures on the document.*

To some extent, you can choose whether to treat a collective noun as singular or plural depending on your meaning. Make sure, however, that you are consistent.

> *its*
> ▶ The jury has reached ~~their~~ decision.

The writer selected the verb *has* to match the singular noun *jury* (see G1), so for consistency the pronoun must be *its.*

Compound antecedents

Treat compound antecedents joined by *and* as plural.

> *Joanne and John* moved to the mountains, where *they* built a log cabin.

With compound antecedents joined by *or* or *nor,* make the pronoun agree with the nearer antecedent.

> Either *Bruce* or *James* should receive first prize for *his* sculpture.

> Neither the *instructor* nor her *students* could find *their* way to the bookstore.

NOTE: If one of the antecedents is singular and the other plural, as in the second example, put the plural one last to avoid awkwardness.

EXCEPTION: If one antecedent is male and the other female, do not follow the traditional rule. The sentence *Either Bruce or Anita should receive the blue ribbon for her sculpture* makes no sense. The best solution is to recast the sentence: *The blue ribbon for best sculpture should go to Bruce or Anita.*

G3-b Make pronoun references clear.

Pronouns substitute for nouns; they are a kind of shorthand. In a sentence like *After Andrew intercepted the ball, he kicked it as hard as he could,* the pronouns *he* and *it* substitute for the nouns *Andrew* and *ball.* The word a pronoun refers to is called its *antecedent.*

A pronoun should refer clearly to its antecedent. A pronoun's reference will be unclear if it is ambiguous, implied, vague, or indefinite.

Ambiguous reference

Ambiguous reference occurs when the pronoun could refer to two possible antecedents.

▶ When Gloria set ~~the pitcher~~ on the glass-topped table, ~~it~~ broke.
it ... *the pitcher*

▶ Tom told James ~~that he had~~ won the lottery."
"You have

What broke — the table or the pitcher? Who won the lottery — Tom or James? The revisions eliminate the ambiguity.

Implied reference

A pronoun must refer to a specific antecedent, not to a word that is implied but not present in the sentence.

▶ After braiding Ann's hair, Sue decorated ~~them~~ with ribbons.
the braids

The pronoun *them* referred to Ann's braids (implied by the term *braiding*), but the word *braids* did not appear in the sentence.

Modifiers, such as possessives, cannot serve as antecedents. A modifier may strongly imply the noun that the pronoun might logically refer to, but it is not itself that noun.

> *his*
> Because of ~~Paul Robeson's~~ outspoken attitude toward fascism, ~~he~~
>   ^   *Paul Robeson*
>   ^
> was labeled a Communist.

The pronoun *he* cannot refer logically to the possessive modifier *Robeson's*.

Broad reference of this, that, which, *and* it

For clarity, the pronouns *this, that, which,* and *it* should ordinarily refer to specific antecedents rather than to whole ideas or sentences. When a pronoun's reference is needlessly broad, either replace the pronoun with a noun or supply an antecedent to which the pronoun clearly refers.

> More and more often, especially in large cities, we are finding
>   *our fate*
> ourselves victims of serious crimes. We learn to accept ~~this~~ with
>   ^
> minor complaints.

> Romeo and Juliet were both too young to have acquired much
>   *a fact*
> wisdom, which accounts for their rash actions.
>   ^

Indefinite reference of they, it, *or* you

The pronoun *they* should refer to a specific antecedent. Do not use *they* to refer indefinitely to persons who have not been specifically mentioned.

> Sometimes a list of ways to save energy is included with the gas
>   *the gas company suggests*
> bill. For example, ~~they suggest~~ setting a moderate temperature for
>   ^
> the hot water heater.

The word *it* should not be used indefinitely in constructions such as "In the article it says that. . . ."

> *The*
> ~~In the~~ encyclopedia ~~it~~ states that male moths can smell female
>   ^
> moths from several miles away.

The pronoun *you* is appropriate when the writer is addressing the reader directly: *Once you have kneaded the dough, let it rise in a warm place.* Except in very informal contexts, however, the indefinite *you* (meaning "anyone in general") is inappropriate.

> *one doesn't*
> In Chad, ~~you don't~~ need much property to be considered well-off.

If the pronoun *one* seems stilted, the writer might recast the sentence: *In Chad, a person doesn't need much property to be considered well-off.*

G3-c Use personal pronouns in the proper case.

The personal pronouns in the following chart change what is known as case form according to their grammatical function in a sentence. Pronouns functioning as subjects or subject complements appear in the *subjective* case; those functioning as objects appear in the *objective* case; and those functioning as possessives appear in the *possessive* case.

SUBJECTIVE CASE	OBJECTIVE CASE	POSSESSIVE CASE
I	me	my
we	us	our
you	you	your
he/she/it	him/her/it	his/her/its
they	them	their

This section explains the difference between the subjective and objective cases; then it alerts you to certain structures that may tempt you to choose the wrong pronoun. Finally, it describes a special use of possessive-case pronouns.

Subjective case

When a pronoun functions as a subject or a subject complement, it must be in the subjective case (*I, we, you, he/she/it, they*).

SUBJECT Sylvia and *he* shared the award.

SUBJECT COMPLEMENT Greg announced that the winners were Sylvia and *he.*

Subject complements — words following linking verbs that complete the meaning of the subject — frequently cause problems for writers, since we rarely hear the correct form in casual speech. (See B2-b.)

▶ Sandra confessed that the artist was ~~her.~~ *she.*

The pronoun *she* follows the linking verb *was* and completes the meaning of the subject *artist*. If *artist was she* seems too stilted, try rewriting the sentence: *Sandra confessed that she was the artist.*

Objective case

When a pronoun functions as a direct object, an indirect object, or the object of a preposition, it must be in the objective case (*me, us, you, him/her/it, them*).

DIRECT OBJECT	Bruce found Tony and brought *him* home.
INDIRECT OBJECT	Alice gave *me* a surprise party.
OBJECT OF A PREPOSITION	Jessica wondered if the call was for *her*.

Compound word groups

When a subject or an object appears as part of a compound structure, you may occasionally become confused. To test for the correct pronoun, mentally strip away all of the compound word group except the pronoun in question.

▶ Everyone laughed when Ellen explained that her brother and ~~her~~ had *she*

seen the Loch Ness monster and fed it sandwiches.

Her brother and she is the subject of the verb *had seen*. Strip away the words *her brother and* to hear the correct pronoun: *she had seen* (not *her had seen*).

▶ The most traumatic experience for her father and ~~I~~ occurred long *me*

after her operation.

Me is the object of the preposition *for*. We would not say *the most traumatic experience for I.*

When in doubt about the correct pronoun, some writers try to evade the choice by using a reflexive pronoun such as *myself*. Such evasions are nonstandard, even though they are used by some educated persons.

► The Egyptian cab driver gave my husband and ~~myself~~ some good

   me

tips on traveling in North Africa.

My husband and me is the indirect object of the verb *gave.* For correct uses of *myself,* see the Glossary of Usage (W1).

Appositives

Appositives are noun phrases that rename nouns or pronouns. A pronoun used as an appositive has the same function as the noun or pronoun it renames.

► The winners of the art competition, Patricia and ~~me~~, will spend a

   I

month studying fresco painting in Florence.

The appositive *Patricia and I* renames the subject *winners.*

► The reporter interviewed only two witnesses, the shopkeeper and ~~I.~~

   me.

The appositive *the shopkeeper and me* renames the direct object *witnesses.*

We *or* us *before a noun*

When deciding whether *we* or *us* should precede a noun, choose the pronoun that would be appropriate if the noun were omitted.

► ~~Us~~ tenants would rather fight than move.

   We

► Management is shortchanging ~~we~~ tenants.

   us

No one would say *Us would rather fight than move* or *Management is shortchanging we.*

Comparisons with *than or* as

Sentence parts, usually verbs, are often omitted in comparisons beginning with *than* or *as.* To test for the correct pronoun, mentally complete the sentence.

▶ My husband is six years older than ~~me.~~ *I.*

I is the subject of the verb *am,* which is understood. If the correct English seems too formal, add the verb: *My husband is six years older than I am.*

▶ We respected no other candidate as much as ~~she.~~ *her.*

Her is the direct object of an understood verb: *We respected no other candidate as much as [we respected] her.*

Subjects of infinitives

An infinitive is the word *to* followed by the base form of a verb. Subjects of infinitives are an exception to the rule that subjects must be in the subjective case. Whenever an infinitive has a subject, the subject must be in the objective case.

▶ We expected Chris and ~~he~~ to win the doubles championship. *him*

Chris and him is the subject of the infinitive *to win.*

Possessive case to modify a gerund

If a pronoun modifies a gerund or a gerund phrase, it should appear in the possessive case (*my, our, your, his/her/its, their*). A gerund is a verb form ending in *-ing* that functions as a noun.

▶ The chances against ~~you~~ being hit by lightning are about two *your*

million to one.

Your modifies the gerund phrase *being hit by lightning.*

Nouns as well as pronouns may modify gerunds. To form the possessive case of a noun, use an apostrophe and an *-s* (*a victim's suffering*) or just an apostrophe (*victims' suffering*). See P5-a.

▶ We had to pay a fifty-dollar fine for ~~Brenda~~ driving without a *Brenda's*

permit.

The possessive noun *Brenda's* modifies the gerund phrase *driving without a permit.*

G3-d Use *who* and *whom* in the proper case.

Who, a subjective-case pronoun, can be used only for subjects and subject complements. *Whom,* an objective-case pronoun, can be used only for objects. (For more about pronoun case, see G3-c.)

Who and *whom* are relative pronouns used to introduce subordinate clauses. (See B3-e.) They are also interrogative pronouns used to open questions.

In subordinate clauses

The case of a relative pronoun in a subordinate clause is determined by its function *within the subordinate clause.*

▶ When medicine is scarce and expensive, physicians must give it to
    whoever
  ~~whomever~~ has the best chance of surviving.
     ^

The writer selected the pronoun *whomever,* thinking that it was the object of the preposition *to.* However, the object of the preposition is the entire subordinate clause *whoever has the best chance of surviving.* The verb of the clause is *has,* and its subject is *whoever.*

When it functions as an object in a subordinate clause, *whom* appears out of order, before both the subject and the verb. To choose the correct pronoun, you can mentally restructure the clause.

                                 whom
▶ You will work with our senior engineers, ~~who~~ you will meet later.
                                       ^

Whom is the direct object of the verb of the subordinate clause, *will meet.* This becomes clear if you mentally restructure the clause: *you will meet whom.*

      whom
▶ The tutor ~~who~~ I was assigned to was very supportive.
       ^

Whom is the object of the preposition *to.* If the correct English seems too formal, drop *whom: The tutor I was assigned to. . . .*

NOTE: Ignore inserted expressions such as *they know* or *I think* when determining the case of a relative pronoun.

                                          who
▶ All of the school bullies want to take on a big guy ~~whom~~ they
                                            ^

  know will not hurt them.

Who is the subject of *will hurt,* not the object of *know.*

In questions

The case of an interrogative pronoun is determined by its function within the question.

> *Who*
> ▶ ~~Whom~~ is responsible for this dastardly deed?
> ⌃

Who is the subject of the verb *is*.

When *whom* appears as an object in a question, it appears out of order, before both the subject and the verb. To choose the correct pronoun, you can mentally restructure the question.

> *Whom*
> ▶ ~~Who~~ did the committee select?
> ⌃

Whom is the direct object of the verb *did select: The committee did select whom?*

G4

Adjectives and adverbs

Adjectives modify nouns or pronouns; adverbs modify verbs, adjectives, or other adverbs. (See B1-d and B1-e.)

Many adverbs are formed by adding *-ly* to adjectives (*formal, formally*). But don't assume that all words ending in *-ly* are adverbs or that all adverbs end in *-ly*. Some adjectives end in *-ly* (*lovely, friendly*) and some adverbs don't (*always, here, there*). When in doubt, consult a dictionary.

ESL NOTE: In English, adjectives are not pluralized to agree with the words they modify: *The red* [not *reds*] *roses were a wonderful surprise.*

G4-a Use adverbs, not adjectives, to modify verbs, adjectives, and adverbs.

When adverbs modify verbs (or verbals), they usually answer one of these questions: When? Where? How? Why? Under what conditions? How often? To what degree?

The incorrect use of adjectives in place of adverbs to modify verbs occurs primarily in casual or nonstandard speech.

> *smoothly   efficiently*
> ▶ The manager must see that the office runs ~~smooth~~ and ~~efficient~~.

The incorrect use of the adjective *good* in place of the adverb *well* is especially common in casual and nonstandard speech.

> *well*
> ▶ Marcia performed very ~~good~~ at her Drama Club audition.

NOTE: The word *well* is an adjective when it means "healthy," "satisfactory," or "fortunate": *I am very well, thank you. All is well. It is just as well.*

Adjectives are sometimes used incorrectly to modify adjectives or other adverbs.

> *really*
> ▶ For a man ninety years old, Joe plays golf ~~real~~ well.

ESL NOTE: Placement of adjectives and adverbs can be a tricky matter for second language speakers. See T3-d.

G4-b Use adjectives, not adverbs, as subject complements.

Adjectives ordinarily precede nouns, but they can also function as subject complements following linking verbs (see B2-b). When an adjective functions as a subject complement, it describes the subject.

Justice is *blind.*

Problems can arise with verbs such as *smell, taste, look,* and *feel,* which may or may not be linking. If the word following one of these verbs describes the subject, use an adjective; if it modifies the verb, use an adverb.

ADJECTIVE   The detective looked *cautious.*

ADVERB   The detective looked *cautiously* for the fingerprints.

Linking verbs suggest states of being, not actions. For example, to look cautious suggests the state of being cautious, whereas to look cautiously is to perform an action in a cautious way.

▶ The lilacs in our backyard smell especially ~~sweetly~~ this year.
sweet

▶ Lori looked ~~well~~ in her new raincoat.
good

▶ All of us on the team felt ~~badly~~ about our performance.
bad

The verbs *smell, looked,* and *felt* suggest states of being, not actions. Therefore, they should be followed by adjectives, not adverbs.

G4-c Use comparatives and superlatives with care.

Most adjectives and adverbs have three forms: the positive, the comparative, and the superlative.

POSITIVE	COMPARATIVE	SUPERLATIVE
soft	softer	softest
fast	faster	fastest
careful	more careful	most careful
bad	worse	worst
good	better	best

Comparative versus superlative

Use the comparative to compare two things, the superlative to compare three or more.

▶ Which of these two brands of toothpaste is ~~best~~?
better?

▶ Though Shaw and Jackson are impressive, Hobbs is the ~~more~~
most

qualified of the three candidates running for mayor.

Form of comparatives and superlatives

To form comparatives and superlatives of most one- and two-syllable adjectives, use the endings *-er* and *-est: smooth, smoother, smoothest; easy, easier, easiest.* With longer adjectives, use *more* and *most: exciting, more exciting, most exciting.*

Some one-syllable adverbs take the endings *-er* and *-est* (*fast, faster, fastest*), but longer adverbs and all of those ending in *-ly* form the comparative and superlative with *more* and *most*.

The comparative and superlative forms of the following adjectives and adverbs are irregular: *good, better, best; bad, worse, worst; badly, worse, worst.*

► The Kirov was the ~~talentedest~~ ballet company we had ever seen.
(most talented)

► Lloyd's luck couldn't have been ~~worser~~ than David's.
(worse)

Double comparatives or superlatives

Do not use double comparatives or superlatives. When you have added *-er* or *-est* to an adjective or adverb, do not also use *more* or *most*.

► Of all her family, Julia is the ~~most~~ happiest about the move.

► That is the most ~~vilest~~ joke I have ever heard.
(vile)

Absolute concepts

Do not use comparatives or superlatives with absolute concepts such as *unique* or *perfect*. Either something is unique or it isn't. It is illogical to suggest that absolute concepts come in degrees.

► That is the most ~~unique~~ wedding gown I have ever seen.
(unusual)

► The painting would have been even more ~~priceless~~ had it been signed.
(valuable)

G4-d Avoid double negatives.

Standard English allows two negatives only if a positive meaning is intended: *The orchestra was not unhappy with its performance.* Double negatives used to emphasize negation are nonstandard.

Negative modifiers such as *never, no,* and *not* should not be paired with other negative modifiers or with negative words such as *neither, none, no one, nobody,* and *nothing.*

anything
▶ Management is not doing ~~nothing~~ to see that the trash is picked up.
          ^

ever
▶ George won't ~~never~~ forget that day.
             ^

The modifiers *hardly, barely,* and *scarcely* are considered negatives in standard English, so they should not be used with negatives
such as *not, no one,* or *never.*

can
▶ Maxine is so weak she ~~can't~~ hardly climb stairs.
                     ^

G5

Sentence fragments

A sentence fragment is a word group that pretends to be a sentence.
Some fragments are clauses that contain a subject and a verb but
begin with a subordinating word. Others are phrases that lack a
subject, a verb, or both.

Sentence fragments are easy to recognize when they appear out
of context, like this one:

> On the old wooden stool in the corner of my grandmother's
> kitchen.

When they appear next to related sentences, however, they are
harder to spot.

> On that morning I sat in my usual spot. On the old wooden stool
> in the corner of my grandmother's kitchen.

To be a sentence, a word group must consist of at least one full
independent clause. An independent clause has a subject and a
verb, and it either stands alone or could stand alone. To test a word
group for sentence completeness, use the flow chart on page 159. For
example, by using the flow chart, you can see exactly why *On the old
wooden stool in the corner of my grandmother's kitchen* is a fragment: It lacks both a verb and a subject.

You can repair most fragments in one of two ways: Either pull the fragment into a nearby sentence, making sure to punctuate the new sentence correctly, or turn the fragment into a sentence. To repair the sample fragment, you would probably choose to combine it with the sentence that precedes it, like this:

> On that morning I sat in my usual spot, on the old wooden stool in the corner of my grandmother's kitchen.

ESL NOTE: Unlike some languages, English does not allow omission of subjects (except in imperative sentences); nor does it allow omission of verbs. See T2-e and T3-a.

G5-a Attach fragmented subordinate clauses or turn them into sentences.

A subordinate clause is patterned like a sentence, with both a subject and verb, but it begins with a word that tells readers it cannot stand alone — a word such as *after, although, because, before, if, though, unless, until, when, where, who, which,* and *that.* (See B3-e.)

Most fragmented subordinate clauses beg to be pulled into a sentence nearby.

▶ With machetes, the explorers cut their way through the tall
grasses to the edge of the canyon/ , ~~Where~~ *where* they began to lay out

their tapes for the survey.

If a fragmented clause cannot be attached to a nearby sentence or if you feel that attaching it would be awkward, try turning it into a sentence. The simplest way to turn a subordinate clause into a sentence is to delete the opening word or words that mark it as subordinate.

▶ Violence has produced a great deal of apprehension among
children and parents. ~~So that self preservation~~, *Self-preservation,* in fact, has

become their primary aim.

G5-b Attach fragmented phrases or turn them into sentences.

Like subordinate clauses, phrases function within sentences as adjectives, as adverbs, or as nouns. They cannot stand alone. Fragmented phrases are often prepositional or verbal phrases; sometimes they are appositives, words or word groups that rename nouns or pronouns. (See B3-a, B3-b, and B3-c.)

Many fragmented phrases may simply be pulled into nearby sentences.

▶ On Sundays Ed read the newspaper's employment sections scrupulously/,
    scrutinizing
                                                                    ∧
~~Scrutinizing~~ every position that held even the remotest possibility.

Scrutinizing every position that held even the remotest possibility is a verbal phrase modifying *Ed*.

                                            a
▶ Mary is suffering from agoraphobia/, Å fear of the outside world.
                                         ∧
A fear of the outside world is an appositive renaming the noun *agoraphobia*.

If a fragmented phrase cannot be pulled into a nearby sentence effectively, turn the phrase into a sentence. You may need to add a subject, a verb, or both.

▶ In the study skills workshop, we learned the value of discipline and
                We also learned
hard work. ~~Also~~ how to organize our time, take meaningful notes,
             ∧
interpret assignments, pinpoint trouble spots, and seek help.

The word group beginning *Also how to organize* is a fragmented verbal phrase. The revision turns the fragment into a sentence by adding a subject and a verb.

G5-c Attach other fragmented word groups or turn them into sentences.

Other word groups that are commonly fragmented include parts of compound predicates, lists, and examples introduced by *such as, for example,* or similar expressions.

Test for sentence completeness

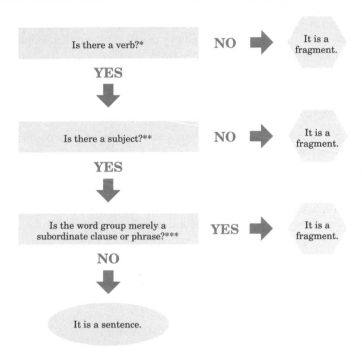

*Do not mistake verbals for verbs. (See B3-b.)
**The subject of a sentence may be *you*, understood. (See B2-a.)
***A sentence may open with a subordinate clause or phrase, but the sentence must also include an independent clause. (See B3.)

If you find any fragments, try one of these methods of revision:
1. Attach the fragment to a nearby sentence.
2. Turn the fragment into a sentence.

Parts of compound predicates

A predicate consists of a verb and its objects, complements, and modifiers (see B2-b). A compound predicate includes two or more predicates joined by a coordinating conjunction such as *and, but,* or *or.* Because the parts of a compound predicate share the same subject, they should appear in the same sentence.

▶ Aspiring bodybuilders must first ascertain their strengths

and weaknesses. And then decide what they want to achieve.
a

Notice that no comma appears between the parts of a compound predicate. (See P2-a.)

Lists

When a list is mistakenly fragmented, it can often be attached to a nearby sentence with a colon or a dash. (See P4-a and P7-d.)

▶ It has been said that there are only three indigenous American
j
art forms. : Jazz, musical comedy, and soap opera.

Examples introduced by such as, for example, *or similar expressions*

Expressions that introduce examples (or explanations) can lead to unintentional fragments. Although you may begin a sentence with some of the following words or phrases, make sure that what you have written is a sentence, not a fragment.

also	especially	in addition	namely	that is
and	for example	like	or	
but	for instance	mainly	such as	

Sometimes fragmented examples can be attached to the preceding sentence.

▶ The South has produced some of our greatest twentieth-century
such
writers. , Such as Flannery O'Connor, William Faulkner,

Alice Walker, Tennessee Williams, and Thomas Wolfe.

At times, however, it may be necessary to turn the fragment into a sentence.

▶ If Eric doesn't get his way, he goes into a fit of rage. For
     he lies   *opens*
example, l̶y̶i̶n̶g̶ on the floor screaming or o̶p̶e̶n̶i̶n̶g̶ the cabinet
                    slams
doors and then s̶l̶a̶m̶m̶i̶n̶g̶ them shut.

The writer corrected this fragment by adding a subject — *he* — and substituting verbs for the verbals *lying, opening,* and *slamming.*

G5-d Exception: Fragments may be used for special purposes.

Skilled writers occasionally use sentence fragments for the following special purposes.

FOR EMPHASIS	Following the dramatic Americanization of their children, even my parents grew more publicly confident. *Especially my mother.* — Richard Rodriguez
TO ANSWER A QUESTION	Are these new drug tests 100 percent reliable? *Not in the opinion of most experts.*
AS A TRANSITION	*And now the opposing arguments.*
EXCLAMATIONS	*Not again!*
IN ADVERTISING	*Fewer calories. Improved taste.*

Although fragments are sometimes appropriate, writers and readers do not always agree on when they are appropriate. Therefore you will find it safer to write in complete sentences.

G6

Comma splices and fused sentences

Comma splices and fused sentences, more commonly known as "run-on sentences," are independent clauses that have not been joined correctly. An independent clause is a word group that can stand alone as a sentence. (See B4-a.) When two independent clauses appear in one sentence, they must be joined in one of these ways:

— with a comma and a coordinating conjunction (*and, but, or, nor, for, so, yet*)
— with a semicolon (or occasionally a colon or a dash)

When a writer puts no mark of punctuation and no coordinating conjunction between independent clauses, the result is a fused sentence.

┌──────────── INDEPENDENT CLAUSE ──────────┐ ┌──
FUSED   Gestures are a means of communication for everyone they

┌──────── INDEPENDENT CLAUSE ────────┐
are essential for the hearing-impaired.

A far more common error is the comma splice — independent clauses joined by a comma without a coordinating conjunction. In some comma splices, the comma appears alone.

COMMA   Gestures are a means of communication for everyone,
SPLICE   they are essential for the hearing-impaired.

In other comma splices, the comma is accompanied by a joining word that is *not* a coordinating conjunction. There are only seven coordinating conjunctions in English: *and, but, or, nor, for, so, yet.* Notice that all of these words are short — only two or three letters long.

COMMA   Gestures are an important means of communication for
SPLICE   everyone, however, they are essential for the hearing-impaired.

In the second example, *however* is a conjunctive adverb, not a coordinating conjunction. When a conjunctive adverb such as *however, therefore,* or *moreover* or a transitional phrase such as *in fact* or *for example* appears between independent clauses, it must be preceded by a semicolon. (See page 165 for a more complete list of these words and phrases.)

Identifying comma splices and fused sentences

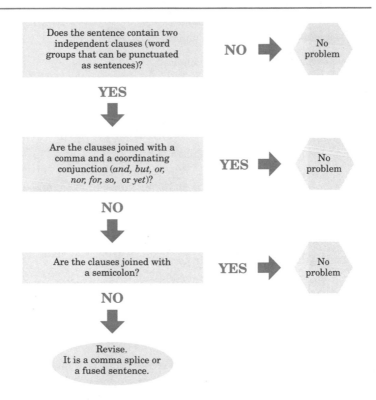

To correct a fused sentence or a comma splice, you have four choices:

1. Use a comma and a coordinating conjunction (*and, but, or, nor, for, so, yet*).

   ▶ Gestures are a means of communication for everyone, ~~they~~ *but* they

   are essential for the hearing-impaired.

2. Use a semicolon (or, if appropriate, a colon or a dash). A semicolon may be used alone; it can also be accompanied by a conjunctive adverb or transitional phrase.

▶ Gestures are a means of communication for everyone/ *;* they

are essential for the hearing-impaired.

                                                 ; however,
▶ Gestures are a means of communication for everyone/ they

are essential for the hearing-impaired.

3. Make the clauses into separate sentences.

                                                 T
▶ Gestures are a means of communication for everyone/. *t*hey

are essential for the hearing-impaired.

4. Restructure the sentence, perhaps by subordinating one of the
   clauses.

   Although gestures
▶ ~~Gestures~~ are a means of communication for everyone, they

are essential for the hearing-impaired.

One of these revision techniques will often work better than the others for a particular sentence. The fourth technique, the one requiring the most extensive revision, is frequently the most effective.

G6-a Consider separating the clauses with a comma and a coordinating conjunction.

There are seven coordinating conjunctions in English: *and, but, or,
nor, for, so,* and *yet.* When a coordinating conjunction joins independent clauses, it must be preceded by a comma. (See P1-a.)

                                       and
▶ The paramedic asked where I was hurt, as soon as I told him, he

cut up the leg of my favorite pair of jeans.

▶ Many government officials privately admit that the polygraph is

       yet
unreliable, ~~however,~~ they continue to use it as a security measure.

G6-b Consider separating the clauses with a semicolon (or, if appropriate, with a colon or a dash).

When the independent clauses are closely related and their relation is clear without a coordinating conjunction, a semicolon is an acceptable method of revision. (See P3-a.)

▶ Suddenly there was a loud silence,/ ; the shelling had stopped.
 ∧

A semicolon is required between independent clauses that have been linked with a conjunctive adverb or transitional phrase.

CONJUNCTIVE ADVERBS AND TRANSITIONAL PHRASES

also	in addition	now
as a result	indeed	of course
besides	in fact	on the other hand
consequently	in other words	otherwise
finally	in the first place	similarly
for example	meanwhile	still
furthermore	moreover	then
hence	nevertheless	therefore
however	next	thus

▶ The timber wolf looks like a large German shepherd,/ ; however,
 ∧
the wolf has longer legs, larger feet, and a wider head.

If the first independent clause introduces the second or if the second clause summarizes or explains the first, a colon or a dash may be an appropriate method of revision. (See P4-b and P7-d.) In formal writing, the colon is usually preferred to the dash.

▶ The experience taught Juanita a lesson,/ ; *She* she could not
 ∧
always rely on her parents to bail her out of trouble.

G6-c Consider making the clauses into separate sentences.

▶ In one episode viewers saw two people smashed by a boat, one

choked, and another shot to death/. ~~what~~ *What* purpose does this

violence serve?

Since one independent clause is a statement and the other is a question, they should be separate sentences.

▶ I gave the necessary papers to the police officer/. ~~t~~ *T*hen he said I

would have to accompany him to the police station, where a

counselor would talk with me and call my parents.

Because the second independent clause is quite long, a sensible revision is to use separate sentences.

G6-d Consider restructuring the sentence, perhaps by subordinating one of the clauses.

If one of the independent clauses is less important than the other, try turning it into a subordinate clause or phrase. (See E6-a.)

▶ Wind power for the home is a supplemental source of energy ~~it~~ *that* can

be combined with electricity, gas, or solar energy.

▶ *When the* ~~The~~ new health plan was explained to the employees in my

division, everyone agreed to give it a try.

▶ Saturday afternoon Julie came running into the house/ ~~she~~

~~wanted~~ to get permission to go to the park.

T

ESL
Trouble Spots

T

ESL Trouble Spots

This section of *A Writer's Reference* has a special audience: speakers of English as a second language (ESL) who have learned English but continue to have difficulty with a few trouble spots.

T1

Articles

Except for occasional difficulty in choosing between *a* and *an*, native speakers of English encounter few problems with articles. To speakers whose native language is not English, however, articles can prove troublesome, for the rules governing their use are surprisingly complex. This section summarizes those rules.

The definite article *the* and the indefinite articles *a* and *an* signal that a noun is about to appear. The noun may follow the article immediately, or modifiers may intervene (see B1-a and B1-d):

> *the candidate, the* exceptionally well qualified *candidate*
> *a sunset, a* spectacular *sunset*
> *an apple, an* appetizing *apple*

Articles are not the only words used to mark nouns. Other noun markers (sometimes called "determiners") include possessive nouns (*Helen's*), numbers, and the following pronouns: *my, your, his, her, its, our, their, whose, this, that, these, those, all, any, each, either, every, few, many, more, most, much, neither, several, some.*

Usually an article is not used with another noun marker. Common exceptions include expressions such as *a few, the most,* and *all the.*

T1-a Use *a* (or *an*) with singular count nouns whose specific identity is not known to the reader.

Count nouns refer to persons, places, or things that can be counted: *one girl, two girls; one city, three cities; one apple, four apples.* Noncount nouns refer to entities or abstractions that cannot be counted: *water, silver, air, furniture, patience, knowledge.* (See pages 170–71 for a more complete list.)

If the specific identity of a singular count noun is not known to the reader — perhaps because it is being mentioned for the first time, perhaps because its specific identity is unknown even to the writer — the noun should be preceded by *a* or *an* unless it has been preceded by another noun marker. *A* (or *an*) usually means "one among many" but can also mean "any one."

▶ Mary Beth arrived in ^a^ limousine.

▶ We are looking for ^an^ apartment close to the lake.

NOTE: *A* is used before a consonant sound: *a banana, a tree, a picture, a hand, a happy child. An* is used before a vowel sound: *an eggplant, an occasion, an uncle, an hour, an honorable person.* Notice that words beginning with *h* can have either a consonant sound (*hand, happy*) or a vowel sound (*hour, honorable*). (See also W1.)

T1-b Do not use *a* (or *an*) with noncount nouns.

A (or *an*) is not used to mark noncount nouns, such as *sugar, gold, honesty,* or *jewelry.*

▶ Claudia asked her mother for ~~an~~ advice.

If you want to express an amount for a noncount noun, you can use *some, any,* or *more: some paper, any information, more pasta.* Or you can add a count noun in front of the noncount noun: *a quart of milk, a piece of furniture, a bar of soap.*

▶ Mother asked us to pick up a ^pound of^ sugar at the corner store.

NOTE: A few noncount nouns may also be used as count nouns: *Bill loves lemonade; Bill offered me a lemonade.*

COMMONLY USED NONCOUNT NOUNS
Food and drink: bacon, beef, bread, broccoli, butter, cabbage, candy, cauliflower, celery, cereal, cheese, chicken, chocolate, coffee, corn, cream, fish, flour, fruit, ice cream, lettuce, meat, milk, oil, pasta, rice, salt, spinach, sugar, tea, water, wine, yogurt

Nonfood substances: air, cement, coal, dirt, gasoline, gold, paper, petroleum, plastic, rain, silver, snow, soap, steel, wood, wool

Abstract nouns: advice, anger, beauty, confidence, courage, employment, fun, happiness, health, honesty, information, intelligence, knowledge, love, poverty, satisfaction, truth, wealth

Other: biology (and other areas of study), clothing, equipment, furniture, homework, jewelry, luggage, lumber, machinery, mail, money, news, poetry, pollution, research, scenery, traffic, transportation, violence, weather, work

T1-c Use *the* with most nouns whose specific identity is known to the reader.

The definite article *the* is used with most nouns whose identity is known to the reader. (For exceptions, see T1-d.) Usually the identity will be clear to the reader for one of the following reasons:

1. The noun has been previously mentioned.
2. A phrase or clause following the noun restricts its identity.
3. A superlative such as *best* or *most intelligent* makes the noun's identity specific.
4. The noun describes a unique person, place, or thing.
5. The context or situation makes the noun's identity clear.

▶ A truck loaded with dynamite cut in front of our van. When *the* truck
skidded a few seconds later, we almost plowed into it.

The noun *truck* is preceded by *A* when it is first mentioned. When the noun is mentioned again, it is preceded by *the* since readers now know the specific truck being discussed.

▶ Bob warned me that *the* gun on the top shelf of the cupboard was
loaded.

The phrase *on the top shelf of the cupboard* identifies the specific gun.

▶ Our petite daughter dated *the* tallest boy in her class.

The superlative *tallest* restricts the identity of the noun *boy*.

▶ During an eclipse, one should not look directly at *the* sun.

There is only one sun in our solar system, so its identity is clear.

> *the*
> ▶ Please don't slam door when you leave.
>   ^

Both the speaker and the listener know which door is meant.

T1-d Do not use *the* with plural or noncount nouns meaning "all" or "in general"; do not use *the* with most singular proper nouns.

When a plural or a noncount noun means "all" or "in general," it is not marked with *the*.

>   F
> ▶ ~~The~~ fountains are an expensive element of landscape design.

> ▶ In some parts of the world, ~~the~~ rice is preferred to all other grains.

Although there are many exceptions, *the* is not used with most singular proper nouns. Do not use *the* with names of persons (Jessica Webner), names of streets, squares, parks, cities, and states (Prospect Street, Union Square, Denali National Park, Miami, Idaho), names of continents and most countries (South America, Italy), and names of bays and single lakes, mountains, and islands (Tampa Bay, Lake Geneva, Mount Everest, Crete).

Exceptions to this rule include names of large regions, deserts, and peninsulas (the East Coast, the Sahara, the Iberian Peninsula) and names of oceans, seas, gulfs, canals, and rivers (the Pacific, the Dead Sea, the Persian Gulf, the Panama Canal, the Amazon).

NOTE: *The* is used to mark plural proper nouns: the United Nations, the Finger Lakes, the Andes, the Bahamas, and so on.

T2

Special problems with verbs

Both native and nonnative speakers of English encounter the following problems with verbs, which are treated elsewhere in this book:

    problems with subject-verb agreement (G1),

    misuse of verb forms (G2-a–G2-d),

    problems with tense, mood, and voice (G2-f, G2-g, G2-h).

This section focuses on features of the English verb system that cause special difficulties for second language speakers.

T2-a Match helping verbs and main verbs appropriately.

Only certain combinations of helping verbs and main verbs make sense in English. The correct combinations are discussed in this section, after the following review of helping verbs and main verbs.

Review of helping verbs and main verbs

Helping verbs always appear before main verbs. (See B1-c.)

>   HV MV   HV   MV
> We *will leave* for the picnic at noon. *Do* you *want* a ride?

Some helping verbs — *have, do,* and *be* — change form to indicate tense; others, known as modals, do not.

> **FORMS OF *HAVE, DO,* AND *BE***
> have, has, had
> do, does, did
> be, am, is, are, was, were, being, been
>
> **MODALS**
> can, could, may, might, must, shall, should, will, would (*also* ought to)

Every main verb has five forms (except *be,* which has eight forms). The following list shows these forms for the regular verb *help* and the irregular verb *give.* (See G2-a for a list of common irregular verbs.)

BASE FORM	help, give
PAST TENSE	helped, gave
PAST PARTICIPLE	helped, given
PRESENT PARTICIPLE	helping, giving
-*S* FORM	helps, gives

Modal + base form

After the modals *can, could, may, might, must, shall, should, will,* and *would,* use the base form of the verb.

▶ My cousin will sends/us photographs from her wedding.

speak
▶ We could ~~spoke~~ Spanish when we were young.
           ^

CAUTION: Do not use *to* in front of a main verb that follows a modal. (*Ought to* is an exception.)

▶ Gina can ~~to~~ drive us home if we miss the bus.

Do, does, *or* did + *base form*

After helping verbs that are a form of *do,* use the base form of the verb.

The helping verbs *do, does,* and *did* are used in three ways: (1) to express a negative meaning with the adverbs *not* or *never,* (2) to ask a question, and (3) to emphasize a main verb used in a positive sense.

▶ Mariko does not wants/any more dessert.

buy
▶ Did Janice ~~bought~~ the gift for Katherine?
           ^

hope
▶ We do ~~hoping~~ that you will come to the party.
        ^

Have, has, *or* had + *past participle (perfect tenses)*

After the helping verb *have, has,* or *had,* use the past participle to form one of the perfect tenses. (See G2-f.) Past participles usually end in *-ed, -d, -en, -n,* or *-t.* (See G2-a.)

offered
▶ On cold nights many churches in the city have ~~offer~~ shelter to the
                                                ^
homeless.

spoken
▶ An-Mei has not ~~speaking~~ Chinese since she was a child.
                 ^

The helping verbs *have, has,* and *had* are sometimes preceded by a modal helping verb such as *will: By nightfall, we will have driven five hundred miles.* (See also perfect tenses, G2-f.)

Form of be + present participle (progressive forms)

After the helping verb *be, am, is, are, was, were,* or *been,* use the present participle (the *-ing* form of the verb) to express a continuing action. (See G2-f.)

> ► Carlos is ~~build~~ *building* his house on a cliff overlooking the ocean.

> ► Uncle Roy was ~~driven~~ *driving* a brand-new red Corvette.

The helping verb *be* must be preceded by a modal (*can, could, may, might, must, shall, should, will,* or *would*): *Edith will be going to Germany soon.* The helping verb *been* must be preceded by *have, has,* or *had: Andy has been studying English for five years.* (See also progressive forms, G2-f.)

CAUTION: Certain verbs are not normally used in the progressive sense in English. In general, these verbs express a state of being or mental activity, not a dynamic action. Common examples are *appear, believe, belong, contain, have, hear, know, like, need, see, seem, taste, think, understand,* and *want.*

> ► I ~~am wanting~~ *want* to see August Wilson's *Fences* at Arena Stage.

Some of these verbs, however, have special uses in which progressive forms are normal (*We are thinking about going to the Bahamas*). You will need to make a note of exceptions as you encounter them.

Form of be + past participle (passive voice)

When a sentence is written in the passive voice, the subject receives the action instead of doing it (*Melissa was given a special award*).

To form the passive voice, use *am, is, are, was, were, being, be,* or *been* followed by a past participle (usually ending in *-ed, -d, -en, -n,* or *-t*). (See G2-h.)

> ► *Bleak House* was ~~write~~ *written* by Charles Dickens.

> ► The scientists were ~~honor~~ *honored* for their work with endangered species.

When the helping verb is *be, being,* or *been,* it must be preceded by another helping verb. *Be* must be preceded by a modal such as *will: Senator Dixon will be defeated. Being* must be preceded by *am, is, are, was,* or *were: The child was being teased. Been* must be preceded by *have, has,* or *had: I have been invited to a party.*

CAUTION: Although they may seem to have passive meanings, verbs such as *occur, happen, sleep, die,* and *fall* may not be used to form the passive voice because they are intransitive. Only transitive verbs, those that take direct objects, may be used to form the passive voice. (See transitive and intransitive verbs, B2-b.)

▶ The earthquake ~~was~~ occurred last Wednesday.

T2-b In conditional sentences, choose verbs with care.

Conditional sentences state that one set of circumstances depends on whether another set of circumstances exists. Choosing verbs in such sentences can be tricky, partly because two clauses are involved: usually an *if* or a *when* or an *unless* clause and an independent clause.

Three kinds of conditional sentences are discussed in this section: factual, predictive, and speculative.

Factual

Factual conditional sentences express factual relationships. These relationships might be scientific truths, in which case the present tense is used in both clauses.

If water *cools* to 32°, it *freezes.*

Or they might be present or past relationships that are habitually true, in which case the same tense is used in both clauses.

When Sue *bicycles* along the canal, her dog *runs* ahead of her.

Whenever the coach *asked* for help, I *volunteered.*

Predictive

Predictive conditional sentences are used to predict the future or to express future plans or possibilities. In such a sentence, an *if* or *unless* clause contains a present-tense verb; the verb in the independent clause usually consists of the modal *will, can, may, should,* or *might* followed by the base form of the verb.

> If you *practice* regularly, your tennis game *will improve.*

> We *will lose* our remaining wetlands unless we *act* now.

Speculative

Speculative conditional sentences are used for three purposes: (1) to speculate about unlikely possibilities in the present or future, (2) to speculate about events that did not happen in the past, and (3) to speculate about conditions that are contrary to fact. Each of these purposes requires its own combination of verbs.

UNLIKELY POSSIBILITIES Somewhat confusingly, English uses the past tense in an *if* clause to speculate about a possible but unlikely condition in the present or future. The verb in the independent clause consists of *would, could,* or *might* plus the base form of the verb.

> If I *had* the time, I *would travel* to Senegal.

> If Stan *studied* harder, he *could master* calculus.

In the *if* clause, the past-tense form *were* is used with subjects that would normally take *was: Even if I were* [not *was*] *invited, I wouldn't go to the picnic.* (See also G2-g.)

EVENTS THAT DID NOT HAPPEN English uses the past perfect tense in an *if* clause to speculate about an event that did not happen in the past or to speculate about a state of being that was unreal in the past. (See past perfect tense, G2-f.) The verb in the independent clause consists of *would have, could have,* or *might have* plus the past participle.

> If I *had saved* enough money, I *would have traveled* to Senegal last year.

> If Grandmother *had been* alive for your graduation, she *would have been* very proud.

CONDITIONS CONTRARY TO FACT To speculate about conditions that are currently unreal or contrary to fact, English usually uses the past-tense verb *were* (never *was*) in an *if* clause. (See G2-g.) The verb in the independent clause consists of *would, could,* or *might* plus the base form of the verb.

> If Grandmother *were* alive today, she *would be* very proud of you.

> I *would make* children's issues a priority if I *were* the president.

T2-c Become familiar with verbs that may be followed by gerunds or infinitives.

A gerund is a verb form that ends in *-ing* and is used as a noun: *sleeping, dreaming.* (See B3-b.) An infinitive is the base form of the verb preceded by the word *to: to sleep, to dream.* The word *to* is not a preposition in this use but an infinitive marker.

A few verbs may be followed by either a gerund or an infinitive; others may be followed by a gerund but not by an infinitive; still others may be followed by an infinitive (either directly or with a noun or pronoun intervening) but not by a gerund.

Verb + *gerund or infinitive*

These commonly used verbs may be followed by a gerund or an infinitive, with little or no difference in meaning:

begin	continue	like	start
can't stand	hate	love	

> I love *skiing.* I love *to ski.*

With a few verbs, however, the choice of a gerund or an infinitive changes the meaning dramatically:

forget	remember	stop	try

> She stopped *speaking* to Lucia. [She no longer spoke to Lucia.]

> She stopped *to speak* to Lucia. [She paused so that she could speak to Lucia.]

Verb + *gerund*

These verbs may be followed by a gerund but not by an infinitive:

admit	discuss	imagine	put off	risk
appreciate	enjoy	miss	quit	suggest
avoid	escape	postpone	recall	tolerate
deny	finish	practice	resist	

Bill enjoys *playing* [not *to play*] the piano.

Verb + infinitive

These verbs may be followed by an infinitive but not by a gerund:

agree	decide	manage	plan	wait
ask	expect	mean	pretend	want
beg	have	need	promise	wish
claim	hope	offer	refuse	

We plan *to visit* [not *visiting*] the Yucatán next week.

Verb + noun (or pronoun) + infinitive

With certain verbs in the active voice, a noun or pronoun must come between the verb and the infinitive that follows it. The noun or pronoun usually names a person who is affected by the action.

advise	command	have	persuade	tell
allow	convince	instruct	remind	urge
cause	encourage	order	require	warn

The class encouraged *Luis to tell* the story of his escape.

A few verbs may be followed either by an infinitive directly or by an infinitive preceded by a noun or pronoun.

ask	expect	need	promise	want	would like

We asked *to speak* to the congregation.

We asked *Rabbi Abrams to speak* to our congregation.

Verb + noun or pronoun + unmarked infinitive

An unmarked infinitive is an infinitive without *to*. A few verbs may be followed by a noun or pronoun and an unmarked (but not a marked) infinitive.

have ("cause")   let ("allow")   make ("force")

Please let *me pay* [not *to pay*] for the tickets.

T2-d Use two-word verbs correctly.

Many verbs in English consist of a verb followed by a preposition or an adverb known as a *particle* (see B1-c). A two-word verb (also known as a *phrasal verb*) often expresses an idiomatic meaning that cannot be understood literally. Consider the verbs in the following sentences, for example.

We *ran across* Dr. Magnotto on the way to the bookstore.

Calvin *dropped in* on his adviser this morning.

Regina told me to *look* her *up* when I got to Seattle.

As you probably know, *ran across* means "encountered," *dropped in* means "paid an unexpected visit," and *look up* means "visit." When you were first learning English, however, these two-word verbs must have suggested strange meanings.

Some two-word verbs are intransitive; they do not take direct objects. (See B2-b.)

This morning I *got up* at dawn.

Transitive two-word verbs (those that take direct objects) have particles that are either separable or inseparable. Separable particles may be separated from the verb by the direct object.

Lucinda *called* the wedding *off*.

When the direct object is a noun, a separable particle may also follow the verb immediately:

At the last minute, Lucinda *called off* the wedding.

When the direct object is a pronoun, however, the particle must be separated from the verb.

Why was there no wedding? Lucinda *called* it *off* [not *called off it*].

Inseparable particles must follow the verb immediately. A direct object cannot come between the verb and the particle.

The police will *look into* the matter [not *look* the matter *into*].

The following list includes common two-word verbs. If a particle can be separated from the verb by a direct object, a pronoun is shown between the verb and the particle: *ask (someone) out.* When in doubt about the meaning of a two-word verb, consult the dictionary.

COMMON TWO-WORD VERBS

ask (someone) out
break down
bring (something or
    someone) up
burn (something) down
burn down
burn (something) up
burn up
call (something) off
call (someone) up
clean (something) up
clean up
come across
cut (something) up
do (something) over
drop in (on someone)
drop (someone or
    something) off
drop out (of something)
fill (something) out
fill (something) up
get along (with someone)
get away (with something)
get up
give (something) away
give (something) back
give in
give up
go out (with someone)
go over (something)
grow up
hand (something) in
hand (something) out
hang on
hang (something) up

help out
help (someone) out
keep on (doing something)
keep up (with someone or
    something)
leave (something) out
look into (something)
look (something) over
look (something) up
make (something) up
pick (something) out
pick (someone) up
pick (something) up
play around
point (something) out
put (something) away
put (something) back
put (something) off
put (something) on
put (something) out
put (something) together
put up (with someone or
    something)
quiet down
run across (someone or
    something)
run into (someone or
    something)
run out (of something)
see (someone) off
shut (something) off
speak to (someone)
speak up
stay away (from someone or
    something)

COMMON TWO-WORD VERBS

stay up	try (something) on
take care of (someone or something)	try (something) out
	turn (something) down
take off	turn (something) on
take (something) off	turn out
take (someone) out	turn up
take (something) over	wake up
think (something) over	wake (someone) up
throw (something) away	wear out
throw (something) out	wrap (something) up

T2-e Do not omit needed verbs.

Some languages allow the omission of the verb when the meaning is clear without it; English does not.

▶ Jim *is* exceptionally intelligent.

▶ Many streets in San Francisco *are* very steep.

▶ Nancy *is* in the backyard.

T3

Other trouble spots

T3-a Do not omit subjects or the expletive *there* or *it*.

English requires a subject for all sentences except imperatives, in which the subject *you* is understood (*Give to the poor*). (See B2-a.) If your native language allows the omission of an explicit subject in other sentences or clauses, be especially alert to this requirement in English.

▶ ~~Have~~ *I have* a large collection of baseball cards.

▶ Your aunt is very energetic; *she* seems young for her age.

When the subject has been moved from its normal position before the verb, English sometimes requires an expletive (*there* or *it*) at the beginning of the sentence or clause. (See B2-a.) *There* is used at the beginning of a sentence or clause that draws the reader's (or listener's) attention to the location or existence of something.

> *There is*
> ▶ ~~Is~~ an apple in the refrigerator.
>   ^

> *there*
> ▶ As you know, are many religious sects in India.
>   ^

Notice that the verb agrees with the subject that follows it: *apple is, sects are.* (See G1-f.)

In one of its uses, the word *it* functions as an expletive, to call attention to a subject following the verb.

> *It is*
> ▶ ~~Is~~ healthy to eat fruit and grains.
>   ^

> *It is*
> ▶ ~~Is~~ clear that we must change our approach.
>   ^

The subjects of these sentences are *to eat fruit and grains* (an infinitive phrase) and *that we must change our approach* (a noun clause). See B3-b and B3-e.

As you probably know, the word *it* is also used as the subject of sentences describing the weather or temperature, stating the time, indicating distance, or suggesting an environmental fact.

It is raining in the valley, and *it* is snowing in the mountains.

In July, *it* is very hot in Arizona.

It is 9:15 A.M.

It is three hundred miles to Chicago.

It gets noisy in our dorm on weekends.

T3-b Do not repeat the subject of a sentence.

English does not allow a subject to be repeated in its own clause.

> ▶ The doctor ~~she~~ advised me to cut down on salt.

The pronoun *she* repeats the subject *doctor.*

The subject of a sentence should not be repeated even if a word group intervenes between the subject and the verb.

▶ The car that had been stolen ~~it~~ was found.

The pronoun *it* repeats the subject *car*.

T3-c Do not repeat an object or adverb in an adjective clause.

In some languages an object or an adverb is repeated later in the adjective clause in which it appears; in English such repetitions are not allowed. Adjective clauses begin with relative pronouns (*who, whom, whose, which, that*) or relative adverbs (*when, where*), and these words always serve a grammatical function within the clauses they introduce. (See B3-e.) Another word in the clause cannot also serve that same grammatical function.

When a relative pronoun functions as the object of a verb or the object of a preposition, do not add another word with the same function later in the clause.

▶ The puppy ran after the car that we were riding in, ~~it~~.
                                                    ^

The relative pronoun *that* is the object of the preposition *in,* so the object *it* is not allowed.

Even when the relative pronoun has been omitted, do not add another word with its same function.

▶ The puppy ran after the car we were riding in, ~~it~~.
                                                 ^

The relative pronoun *that* is understood even though it is not present in the sentence.

Like a relative pronoun, a relative adverb should not be echoed later in its clause.

▶ The place where I work ~~there~~ is one hour from the city.

The adverb *there* should not echo the relative adverb *where.*

T3-d Place adjectives and adverbs with care.

Adjectives modify nouns or pronouns; adverbs modify verbs, adjectives, or other adverbs (see B1-d, B1-e). Both native and nonnative speakers encounter problems in the use of adjectives and adverbs (see G4). For nonnative speakers, the placement of adjectives and adverbs can also be troublesome.

Placement of adjectives

No doubt you have already learned that in English adjectives usually precede the nouns they modify and that they may also appear following linking verbs. (See B1-d and B2-b.)

> Janine wore a *new* necklace. Janine's necklace was *new*.

When adjectives pile up in front of a noun, however, you may sometimes have difficulty arranging them. English is quite particular about the order of cumulative adjectives, those not separated by commas. (See P2-d.)

> Janine was wearing *a beautiful antique silver* necklace [not *a silver antique beautiful* necklace].

The chart on the next page shows the order in which cumulative adjectives ordinarily appear in front of the noun they modify. This list is just a general guide; don't be surprised when you encounter exceptions.

NOTE: Long strings of cumulative adjectives tend to be awkward. As a rule, use no more than two or three of them between the article (or other noun marker) and the noun modified.

> a beautiful old pine table   Susan's large round painting
> two enormous French urns   some small blue medicine bottles
> an exotic purple jungle flower

Placement of adverbs

Adverbs modifying verbs appear in various positions: at the beginning or end of the sentence, before or after the verb, or between a helping verb and its main verb.

Usual order of cumulative adjectives

ARTICLE OR OTHER NOUN MARKER

a, an, the, her, Joe's, two, many, some

EVALUATIVE WORD

attractive, dedicated, delicious, ugly, disgusting

SIZE

large, enormous, small, little

LENGTH OR SHAPE

long, short, round, square

AGE

new, old, young, antique

COLOR

yellow, blue, crimson

NATIONALITY

French, Scandinavian, Vietnamese

RELIGION

Catholic, Protestant, Jewish, Muslim

MATERIAL

silver, walnut, wool, marble

NOUN/ADJECTIVE

tree (as in *tree house*), kitchen (as in *kitchen table*)

THE NOUN MODIFIED

house, sweater, bicycle, bread, woman, priest

Slowly, we drive along the rain-slick road.

Mother wrapped the gift *carefully.*

Martin *always* wins our tennis matches.

Christina is *rarely* late for our lunch dates.

My daughter has *often* spoken of you.

An adverb may not, however, be placed between a verb and its direct object.

    carefully
▶ Mother wrapped ~~carefully~~ the gift.
       ^

The adverb *carefully* may be placed at the beginning or at the end of this sentence or before the verb. It cannot appear after the verb because the verb is followed by the direct object *the gift.*

T3-e Distinguish between present participles and past participles used as adjectives.

Both present and past participles may be used as adjectives. The present participle always ends in *-ing.* Past participles usually end in *-ed, -d, -en, -n,* or *-t.* (See G2-a.)

PRESENT PARTICIPLES confusing, speaking

PAST PARTICIPLES confused, spoken

Participles used as adjectives can precede the nouns they modify; they can also follow linking verbs, in which case they describe the subject of the sentence. (See B2-b.)

It was a *depressing* movie. Jim was a *depressed* young man.

The essay was *confusing.* The student was *confused.*

A present participle should describe a person or thing causing or stimulating an experience; a past participle should describe a person or thing undergoing an experience.

The lecturer was *boring* [not *bored*].

The audience was *bored* [not *boring*].

In the first example, the lecturer is causing boredom, not experiencing it. In the second example, the audience is experiencing boredom, not causing it.

The participles that cause the most trouble for nonnative speakers are those describing mental states:

annoying/annoyed	exhausting/exhausted
boring/bored	fascinating/fascinated
confusing/confused	frightening/frightened
depressing/depressed	satisfying/satisfied
exciting/excited	surprising/surprised

When you come across these words in your drafts, check to see that you have used them correctly.

T3-f Become familiar with common prepositions that show time and place.

The most frequently used prepositions in English are *at, by, for, from, in, of, on, to,* and *with*. Each of these prepositions has a variety of uses that must be learned gradually, in context.

Prepositions that indicate time and place can be difficult to master because the differences among them are subtle and idiomatic. The chart in this section limits itself to three troublesome prepositions that show time and place: *at, on,* and *in*.

Not every possible use is listed in the chart, so don't be surprised when you encounter exceptions and idiomatic uses that you must learn one at a time. For example, in English we ride *in* a car but *on* a bus, train, or subway. And when we fly *on* (not *in*) a plane, we are not sitting on top of the plane.

At, on, and *in* to show time and place

Showing time

AT *at* a specific time: *at* 7:00, *at* dawn, *at* dinner

ON *on* a specific day or date: *on* Tuesday, *on* June 4

IN *in* a part of a 24-hour period: *in* the afternoon, *in* the daytime [but *at* night]

in a year or month: *in* 1999, *in* July

in a period of time: finished *in* three hours

Showing place

AT *at* a meeting place or location: *at* home, *at* the club
at the edge of something: sitting *at* the desk
at the corner of something: turning *at* the intersection
at a target: throwing the snowball *at* Lucy

ON *on* a surface: placed *on* the table, hanging *on* the wall
on a street: the house *on* Spring Street

IN *in* an enclosed space: *in* the garage, *in* the envelope
in a geographic location: *in* San Diego, *in* Texas

P

Punctuation

P

Punctuation

P1

The comma

The comma was invented to help readers. Without it, sentence parts can collide into one another unexpectedly, causing misreadings.

> CONFUSING   If you cook Elmer will do the dishes.

> CONFUSING   While we were eating a rattlesnake approached our campsite.

Add commas in the logical places (after *cook* and *eating*), and suddenly all is clear. No longer is Elmer being cooked, the rattlesnake being eaten.

Various rules have evolved to prevent such misreadings and to speed readers along through complex grammatical structures. Those rules are detailed in this section.

P1-a   Use a comma before a coordinating conjunction joining independent clauses.

When a coordinating conjunction connects two or more independent clauses — word groups that could stand alone as separate sentences — a comma must precede it. There are seven coordinating conjunctions in English: *and, but, or, nor, for, so,* and *yet.*

A comma tells readers that one independent clause has come to a close and that another is about to begin.

▶ Nearly everyone has heard of love at first sight‸ but I fell in love

  at first dance.

EXCEPTION: If the two independent clauses are short and there is no danger of misreading, the comma may be omitted.

   The plane took off and we were on our way.

CAUTION: Do *not* use a comma to separate compound elements that are not independent clauses. See P2-a.

▶ A good money manager controls expenses, and invests surplus

dollars to meet future needs.

The word group following *and* is not an independent clause; it is the second half of a compound predicate.

P1-b Use a comma after an introductory word group.

The most common introductory word groups are clauses and phrases functioning as adverbs. Such word groups usually tell when, where, how, why, or under what conditions the main action of the sentence occurred. (See B3-a, B3-b, and B3-e.)

A comma tells readers that the introductory clause or phrase has come to a close and that the main part of the sentence is about to begin.

▶ When Irwin was ready to eat, his cat jumped onto the table.

▶ Near a small stream at the bottom of the canyon, we discovered

an abandoned shelter.

EXCEPTION: The comma may be omitted after a short adverb clause or phrase if there is no danger of misreading.

In no time we were at 2,800 feet.

Sentences also frequently begin with participial phrases describing the noun or pronoun immediately following them. The comma tells readers that they are about to learn the identity of the person or thing described; therefore, the comma is usually required even when the phrase is short. (See B3-b.)

▶ Knowing that he couldn't outrun a car, Kevin took to the fields.

▶ Excited about the move, Alice and Don began packing their books.

NOTE: Other introductory word groups include conjunctive adverbs, transitional expressions, and absolute phrases. (See P1-f.)

P1-c Use a comma between all items in a series.

When three or more items are presented in a series, those items should be separated from one another with commas. Items in a series may be single words, phrases, or clauses.

▶ For breakfast the children ordered cornflakes, English muffins with

peanut butter, and cherry Cokes.

Although some writers view the comma between the last two items as optional, most experts advise using it because its omission can result in ambiguity or misreading.

▶ My uncle willed me all of his property, houses, and warehouses.

Did the uncle will his property *and* houses *and* warehouses — or simply his property, consisting of houses and warehouses? If the first meaning is intended, a comma is necessary to prevent ambiguity.

▶ The activities include a search for lost treasure, dubious financial

dealings, much discussion of ancient heresies, and midnight orgies.

Without the comma, the people seem to be discussing orgies, not participating in them. The comma makes it clear that *midnight orgies* is a separate item in the series.

P1-d Use a comma between coordinate adjectives not joined by *and*. Do not use a comma between cumulative adjectives.

When two or more adjectives each modify a noun separately, they are *coordinate*.

Mother has become a *strong, confident, independent* woman.

Adjectives are coordinate if they can be joined with *and* (strong *and* confident *and* independent) or if they can be scrambled (an *independent, strong, confident* woman).

Two or more adjectives that do not modify the noun separately are cumulative.

Three large gray shapes moved slowly toward us.

Beginning with the adjective closest to the noun *shapes,* these modifiers lean on one another, piggyback style, with each modifying a larger word group. *Gray* modifies *shapes, large* modifies *gray shapes,* and *three* modifies *large gray shapes.* We cannot insert the word *and* between cumulative adjectives (three *and* large *and* gray shapes). Nor can we scramble them (*gray three large* shapes).

COORDINATE ADJECTIVES

▶ Robert is a warm‚ gentle‚ affectionate father.

CUMULATIVE ADJECTIVES

▶ Ira ordered a rich⁄ chocolate⁄ layer cake.

P1-e Use commas to set off nonrestrictive elements. Do not use commas to set off restrictive elements.

Word groups describing nouns or pronouns (adjective clauses, adjective phrases, and appositives) are restrictive or nonrestrictive. A *restrictive* element defines or limits the meaning of the word it modifies and is therefore essential to the meaning of the sentence. Because it contains essential information, a restrictive element is not set off with commas.

RESTRICTIVE
For camp the children needed clothes *that were washable.*

If you remove a restrictive element from a sentence, the meaning changes significantly, becoming more general than you intended. The writer of the example sentence does not mean that the children needed clothes in general. The intended meaning is more limited: The children needed *washable* clothes.

A *nonrestrictive* element describes a noun or pronoun whose meaning has already been clearly defined or limited. Because it contains nonessential or parenthetical information, a nonrestrictive element is set off with commas.

NONRESTRICTIVE

For camp the children needed sturdy shoes, *which were expensive.*

If you remove a nonrestrictive element from a sentence, the meaning does not change dramatically. Some meaning is lost, to be sure, but the defining characteristics of the person or thing described remain the same as before. The children needed *sturdy shoes,* and these happened to be expensive.

Often it is difficult to tell whether a word group is restrictive or nonrestrictive without seeing it in context and considering your meaning. Should you write "The dessert made with fresh raspberries was delicious" or "The dessert, made with fresh raspberries, was delicious"? That depends. If the phrase *made with fresh raspberries* tells readers which of several desserts you're referring to, you would omit the commas. If the phrase merely adds information about one dessert, you would use the commas.

Adjective clauses

Adjective clauses are patterned like sentences, containing subjects and verbs, but they function within sentences as modifiers of nouns or pronouns. Adjective clauses begin with a relative pronoun (*who, whom, whose, which, that*) or with a relative adverb (*where, when*).

Nonrestrictive adjective clauses are set off with commas; restrictive adjective clauses are not.

NONRESTRICTIVE CLAUSE

▶ Ed's country house, which is located on thirteen acres, was completely furnished with bats in the rafters and mice in the kitchen.

The clause *which is located on thirteen acres* does not restrict the meaning of *Ed's country house,* so the information is nonessential.

RESTRICTIVE CLAUSE

▶ An office manager for a corporation/ that had government contracts/ asked her supervisor for permission to reprimand her co-workers for smoking.

Because the adjective clause *that had government contracts* identifies the corporation, the information is essential.

NOTE: Use *that* only with restrictive clauses. Many writers prefer to use *which* only with nonrestrictive clauses, but usage varies.

Phrases functioning as adjectives

Prepositional or verbal phrases functioning as adjectives may be restrictive or nonrestrictive. Nonrestrictive phrases are set off with commas; restrictive phrases are not.

NONRESTRICTIVE PHRASE

▶ The helicopter‚ with its 100,000-candlepower spotlight

illuminating the area‚ circled above.

The *with* phrase is nonessential because its purpose is not to specify which of two or more helicopters is being discussed.

RESTRICTIVE PHRASE

▶ One corner of the attic was filled with newspapers⁄ dating from

the turn of the century.

Dating from the turn of the century restricts the meaning of *newspapers,* so the comma should be omitted.

Appositives

An appositive is a noun or noun phrase that renames a nearby noun. Nonrestrictive appositives are set off with commas; restrictive appositives are not.

NONRESTRICTIVE APPOSITIVE

▶ Norman Mailer's first novel‚ *The Naked and the Dead‚* was a best-seller.

The term *first* restricts the meaning to one novel, so the appositive *The Naked and the Dead* is nonrestrictive.

RESTRICTIVE APPOSITIVE

▶ The song⁄ "Fire It Up⁄" was blasted out of amplifiers ten feet tall.

Once they've read *song,* readers still don't know precisely which song the writer means. The appositive following *song* restricts its meaning.

P1-f Use commas to set off transitional and parenthetical expressions, absolute phrases, and contrasted elements.

Transitional expressions

Transitional expressions serve as bridges between sentences or parts of sentences. They include conjunctive adverbs such as *however, therefore,* and *moreover* and transitional phrases such as *for example, as a matter of fact,* and *in other words.* (For a more complete list, see P3-b.)

When a transitional expression appears between independent clauses in a compound sentence, it is preceded by a semicolon and is usually followed by a comma.

▶ Minh did not understand our language; moreover, he was

unfamiliar with our customs.

▶ Natural foods are not always salt free; for example, celery

contains more sodium than most people would imagine.

When a transitional expression appears at the beginning of a sentence or in the middle of an independent clause, it is usually set off with commas.

▶ As a matter of fact, American football was established by fans who

wanted to play a more organized game of rugby.

▶ The prospective babysitter looked very promising; she was busy,

however, throughout the month of January.

EXCEPTION: If a transitional expression blends smoothly with the rest of the sentence, calling for little or no pause in reading, it does not need to be set off with commas. Expressions such as *also, at least, certainly, consequently, indeed, of course, no doubt, perhaps, then,* and *therefore* do not always call for a pause.

Bill's bicycle is broken; *therefore* you will need to borrow Sue's.

Bill's bicycle is broken; you will *therefore* need to borrow Sue's.

Parenthetical expressions

Expressions that are distinctly parenthetical should be set off with commas. Providing supplemental comments or information, they interrupt the flow of a sentence or appear as afterthoughts.

▶ Evolution ⌄so far as we know⌄doesn't work this way.

▶ The bluefish weighed about twelve pounds ⌄give or take a few ounces.

Absolute phrases

Absolute phrases should be set off with commas. An absolute phrase, which modifies the whole sentence, usually consists of a noun followed by a participle or participial phrase. (See B3-d.)

▶ His tennis game at last perfected ⌄Chris won the cup.

▶ Brenda was forced to rely on public transportation ⌄her car having been wrecked the week before.

Contrasted elements

Sharp contrasts beginning with words such as *not* and *unlike* are set off with commas.

▶ Now that I am married, Jane talks to me as an adult ⌄not as her little sister.

▶ Celia ⌄unlike Robert ⌄had no loathing for dance contests.

P1-g Use commas to set off nouns of direct address, the words *yes* and *no*, interrogative tags, and mild interjections.

▶ Forgive us ⌄Dr. Spock ⌄for spanking Brian.

▶ Yes ⌄the loan will probably be approved.

▶ The film was faithful to the book ⌄wasn't it?

▶ Well, cases like these are difficult to decide.
     ∧

P1-h Use commas with expressions such as *he said* to set off direct quotations. (See also P6-f.)

▶ Naturalist Arthur Cleveland Bent remarked, "In part the
     ∧
peregrine declined unnoticed because it is not adorable."

▶ "Convictions are more dangerous foes of truth than lies," wrote
                                                            ∧
philosopher Friedrich Nietzsche.

P1-i Use commas with dates, addresses, titles, and numbers.

Dates

In dates, the year is set off from the rest of the sentence with a pair of commas.

▶ On December 12, 1890, orders were sent out for the arrest of
                 ∧   ∧
Sitting Bull.

EXCEPTIONS: Commas are not needed if the date is inverted or if only the month and year are given.

The recycling plan went into effect on 15 April 1993.

January 1994 was an extremely cold month.

Addresses

The elements of an address or place name are followed by commas. A zip code, however, is not preceded by a comma.

▶ John Lennon was born in Liverpool, England, in 1940.
                                    ∧   ∧

▶ Please send the package to Greg Tarvin at 708 Spring Street,
                                                              ∧
Washington, Illinois 61571.
           ∧

Titles

If a title follows a name, separate it from the rest of the sentence with a pair of commas.

▶ Sandra Barnes, M.D., performed the surgery.
　　　　　　　^　　　^

Numbers

In numbers more than four digits long, use commas to separate the numbers into groups of three, starting from the right. In numbers four digits long, a comma is optional.

```
    3,500 [or 3500]
  100,000
5,000,000
```

EXCEPTIONS: Do not use commas in street numbers, zip codes, telephone numbers, or years.

P1-j Use a comma to prevent confusion.

In certain contexts, a comma is necessary to prevent confusion. If the writer has omitted a word or phrase, for example, a comma may be needed to signal the omission.

▶ To err is human; to forgive, divine.
　　　　　　　　　　　　　　^

If two words in a row echo each other, a comma may be needed for ease of reading.

▶ All of the catastrophes that we had feared might happen,
　　　　　　　　　　　　　　　　　　　　　　　　　　　　　　^

　happened.

Sometimes a comma is needed to prevent readers from grouping words in ways that do not match the writer's intention.

▶ Patients who can, walk up and down the halls several times
　　　　　　　　　　^

　a day.

P2

Unnecessary commas

P2-a Do not use a comma between compound elements that are not independent clauses.

Although a comma is used before a coordinating conjunction joining independent clauses (see P1-a), this rule should not be extended to other compound word groups.

▶ Male supremacy was assumed by my father,/and accepted by my

mother.

And links the two parts of a compound predicate: *was assumed* and *accepted*.

▶ Jake still does not realize that his illness is serious,/and that he

will have to alter his diet to improve.

And connects two subordinate clauses, each beginning with *that*.

P2-b Do not use a comma to separate a verb from its subject or object.

A sentence should flow from subject to verb to object without unnecessary pauses. Commas may appear between these major sentence elements only when a specific rule calls for them.

▶ Zoos large enough to give the animals freedom to roam,/are

becoming more popular.

▶ Captain Spurlock observed,/that the vast majority of crimes in our

city are committed by repeat offenders.

The subject *Zoos* should not be separated from its verb, *are becoming*. The verb *observed* should not be separated from its direct object, the subordinate clause beginning with *that*.

P2-c Do not use a comma before the first or after the last
item in a series.

Though commas are required between items in a series (see P1-c),
do not place them either before or after the series.

▶ Other causes of asthmatic attacks are⁄ stress, change in

temperature, humidity, and cold air.

▶ Ironically, this job that appears so glamorous, carefree, and easy⁄

carries a high degree of responsibility.

P2-d Do not use a comma between cumulative adjectives,
between an adjective and a noun, or between an adverb
and an adjective.

Though commas are required between coordinate adjectives (those
that can be joined with *and*), they do not belong between cumulative
adjectives (those that cannot be joined with *and*). (For a full discussion, see P1-d.)

▶ In the corner of the closet we found an old⁄ maroon hatbox

from Sears.

▶ Sandra was wearing a slinky⁄ red silk gown.

A comma should never be used to separate an adjective from
the noun that follows it.

▶ It was a senseless, dangerous⁄ mission.

Nor should a comma be used to separate an adverb from an adjective that follows it.

▶ The Hurst Home is unsuitable as a mental facility for severely⁄

disturbed youths.

P2-e Do not use commas to set off restrictive or mildly parenthetical elements.

Restrictive elements are modifiers or appositives necessary for identifying the nouns they follow; therefore, they are essential to the meaning of the sentence and should not be set off with commas. (For a full discussion, see P1-e.)

> ▶ Drivers,/who think they own the road,/make cycling a dangerous
>
> sport.
>
> The *who clause* restricts the meaning of *Drivers* and is therefore essential to the meaning of the sentence. Putting commas around the *who* clause falsely suggests that all drivers think they own the road.

> ▶ Margaret Mead's book,/*Coming of Age in Samoa*,/stirred up
>
> considerable controversy when it was published.
>
> Since Margaret Mead wrote more than one book, the appositive contains information essential to the meaning of the sentence.

Although commas should be used with distinctly parenthetical expressions (see P1-f), do not use them to set off elements that are only mildly parenthetical.

> ▶ As long as patients are treated in a professional yet
>
> compassionate manner, most,/eventually,/learn to deal
>
> with their illness.

P2-f Do not use a comma to set off a concluding adverb clause that is essential to the meaning of the sentence.

When adverb clauses introduce a sentence, they are nearly always followed by a comma (see P1-b). When they conclude a sentence, however, they are not set off by commas if their content is essential to the meaning of the earlier part of the sentence. Adverb clauses beginning with *after, as soon as, before, because, if, since, unless, until,* and *when* are usually essential.

▶ Don't visit Paris at the height of the tourist season/ unless

you have booked hotel reservations.

> Without the concluding *unless* clause, the meaning of the sentence would be broader than the writer intended.

When a concluding adverb clause is nonessential, it should be preceded by a comma. Clauses beginning with *although, even though, though,* and *whereas* are usually nonessential.

> The lecture seemed to last only a short time, although the clock said it had gone on for more than an hour.

P2-g Avoid other common misuses of the comma.

Do not use a comma in the following situations.

AFTER A COORDINATING CONJUNCTION (*AND, BUT, OR, NOR, FOR, SO, YET*)

▶ Occasionally soap operas are performed live, but/ more often they are

taped.

AFTER *SUCH AS* OR *LIKE*

▶ Many shade-loving plants, such as/ begonias, impatiens, and

coleus, can add color to a shady garden.

BEFORE *THAN*

▶ Touring Crete was more thrilling for us/ than visiting the Greek

islands frequented by the jet set.

AFTER *ALTHOUGH*

▶ Although/ the air was balmy, the water was too cold for

swimming.

BEFORE A PARENTHESIS

▶ At MCI Sylvia began at the bottom/(with only three and a half walls and a swivel chair), but within five years she had been promoted to supervisor.

TO SET OFF AN INDIRECT (REPORTED) QUOTATION

▶ Samuel Goldwyn once said/that a verbal contract isn't worth the paper it's written on.

WITH A QUESTION MARK OR AN EXCLAMATION POINT

▶ "Why don't you try it?/" she coaxed.

P3

The semicolon

The semicolon is used to separate major sentence elements of equal grammatical rank.

P3-a Use a semicolon between closely related independent clauses not joined by a coordinating conjunction.

When related independent clauses appear in one sentence, they are ordinarily connected with a comma and a coordinating conjunction (*and, but, or, nor, for, so, yet*). The conjunction expresses the relation between the clauses. If the relation is clear without the conjunction, a writer may choose to connect the clauses with a semicolon instead.

> Injustice is relatively easy to bear; what stings is justice.
> — H. L. Mencken

A semicolon must be used whenever a coordinating conjunction has been omitted between independent clauses. To use merely a comma creates an error known as a comma splice. (See G6.)

▶ Most U.S. hospitals offer only Western methods of treatment/**;** hospitals in China provide both Western and traditional Chinese medicine.

CAUTION: Do not overuse the semicolon as a means of revising comma splices. For other revision strategies, see G6.

P3-b Use a semicolon between independent clauses linked with a transitional expression.

Transitional expressions include conjunctive adverbs and transitional phrases.

CONJUNCTIVE ADVERBS
accordingly, also, anyway, besides, certainly, consequently, conversely, finally, furthermore, hence, however, incidentally, indeed, instead, likewise, meanwhile, moreover, nevertheless, next, nonetheless, otherwise, similarly, specifically, still, subsequently, then, therefore, thus

TRANSITIONAL PHRASES
after all, as a matter of fact, as a result, at any rate, at the same time, even so, for example, for instance, in addition, in conclusion, in fact, in other words, in the first place, on the contrary, on the other hand

When a transitional expression appears between independent clauses, it is preceded by a semicolon and often followed by a comma.

▶ I learned all the rules and regulations/**;**however, I never really learned to control the ball.

When a transitional expression appears in the middle or at the end of the second independent clause, the semicolon goes *between the clauses.*

Most singers gain fame through hard work and dedication; Evita, however, found other means.

Transitional expressions should not be confused with the coordinating conjunctions *and, but, or, nor, for, so,* and *yet,* which are preceded by a comma when they link independent clauses. (See P1-a and G6-a.)

P3-c Use a semicolon between items in a series containing internal punctuation.

▶ Classic science fiction sagas are *Star Trek,* with Mr. Spock and his large pointed ears/; *Battlestar Galactica,* with its Cylon Raiders/; and *Star Wars,* with Han Solo, Luke Skywalker, and Darth Vader.

Without the semicolons the reader must sort out the major groupings, distinguishing between important and less important pauses according to the logic of the sentence. By inserting semicolons at the major breaks, the writer does this work for the reader.

P3-d Avoid common misuses of the semicolon.

Do not use a semicolon in the following situations.

BETWEEN A SUBORDINATE CLAUSE AND THE REST OF THE SENTENCE

▶ Unless you brush your teeth within ten or fifteen minutes after eating/, brushing does almost no good.

BETWEEN AN APPOSITIVE AND THE WORD IT REFERS TO

▶ Another delicious dish is the chef's special/, a roasted duck rubbed with spices and stuffed with wild rice.

TO INTRODUCE A LIST

▶ Some of my favorite artists are featured on *Red, Hot, and Blue*/: the Neville Brothers, Annie Lennox, and Neneh Cherry.

BETWEEN INDEPENDENT CLAUSES JOINED BY *AND, BUT, OR, NOR, FOR, SO,* OR *YET*

▶ Five of the applicants had worked with spreadsheets ; but only
one was familiar with database management.

P4

The colon

The colon is used primarily to call attention to the words that follow it.

P4-a Use a colon after an independent clause to direct attention to a list, an appositive, or a quotation.

A LIST
The daily routine should include at least the following: twenty knee bends, fifty sit-ups, fifteen leg lifts, and five minutes of running in place.

AN APPOSITIVE
My roommate is guilty of two of the seven deadly sins: gluttony and sloth.

A QUOTATION
Consider the words of John F. Kennedy: "Ask not what your country can do for you; ask what you can do for your country."

For other ways of introducing quotations, see P6-f.

P4-b Use a colon between independent clauses if the second summarizes or explains the first.

Minds are like parachutes: They function only when open.

NOTE: When an independent clause follows a colon, it may begin with a lowercase or a capital letter.

P4-c Use a colon after the salutation in a formal letter, to indicate hours and minutes, to show proportions, between a title and subtitle, and to separate city from publisher and date in bibliographic entries.

Dear Sir or Madam:

5:30 P.M. (or p.m.)

The ratio of women to men was 2:1.

The Glory of Hera: Greek Mythology and the Greek Family

Boston: Bedford, 1995

NOTE: In biblical references, a colon is ordinarily used between chapter and verse (Luke 2:14). The Modern Language Association recommends a period instead (Luke 2.14).

P4-d Avoid common misuses of the colon.

A colon must be preceded by a full independent clause. Therefore, avoid using it in the following situations.

BETWEEN A VERB AND ITS OBJECT OR COMPLEMENT

▶ Some important vitamins found in vegetables are ꞉/vitamin A, thiamine, niacin, and vitamin C.

BETWEEN A PREPOSITION AND ITS OBJECT

▶ The area to be painted consisted of ꞉/three gable ends, trim work, sixteen windows, and a front and back porch.

AFTER *SUCH AS, INCLUDING,* OR *FOR EXAMPLE*

▶ The trees on our campus include many fine Japanese specimens such as ꞉/black pines, ginkgos, weeping cherries, and cutleaf maples.

P5

The apostrophe

P5-a Use an apostrophe to indicate that a noun is possessive.

Possessive nouns usually indicate ownership, as in *Tim's hat* or *the lawyer's desk*. Frequently, however, ownership is only loosely implied: *the tree's roots, a day's work*. If you are not sure whether a noun is possessive, try turning it into an *of* phrase: *the roots of the tree, the work of a day*.

When to add -'s

    1. If the noun does not end in *-s*, add *-'s*.

    Roy managed to climb out on the driver's side.

    Thank you for refunding the children's money.

    2. If the noun is singular and ends in *-s*, add *-'s*.

    Lois's sister spent last year in India.

EXCEPTION: If pronunciation would be awkward with the added *-'s*, some writers use only the apostrophe. Either use is acceptable.

    Sophocles' plays are among my favorites.

When to add only an apostrophe

If the noun is plural and ends in *-s*, add only an apostrophe.

    Both diplomats' briefcases were stolen.

Joint possession

To show joint possession, use *-'s* (or *-s'*) with the last noun only; to show individual possession, make all nouns possessive.

    Have you seen Joyce and Greg's new camper?

John's and Marie's expectations of marriage couldn't have been more different.

In the first sentence, Joyce and Greg jointly own one camper. In the second sentence, John and Marie individually have different expectations.

Compound nouns

If a noun is compound, use *-'s* (or *-s'*) with the last element.

Her father-in-law's sculpture won first place.

P5-b Use an apostrophe and *-s* to indicate that an indefinite pronoun is possessive.

Indefinite pronouns are pronouns that refer to no specific person or thing: *everyone, someone, no one, something.* (See B1-b.)

Someone's raincoat has been left behind.

This diet will improve almost anyone's health.

P5-c Use an apostrophe to mark contractions.

In contractions the apostrophe takes the place of missing letters. In the following sentence, *It's* stands for *It is* and *can't* stands for *cannot.*

It's a shame that Frank can't go on the tour.

The apostrophe is also used to mark the omission of the first two digits of a year (the class of '91) or years (the '60s generation).

P5-d Use an apostrophe and *-s* to pluralize numbers mentioned as numbers, letters mentioned as letters, words mentioned as words, and abbreviations.

Peggy skated nearly perfect figure 8's.

The bleachers in our section were marked with large red *J*'s.

We've heard enough *maybe*'s.

You must ask to see their I.D.'s.

Notice that the *-s* is not italicized when used with an italicized letter or word.

EXCEPTION: An *-s* alone is often added to the years in a decade: the 1980s.

NOTE: The Modern Language Association recommends no apostrophe in plurals of numbers and abbreviations: figure 8s, VCRs.

P5-e Avoid common misuses of the apostrophe.

Do not use an apostrophe in the following situations.

WITH NOUNS THAT ARE NOT POSSESSIVE

▶ Some ~~outpatient's~~ *outpatients* are given special parking permits.

IN THE POSSESSIVE PRONOUNS *ITS, WHOSE, HIS, HERS, OURS, YOURS,*
AND *THEIRS*

▶ Each area has ~~it's~~ *its* own conference room.

It's means *it is*. The possessive pronoun *its* contains no apostrophe despite the fact that it is possessive.

P6

Quotation marks

P6-a Use quotation marks to enclose direct quotations.

Direct quotations of a person's words, whether spoken or written, must be in quotation marks.

"A foolish consistency is the hobgoblin of little minds," wrote Ralph Waldo Emerson.

CAUTION: Do not use quotation marks around indirect quotations. An indirect quotation reports someone's ideas without using that person's exact words.

> Ralph Waldo Emerson believed that consistency for its own sake is the mark of a small mind.

NOTE: In dialogue, begin a new paragraph to mark a change in speaker.

> "Mom, his name is Willie, not William. A thousand times I've told you, it's *Willie.*"
> "Willie is a derivative of William, Lester. Surely his birth certificate doesn't have Willie on it, and I like calling people by their proper names."
> "Yes, it does, ma'am. My mother named me Willie K. Mason."
> — Gloria Naylor

If a single speaker utters more than one paragraph, introduce each paragraph with quotation marks, but do not use closing quotation marks until the end of the speech.

P6-b Set off long quotations of prose or poetry by indenting.

When a quotation of prose runs to more than four typed lines in your paper, set it off by indenting ten spaces from the left margin. Quotation marks are not required because the indented format tells readers that the quotation is taken word for word from a source. Long quotations are ordinarily introduced by a sentence ending with a colon.

> After making an exhaustive study of the historical record, James Horan evaluates Billy the Kid like this:
>
> > The portrait that emerges of [the Kid] from the thousands of pages of affidavits, reports, trial transcripts, his letters, and his testimony is neither the mythical Robin Hood nor the stereotyped adenoidal

```
moron and pathological killer.   Rather Billy
appears as a disturbed, lonely young man,
honest, loyal to his friends, dedicated to
his beliefs, and betrayed by our institu-
tions and the corrupt, ambitious, and com-
promising politicians of his time. (158)
```

The number in parentheses is a citation handled according to the Modern Language Association style. (See M1.)

NOTE: When you quote two or more paragraphs from the source, indent the first line of each paragraph an additional three spaces.

When quoting more than three lines of a poem, set the quoted lines off from the text by indenting ten spaces from the left margin. Use no quotation marks unless they appear in the poem itself. (To punctuate two or three lines of poetry, see P7-h.)

```
Although many anthologizers "modernize" her punctua-
tion, Emily Dickinson relied heavily on dashes, using
them, perhaps, as a musical device.   Here, for example,
is the original version of the opening stanza from
"The Snake":
            A narrow Fellow in the Grass
            Occasionally rides--
            You may have met Him--did you not
            His notice sudden is--
```

NOTE: The American Psychological Association has slightly different guidelines for setting off long quotations. See D2-b.

P6-c Use single quotation marks to enclose a quotation within a quotation.

> According to Paul Eliott, Eskimo hunters "chant an ancient magic song to the seal they are after: 'Beast of the sea! Come and place yourself before me in the early morning!' "

P6-d Use quotation marks around the titles of newspaper and magazine articles, poems, short stories, songs, episodes of television and radio programs, and chapters or subdivisions of books.

> Even after forty minutes of discussion, our class could not agree on an interpretation of Robert Frost's poem "The Road Not Taken."

NOTE: Titles of books, plays, and films and names of magazines and newspapers are put in italics or underlined. (See S6-a.)

P6-e Quotation marks may be used to set off words used as words.

Although words used as words are ordinarily underlined to indicate italics (see S6-d), quotation marks are also acceptable.

> The words "flaunt" and "flout" are frequently confused.

> The words *flaunt* and *flout* are frequently confused.

P6-f Use punctuation with quotation marks according to convention.

This section describes the conventions used by American publishers in placing various marks of punctuation inside or outside quotation marks. It also explains how to punctuate when introducing quoted material.

Periods and commas

Always place periods and commas inside quotation marks.

> "This is a stick-up," said the well-dressed young couple. "We want all your money."

This rule applies to single quotation marks as well as double quotation marks. (See P6-c.) It also applies to all uses of quotation marks: for quoted material, for titles of works, and for words used as words.

EXCEPTION: In the Modern Language Association's style of parenthetical in-text citations (see M1), the period follows the citation in parentheses.

> James M. McPherson acknowledges that the Whigs "were not averse to extending the blessings of American liberty, even to Mexicans and Indians" (48).

Colons and semicolons

Put colons and semicolons outside quotation marks.

> Harold wrote, "I regret that I am unable to attend the fundraiser for AIDS research"; his letter, however, contained a substantial contribution.

Question marks and exclamation points

Put question marks and exclamation points inside quotation marks unless they apply to the sentence as a whole.

> Contrary to tradition, bedtime at my house is marked by "Mommy, can I tell you a story now?"

> Have you heard the old proverb "Do not climb the hill until you reach it"?

In the first sentence, the question mark applies only to the quoted question. In the second sentence, the question mark applies to the whole sentence.

NOTE: MLA parenthetical citations create a special problem. According to MLA, the question mark or exclamation point should appear before the quotation mark, and a period should follow the parenthetical citation: *Rosie Thomas asks, "Is nothing in life ever straight and clear, the way children see it?" (77).*

Introducing quoted material

After a word group introducing a quotation, choose a colon, a comma, or no punctuation at all, whichever is appropriate in context.

If a quotation has been formally introduced, a colon is appropriate. A formal introduction is a full independent clause, not just an expression such as *he said* or *she remarked*.

Morrow views personal ads in the classifieds as an art form: "The personal ad is like a haiku of self-celebration, a brief solo played on one's own horn."

If a quotation is introduced with an expression such as *he said* or *she remarked* — or if it is followed by such an expression — a comma is needed.

My commanding officer said, "If we wanted you to have children, we would have issued them to you."

"You can be a little ungrammatical if you come from the right part of the country," said Robert Frost.

When a quotation is blended into the writer's own sentence, either a comma or no punctuation is appropriate, depending on the way in which the quotation fits into the sentence structure.

The future champion could, as he put it, "float like a butterfly and sting like a bee."

Charles Hudson noted that the prisoners escaped "by squeezing through a tiny window eighteen feet above the floor of their cell."

If a quotation appears at the beginning of a sentence, set it off with a comma unless the quotation ends with a question mark or an exclamation point.

"We shot them like dogs," boasted Davy Crockett, who was among Jackson's troops.

"What is it?" I asked, bracing myself.

If a quoted sentence is interrupted by explanatory words, use commas to set off the explanatory words.

"A great many people think they are thinking," wrote William James, "when they are merely rearranging their prejudices."

If two successive quoted sentences from the same source are interrupted by explanatory words, use a comma before the explanatory words and a period after them.

"I was a flop as a daily reporter," admitted E. B. White. "Every piece had to be a masterpiece — and before you knew it, Tuesday was Wednesday."

P6-g Avoid common misuses of quotation marks.

1. Do not use quotation marks to draw attention to familiar slang, to disown trite expressions, or to justify an attempt at humor.

▶ Between Thanksgiving and Super Bowl Sunday, many American

wives become ⌐football widows.⌐

2. Do not use quotation marks around indirect quotations. (See also P6-a.)

▶ After leaving the scene of the domestic quarrel, the officer said

that ⌐he was due for a coffee break.⌐

3. Do not use quotation marks around the title of your own essay.

P7

Other marks

P7-a The period

1. Use a period to end all sentences except direct questions or genuine exclamations.

Everyone knows that a period should be used to end most sentences. The only problems that arise concern the choice between a period and a question mark or between a period and an exclamation point.

If a sentence reports a question instead of asking it directly, it should end with a period, not a question mark.

Celia asked whether the picnic would be canceled.

If a declarative or an imperative sentence is not a genuine exclamation, it should end with a period, not an exclamation point.

After years of working her way through school, Pat finally graduated with high honors.

2. Use periods in abbreviations according to convention. A period is conventionally used in abbreviations such as the following:

Mr.	B.A.	B.C.	i.e.	A.M. (or a.m.)
Mrs.	M.A.	B.C.E.	e.g.	P.M. (or p.m.)
Ms.	Ph.D.	A.D.	etc.	
Dr.	R.N.	C.E.		

A period is not used with U.S. Postal Service abbreviations for states: MD, TX, CA.

Ordinarily a period is not used in abbreviations of organization names:

NATO	UNESCO	AFL-CIO	FCC
TVA	IRS	SEC	IBM
USA	NAACP	PUSH	FTC
(or U.S.A.)	UCLA	NBA	NIH

Usage varies, however. When in doubt, consult a dictionary, a style manual, or a publication by the agency in question. Even the yellow pages can help.

NOTE: If a sentence ends with a period marking an abbreviation, do not add a second period.

P7-b The question mark

1. Use a question mark after a direct question.

Obviously a direct question should be followed by a question mark.

What is the horsepower of a 747 engine?

If a polite request is written in the form of a question, it too is usually followed by a question mark, although usage varies.

Would you please send me your catalog of lilies?

CAUTION: Do not use a question mark after an indirect question (one that is reported rather than asked directly). Use a period instead.

He asked me where the nearest pastry shop was.

2. Questions in a series may be followed by question marks even when they are not complete sentences.

We wondered where Calamity had hidden this time. Under the sink? Behind the furnace? On top of the bookcase?

P7-c The exclamation point

1. Use an exclamation point after a word group or sentence that expresses exceptional feeling or deserves special emphasis.

The medic shook me and kept yelling, "He's dead! He's dead! Can't you see that?"

2. Do not overuse the exclamation point.

▶ In the fisherman's memory the fish lives on, increasing in length and weight with each passing year, until at last it is big enough to shade a fishing boat/.

This sentence doesn't need to be pumped up with an exclamation point. It is emphatic enough without it.

▶ Whenever I see Steffi lunging forward to put away an overhead smash, it might as well be me/. She does it just the way that I would!

The first exclamation point should be deleted so that the second one will have more force.

P7-d The dash

When typing, use two hyphens to form a dash (--). Do not put spaces before or after the dash.

1. Use dashes to set off parenthetical material that deserves emphasis.

> Everything that went wrong — from the peeping Tom at her window to my head-on collision — was blamed on our move.

2. Use dashes to set off appositives that contain commas.

An appositive is a noun or noun phrase that renames a nearby noun. Ordinarily most appositives are set off with commas (see P1-e), but when the appositive contains commas, a pair of dashes helps readers see the relative importance of all the pauses.

> Gumbo — a New Orleans dish of rice, okra, beans, and spicy seasonings — is our traditional New Year's Day dinner.

3. Use a dash to prepare for a list, a restatement, an amplification, or a dramatic shift in tone or thought.

> Along the wall are the bulk liquids — sesame seed oil, honey, safflower oil, and that half-liquid "peanuts only" peanut butter.

> Consider the amount of sugar in the average person's diet — 104 pounds per year, 90 percent more than that consumed by our ancestors.

> Everywhere we looked there were little kids — a box of Cracker Jacks in one hand and mommy's or daddy's sleeve in the other.

> Kiere took a few steps back, came running full speed, kicked a mighty kick — and missed the ball.

In the first two examples, the writer could also use a colon. (See P4-a.) The colon is more formal than the dash and not quite as dramatic.

4. Do not overuse the dash.

Unless there is a specific reason for using the dash, avoid it. Unnecessary dashes create a choppy effect.

▶ Seeing that our young people learn to use computers as

instructional tools ⫽ for information retrieval ⫽ makes good sense.

Herding them ⫽ sheeplike ⫽ into computer technology does not.

P7-e Parentheses

1. Use parentheses to enclose supplemental material, minor digressions, and afterthoughts.

> After taking her temperature, pulse, and blood pressure (routine vital signs), the nurse made Becky as comfortable as possible.

> The weights James was first able to move (not lift, mind you) were measured in ounces.

2. Use parentheses to enclose letters or numbers labeling items in a series.

> Regulations stipulated that only the following equipment could be used on the survival mission: (1) a knife, (2) thirty feet of parachute line, (3) a book of matches, (4) two ponchos, (5) an *E* tool, and (6) a signal flare.

3. Do not overuse parentheses.

Rough drafts are likely to contain more afterthoughts than necessary. As writers head into a sentence, they often think of additional details, occasionally working them in as best they can with parentheses. Usually such sentences should be revised so that the additional details no longer seem to be afterthoughts.

> ▶ Researchers have said that ~~ten million (estimates run as high as~~ *from ten to fifty million*
> ^
> ~~fifty million)~~ Americans have hypoglycemia.

P7-f Brackets

Use brackets to enclose any words or phrases that you have inserted into an otherwise word-for-word quotation.

> *Audubon* reports that "if there are not enough young to balance deaths, the end of the species [California condor] is inevitable."

The *Audubon* article did not contain the words *California condor* in the sentence quoted, since the context made clear what species was meant, so the writer in this example needed to add the name in brackets.

The Latin word *sic* in brackets indicates that an error in a quoted sentence appears in the original source.

> According to the review, Darci Kistler's performance was brilliant, "exceding [*sic*] the expectations of even her most loyal fans."

Do not overuse *sic,* however, since calling attention to others' mistakes can appear snobbish. The quotation above, for example, might have been handled like this instead: *According to the review, Darci Kistler's performance was so brilliant that it exceeded "the expectations of even her most loyal fans."*

P7-g The ellipsis mark

The ellipsis mark consists of three spaced periods. Use an ellipsis mark to indicate that you have deleted material from an otherwise word-for-word quotation.

> Reuben reports that "when the amount of cholesterol circulating in the blood rises over . . . 300 milligrams per 100, the chances of a heart attack increase dramatically."

If you delete a full sentence or more in the middle of a quoted passage, use a period before the three ellipsis dots.

CAUTION: Do not use the ellipsis mark at the beginning of a quotation; do not use it at the end of a quotation unless you have cut some words from the end of the final sentence quoted.

In quoted poetry, use a full line of dots to indicate that you have dropped a line or more from the poem:

> Had we but world enough, and time,
> This coyness, lady, were no crime.
> . . . .
> But at my back I always hear
> Time's wingèd chariot hurrying near;   — Andrew Marvell

The ellipsis mark may also be used to mark a hesitation or an interruption in speech or to suggest unfinished thoughts.

> Before falling into a coma, the victim whispered,
> "It was a man with a tattoo on his. . . ."

P7-h The slash

Use the slash to separate two or three lines of poetry that have been run in with your text. Add a space both before and after the slash.

> In the opening lines of "Jordan," George Herbert pokes gentle fun at popular poems of his time: "Who says that fictions only and false hair / Become a verse? Is there in truth no beauty?"

More than three lines of poetry should be handled as a block quotation set off from the text. (See P6-b.)

The slash may occasionally be used to separate paired terms such as *pass/fail* and *producer/director*. Do not use a space before or after the slash.

> Roger Sommers, the team's manager/owner, announced a change in the lineup.

Be sparing, however, in this use of the slash. In particular, avoid the use of *and/or, he/she,* and *his/her.*

S

Spelling and Mechanics

S

Spelling and Mechanics

S1

Spelling

You learned to spell from repeated experience with words in both reading and writing, but especially writing. Words have a look, a sound, and even a feel to them as the hand moves across the page. As you proofread, you can probably tell if a word doesn't look quite right. In such cases, the solution is obvious: Look up the word in the dictionary. (See W5-a.)

A word processor equipped with a spelling checker is a useful alternative to a dictionary, but only up to a point. A spelling checker will not tell you how to spell words not listed in its dictionary; nor will it help you catch words commonly confused, such as *accept* and *except,* or common typographical errors, such as *own* for *won.* You will still need to proofread, and for some words you may need to turn to the dictionary.

S1-a Become familiar with the major spelling rules.

1. Use *i* before *e* except after *c* or when sounded like *ay,* as in *neighbor* and *weigh.*

I BEFORE *E*   relieve, believe, sieve, niece, fierce, frieze

E BEFORE *I*   receive, deceive, sleigh, freight, eight

EXCEPTIONS   seize, either, weird, height, foreign, leisure

2. Generally, drop a final silent *e* when adding a suffix that begins with a vowel. Keep the final *e* if the suffix begins with a consonant.

combine, combination	achieve, achievement
desire, desiring	care, careful
prude, prudish	entire, entirety
remove, removable	gentle, gentleness

Words such as *changeable, judgment, argument,* and *truly* are exceptions.

3. When adding -*s* or -*ed* to words ending in *y,* ordinarily change *y* to *i* when the *y* is preceded by a consonant but not when it is preceded by a vowel.

comedy, comedies   monkey, monkeys
dry, dried   play, played

With proper names ending in *y,* however, do not change the *y* to *i* even if it is preceded by a consonant: *the Dougherty family, the Doughertys.*

4. If a final consonant is preceded by a single vowel *and* the consonant ends a one-syllable word or a stressed syllable, double the consonant when adding a suffix beginning with a vowel.

bet, betting   occur, occurrence
commit, committed

5. Add -*s* to form the plural of most nouns; add -*es* to singular nouns ending in -*s, -sh, -ch,* and -*x.*

table, tables   church, churches
paper, papers   dish, dishes

Ordinarily add -*s* to nouns ending in -*o* when the *o* is preceded by a vowel. Add -*es* when it is preceded by a consonant.

radio, radios   hero, heroes
video, videos   tomato, tomatoes

To form the plural of a hyphenated compound word, add the -*s* to the chief word even if it does not appear at the end.

mother-in-law, mothers-in-law

NOTE: English words derived from other languages such as Latin or French sometimes form the plural as they would in their original language.

medium, media   chateau, chateaux
criterion, criteria

ESL NOTE: Spelling may vary slightly among English-speaking countries. This can prove particularly confusing for ESL students, who may have learned British or Canadian English. Following is a list of some common words spelled differently in American and British English. Consult a dictionary for others.

AMERICAN	BRITISH
canceled, traveled	cancelled, travelled
color, humor	colour, humour
judgment	judgement
check	cheque
realize, apologize	realise, apologise
defense	defence
anemia, anesthetic	anaemia, anaesthetic
theater, center	theatre, centre
fetus	foetus
mold, smolder	mould, smoulder
civilization	civilisation
connection, inflection	connexion, inflexion
licorice	liquorice

S1-b Discriminate between words that sound alike but have different meanings.

Words that sound alike or nearly alike but have different meanings and spellings are called homophones. The following homophones are so commonly confused that a good proofreader will double-check their every use.

affect (verb: "to exert an influence")
effect (verb: "to accomplish"; noun: "result")

its (possessive pronoun: "of or belonging to it")
it's (contraction for "it is")

loose (adjective: "free, not securely attached")
lose (verb: "to fail to keep, to be deprived of")

principal (adjective: "most important"; noun: "head of a school")
principle (noun: "a general or fundamental truth")

their (possessive pronoun: "belonging to them")
they're (contraction for "they are")
there (adverb: "that place or position")

who's (contraction for "who is")
whose (possessive form of "who")

your (possessive form of "you")
you're (contraction of "you are")

To check for correct use of these and other homophones, consult the Glossary of Usage in this book (W1). There you will find definitions and examples for all of the following sets of words.

HOMOPHONES IN THE GLOSSARY OF USAGE (See W1.)

accept, except	elicit, illicit
adverse, averse	eminent, imminent
advice, advise	everyone, every one
affect, effect	ingenious, ingenuous
all ready, already	its, it's
all together, altogether	lead, led
allusion, illusion	loose, lose
anyone, any one	maybe, may be
awhile, a while	passed, past
beside, besides	principal, principle
capital, capitol	sometime, some time, sometimes
censor, censure	than, then
cite, site	their, there, they're
climactic, climatic	to, too, two
coarse, course	weather, whether
complement, compliment	who's, whose
conscience, conscious	your, you're

S1-c Be alert to the following **commonly misspelled words.**

absence	almost	argument	benefited
academic	although	arising	brilliant
accidentally	altogether	arithmetic	Britain
accommodate	always	arrangement	bureau
accomplish	amateur	ascend	business
accumulate	among	association	cafeteria
achievement	analyze	athlete	calendar
acknowledge	annual	athletics	candidate
acquaintance	answer	attendance	category
acquire	apology	audience	cemetery
across	apparently	bachelor	changeable
address	appearance	basically	changing
aggravate	appropriate	beginning	characteristic
all right	arctic	believe	chosen

column
coming
commitment
committed
committee
comparative
competitive
conceivable
conference
conferred
conqueror
conscience
conscientious
conscious
convenient
courteous
criticism
criticize
curiosity
dealt
decision
definitely
descendant
describe
description
despair
desperate
develop
dictionary
dining
disagree
disappear
disappoint
disastrous
dissatisfied
eighth
eligible
eliminate
embarrass
eminent
emphasize
entirely
entrance
environment
equivalent
especially
exaggerated

exercise
exhaust
existence
experience
explanation
extraordinary
extremely
familiar
fascinate
February
foreign
forty
fourth
friend
government
grammar
guard
guidance
harass
height
humorous
illiterate
imaginary
imagination
immediately
incidentally
incredible
indefinitely
indispensable
inevitable
infinite
intelligence
interesting
irrelevant
irresistible
knowledge
laboratory
legitimate
license
lightning
literature
loneliness
maintenance
maneuver
marriage
mathematics
mischievous

necessary
nevertheless
noticeable
obstacle
occasion
occasionally
occur
occurred
occurrence
optimistic
original
outrageous
pamphlet
parallel
particularly
pastime
perform
performance
permissible
perseverance
perspiration
phenomenon
physically
picnicking
playwright
politics
practically
precede
precedence
preference
preferred
prejudice
preparation
prevalent
primitive
privilege
probably
proceed
professor
prominent
pronunciation
quantity
quiet
quite
quizzes
receive
recognize

recommend
reference
referred
regard
religion
repetition
restaurant
rhythm
rhythmical
ridiculous
roommate
sandwich
schedule
secretary
seize
separate
sergeant
several
siege
similar
sincerely
soliloquy
sophomore
specimen
strictly
subtly
succeed
surprise
temperature
thorough
tragedy
transferred
tries
truly
unanimous
unnecessarily
until
usually
vacuum
vengeance
villain
weird
whether
writing

S2

The hyphen

S2-a Consult the dictionary to determine how to treat a compound word.

The dictionary will tell you whether to treat a compound word as a hyphenated compound (*water-repellent*), one word (*waterproof*), or two words (*water table*). If the compound word is not in the dictionary, treat it as two words.

▶ The prosecutor chose not to cross‸examine any witnesses.

▶ Grandma kept a small note book in her apron pocket.

▶ Alice walked through the looking⁄glass into a backward world.

S2-b Use a hyphen to connect two or more words functioning together as an adjective before a noun.

▶ Mrs. Douglas gave Mary a seashell and some newspaper‸wrapped

fish to take home to her mother.

▶ Priscilla Hobbes is not yet a well‸known candidate.

Newspaper-wrapped and *well-known* are adjectives used before the nouns *fish* and *candidate*.

Generally, do not use a hyphen when such compounds follow the noun.

▶ After our television campaign, Priscilla Hobbes will be well⁄known.

Do not use a hyphen to connect -*ly* adverbs to the words they modify.

▶ A slowly⁄moving truck tied up traffic.

NOTE: In a series, hyphens are suspended.

> Do you prefer first-, second-, or third-class tickets?

S2-c Hyphenate the written form of fractions and of compound numbers from twenty-one to ninety-nine.

▶ One-fourth of my income goes to pay off the national debt.

S2-d Use a hyphen with the prefixes *all-, ex-,* and *self-* and with the suffix *-elect*.

▶ The charity is funneling more money into self-help projects.

▶ Carmen is our club's president-elect.

S2-e A hyphen is used in some words to avoid ambiguity or to separate awkward double or triple letters.

Without the hyphen there would be no way to distinguish between words such as *re-creation* and *recreation*.

> Bicycling in the country is my favorite recreation.

> The film was praised for its astonishing re-creation of nineteenth-century London.

Hyphens are sometimes used to separate awkward double or triple letters in compound words (*anti-intellectual, cross-stitch*). Check a dictionary for the standard form of the word.

S2-f If a word must be divided at the end of a line, divide it correctly.

1. Divide words between syllables.

▶ When I returned from overseas, I didn't recognize
gnize one face on the magazine covers.

2. Never divide one-syllable words.

▶ Grandfather didn't have the courage or the ~~stren-~~
strength
~~gth~~ to open the door.
　^

3. Never divide a word so that a single letter stands alone at the end of a line or fewer than three letters begin a line.

▶ She'll bring her brother with her when she comes ~~a-~~
again.
~~gain.~~
^

▶ As audience to *The Mousetrap,* Hamlet is a ~~watch-~~
watcher
~~er~~ watching watchers.
^

4. When dividing a compound word at the end of a line, either make the break between the words that form the compound or put the whole word on the next line.

▶ My niece Monica is determined to become a long-~~dis-~~
distance
~~tance~~ runner when she grows up.
　^

S3

Capitalization

In addition to the following rules, a good dictionary can often tell you when to use capital letters.

S3-a Capitalize proper nouns and words derived from them; do not capitalize common nouns.

Proper nouns are the names of specific persons, places, and things. All other nouns are common nouns. The following types of words are usually capitalized: names for the deity, religions, religious followers, sacred books; words of family relationship used as names; particular places; nationalities and their languages, races, tribes; educational institutions, departments, degrees, particular courses; government departments, organizations, political parties; and historical movements, periods, events, documents.

PROPER NOUNS	COMMON NOUNS
God (used as a name)	a god
Book of Jeremiah	a book
Uncle Pedro	my uncle
Father (used as a name)	my father
Lake Superior	a picturesque lake
the Capital Center	a center for advanced studies
the South	a southern state
Japan, a Japanese garden	an ornamental garden
University of Wisconsin	a good university
Geology 101	geology
Environmental Protection Agency	a federal agency
Phi Kappa Psi	a fraternity
a Democrat	an independent
the Enlightenment	the eighteenth century
Great Depression	a recession
the Declaration of Independence	a treaty

Months, holidays, and days of the week are treated as proper nouns; the seasons and numbers of the days of the month are not.

Our town fair begins on the first Friday in June, right after Memorial Day.

My mother's birthday is in early spring, on the fifth of April.

Names of school subjects are capitalized only if they are names of languages. Names of particular courses are capitalized.

This semester Austin is taking math, geography, geology, French, and English.

Professor Anderson offers Modern American Fiction 501 to graduate students.

CAUTION: Do not capitalize common nouns to make them seem important. *Our company is currently hiring computer programmers* [not *Company, Computer Programmers*].

S3-b Capitalize titles of persons when used as part of a proper name but usually not when used alone.

> Prof. Margaret Barnes; Dr. Harold Stevens; John Scott Williams, Jr.; Anne Tilton, LL.D.

> District Attorney Marshall was reprimanded for badgering the witness.

> The district attorney was elected for a two-year term.

Usage varies when the title of an important public figure is used alone. *The president* [or *President*] *vetoed the bill.*

S3-c Capitalize the first, last, and all major words in titles and subtitles of works such as books, articles, and songs.

In both titles and subtitles, major words — nouns, verbs, adjectives, and adverbs — should be capitalized. Minor words — articles, prepositions, and coordinating conjunctions — are not capitalized unless they are the first or last word of a title or subtitle. Capitalize the second part of a hyphenated term in a title if it is a major word but not if it is a minor word.

> *The Country of the Pointed Firs*
> "A Valediction: Of Weeping"
> *The F-Plan Diet*

Capitalize chapter titles and the titles of other major divisions of a work following the same guidelines used for titles of complete works.

> "Work and Play" in Santayana's *The Nature of Beauty*

S3-d Capitalize the first word of a sentence.

Obviously the first word of a sentence should be capitalized.

> When lightning struck the house, the roof and the chimney collapsed.

When a sentence appears within parentheses, capitalize its first word unless the parentheses appear within another sentence.

> Early detection of breast cancer significantly increases survival rates. (See table 2.)

> Early detection of breast cancer significantly increases survival rates (see table 2).

S3-e Capitalize the first word of a quoted sentence unless it is blended into the sentence that introduces it.

> In *Time* magazine Robert Hughes writes, "There are only about sixty Watteau paintings on whose authenticity all experts agree."

> Russell Baker has written that in our country "it is sport that is the opiate of the masses."

If a quoted sentence is interrupted by explanatory words, do not capitalize the first word after the interruption.

> "If you wanted to go out," he said sharply, "you should have told me."

When quoting poetry, copy the poet's capitalization exactly. Many poets capitalize the first word of every line of poetry; a few contemporary poets dismiss capitalization altogether.

> When I consider everything that grows
> Holds in perfection but a little moment   — Shakespeare

> it was the week   that
> i felt the city's narrow breezes rush about
> me   — Don L. Lee

S3-f Do not capitalize the first word after a colon unless it begins an independent clause, in which case capitalization is optional.

> Most bar patrons can be divided into two groups: the occasional after-work socializers and the nothing-to-go-home-to regulars.

> This we are forced to conclude: The [*or* the] federal government is needed to protect the rights of minorities.

S3-g Capitalize abbreviations for departments and agencies of government, other organizations, and corporations; capitalize trade names and the call letters of radio and television stations.

EPA, FBI, OPEC, IBM, Xerox, WCRB, KNBC-TV

S4

Abbreviations

S4-a Use standard abbreviations for titles immediately before and after proper names.

TITLES BEFORE PROPER NAMES	TITLES AFTER PROPER NAMES
Mr. Raphael Zabala	William Albert, Sr.
Ms. Nancy Linehan	Thomas Hines, Jr.
Mrs. Edward Horn	Anita Lor, Ph.D.
Dr. Margaret Simmons	Robert Simkowski, M.D.
Rev. John Stone	William Lyons, M.A.
St. Joan of Arc	Margaret Chin, LL.D.
Prof. James Russo	Polly Stein, D.D.S.

Do not abbreviate a title if it is not used with a proper name.

▶ My history ~~prof.~~ professor was a specialist on America's use of the atomic

bomb in World War II.

Avoid redundant titles such as *Dr. Susan Hassel, M.D.* Choose one title or the other: *Dr. Susan Hassel* or *Susan Hassel, M.D.*

S4-b Use familiar abbreviations for the names of organizations, corporations, and countries.

Familiar abbreviations, often written without periods, are acceptable.

CIA, FBI, AFL-CIO, NAACP, IBM, UPI, CBS, USA (or U.S.A.)

The YMCA has opened a new gym close to my office.

NOTE: When using an unfamiliar abbreviation (such as CBE for Council of Biology Editors) throughout a document, write the full name followed by the abbreviation in parentheses at the first mention of the name. You may use the abbreviation alone from then on.

S4-c Use B.C., A.D., A.M., P.M., No., and $ only with specific dates, times, numbers, and amounts.

The abbreviation B.C. ("before Christ") follows a date, and A.D. (*anno Domini*) precedes a date. Acceptable alternatives are B.C.E. ("before the common era") and C.E. ("common era").

40 B.C. (or B.C.E.)	4:00 A.M. (or a.m.)	No. 12 (or no. 12)
A.D. 44 (or C.E.)	6:00 P.M. (or p.m.)	$150

Avoid using A.M., P.M., No., or $ when not accompanied by a specific figure.

▶ We set off for the lake early in the ~~A.M.~~ *morning.*

▶ There were a ~~no.~~ *number* of old hats in the trunk.

S4-d Be sparing in your use of Latin abbreviations.

Latin abbreviations are appropriate in footnotes and bibliographies and in informal writing.

cf. (Latin *confer,* "compare")
e.g. (Latin *exempli gratia,* "for example")
et al. (Latin *et alii,* "and others")
etc. (Latin *et cetera,* "and so forth")
i.e. (Latin *id est,* "that is")
N.B. (Latin *nota bene,* "note well")
P.S. (Latin *postscriptum*, "postscript")

She hated the slice-and-dice genre of horror movies (e.g., *Happy Birthday to Me, The Texas Chainsaw Massacre, Friday the Thirteenth*).

Harold Simms et al., *The Race for Space*

In formal writing use the appropriate English phrases.

> Many obsolete laws remain on the books, ~~e.g.,~~ a law in Vermont
> *for example,*
>
> forbidding an unmarried man and woman to sit less than six
>
> inches apart on a park bench.

S4-e Avoid inappropriate abbreviations.

In formal writing, abbreviations for the following are not commonly accepted: personal names, units of measurement, days of the week, holidays, months, courses of study, divisions of written works, states and countries (except in addresses and except Washington, D.C.).

In company names, use abbreviated forms such as *Co., Inc.,* and & if they are part of the official name: *Temps & Co., Bogart Inc.* Do not abbreviate such forms if they are not part of the official name: *Dunn Photographic Associates* (not *Dunn Photo. Assoc.*). When in doubt about a company's official name, consult a business card, company letterhead stationery, or the yellow pages.

PERSONAL NAME Charles (not Chas.)

UNITS OF MEASUREMENT pound (not lb.)

DAYS OF THE WEEK Monday through Friday (not Mon. through Fri.)

HOLIDAYS Christmas (not Xmas)

MONTHS January, February, March (not Jan., Feb., Mar.)

COURSES OF STUDY political science, psychology (not poli. sci., psych.)

DIVISIONS OF WRITTEN WORKS chapter, page (not ch., p.)

STATES AND COUNTRIES Massachusetts (not MA or Mass.)

PARTS OF A BUSINESS NAME Adams Lighting Company (not Adams Lighting Co.); Kim and Brothers (not Kim and Bros.)

> Eliza promised to buy me one ~~lb.~~ of Godiva chocolate for my
> *pound*
>
> birthday, which was last ~~Fri.~~
> *Friday.*

S5

Numbers

S5-a Spell out numbers of one or two words or those that begin a sentence. Use figures for numbers that require more than two words to spell out.

▶ Now, some *eight* ~~8~~ years later, Muffin is still with us.

▶ I counted ~~one hundred seventy-six~~ *176* CD's on the shelf.

If a sentence begins with a number, spell out the number or rewrite the sentence.

▶ *One hundred fifty* ~~150~~ children in our program need expensive dental treatment.

Rewriting the sentence may be less awkward if the number is long: *In our program 150 children need expensive dental treatment.*

EXCEPTIONS: In technical and some business writing, figures are preferred even when spellings would be brief, but usage varies.

When several numbers appear in the same passage, many writers choose consistency rather than strict adherence to the rule.

When one number immediately follows another, spell out one and use figures for the other: *three 100-meter events, 60 four-poster beds.*

S5-b Generally, figures are acceptable for dates, addresses, percentages, fractions, decimals, scores, statistics and other numerical results, exact amounts of money, divisions of books and plays, pages, identification numbers, and the time.

DATES   July 4, 1776, 56 B.C., A.D. 30

ADDRESSES   77 Latches Lane, 519 West 42nd Street

PERCENTAGES   55 percent (or 55%)

FRACTIONS, DECIMALS   ½, 0.047

SCORES   7 to 3, 21–18

STATISTICS   average age 37, average weight 180

SURVEYS   4 out of 5

EXACT AMOUNTS OF MONEY $105.37, $106,000, $0.05

DIVISIONS OF BOOKS   volume 3, chapter 4, page 189

DIVISIONS OF PLAYS   act III, scene iii (or act 3, scene 3)

IDENTIFICATION NUMBERS   serial number 10988675

TIME OF DAY   4:00 P.M., 1:30 A.M.

▶ Several doctors put up ~~two hundred fifty-five thousand dollars~~ *$255,000* for

the construction of a golf course.

▶ Though I was working on a ~~nineteen thirty-nine~~ *1939* sewing machine,

my costume turned out well.

NOTE: When not using A.M. or P.M., write out the time in words (*four o'clock in the afternoon, twelve noon, seven in the morning*).

S6

Italics (underlining)

In handwritten or typed papers <u>underlining</u> represents *italics,* a slanting typeface used in printed <u>material</u>.

S6-a Underline the titles of works according to convention.

Titles of the following works are underlined to indicate italics:

TITLES OF BOOKS   *The Great Gatsby, A Distant Mirror*

MAGAZINES   *Time, Scientific American*

NEWSPAPERS   the *St. Louis Post-Dispatch*

PAMPHLETS   *Common Sense, Facts about Marijuana*

LONG POEMS   *The Waste Land, Paradise Lost*

PLAYS   *King Lear, A Raisin in the Sun*

FILMS   *Schindler's List*

TELEVISION PROGRAMS   *Murphy Brown, 60 Minutes*

RADIO PROGRAMS   *All Things Considered*

MUSICAL COMPOSITIONS   Gershwin's *Porgy and Bess*

CHOREOGRAPHIC WORKS   Twyla Tharp's *Push Comes to Shove*

WORKS OF VISUAL ART   Rodin's *The Thinker*

COMIC STRIPS   *Calvin and Hobbes*

SOFTWARE   *WordPerfect*

The titles of other works, such as short stories, essays, songs, and short poems, are enclosed in quotation marks. (See P6-d.)

NOTE: Do not underline the Bible or the titles of books in the Bible (Genesis, not *Genesis*); the titles of legal documents (the Constitution, not the *Constitution*); or the titles of your own papers.

S6-b Underline the names of spacecraft, aircraft, ships, and trains.

Challenger, Spirit of St. Louis, Queen Elizabeth II, Silver Streak

▶ The success of the Soviet's <u>Sputnik</u> galvanized the U.S. space program.

S6-c Underline foreign words in an English sentence.

▶ Although Joe's method seemed to be successful, I decided to

establish my own <u>modus operandi</u>.

EXCEPTION: Do not underline foreign words that have become part of the English language — "laissez-faire," "fait accompli," "habeas corpus," and "per diem," for example.

S6-d Underline words, letters, and numbers mentioned as themselves.

▶ Tim assured us that the howling probably came from his bloodhound, Hill Billy, but his <u>probably</u> stuck in our minds.

▶ Sarah called her father by his given name, Johnny, but she was unable to pronounce the <u>J</u>.

▶ A big <u>3</u> was painted on the door.

NOTE: Quotation marks may be used instead of underlining to set off words mentioned as words. (See P6-e.)

S6-e Avoid excessive underlining for emphasis.

Frequent underlining to emphasize words or ideas is distracting and should be used sparingly.

▶ Tennis is a sport that has become an addiction.

R

Research
Writing

R

Research Writing

You will find that writing a research paper is much like planning, drafting, and revising any other kind of writing. (See C1–C4.) Because you will be using quotations and ideas from other writers, however, the process of research writing is somewhat more complex. This section focuses on the special demands of research writing: conducting research, citing sources, avoiding plagiarism, and integrating quotations.

NOTE: For more detailed advice on citing sources with the MLA system, used in English and the humanities, turn to section M; a sample MLA research paper also appears in that section. If you have been asked to use another system of documentation, such as APA style or endnotes, turn to section A, where you will also find a sample APA paper.

R1

Conducting research

Most college research assignments ask you to pose a question worth exploring, to read widely in search of possible answers, and to draw your own conclusions based on a rational assessment of the evidence.

R1-a Pose a question worth exploring.

Working within the guidelines of your assignment, jot down a few questions that seem worth researching; then choose the one that interests you the most. Here are some questions from students who were asked to write about a political or social issue:

Should the use of lie detectors be banned?

What are the hazards of fad diets?

How widespread is the problem of computer crime?

What was Marcus Garvey's contribution to the fight for racial equality?

Does investing in wind energy make economic sense?

Which geological formations are the safest repositories for nuclear waste?

How can governments and zoos help preserve China's endangered giant panda?

R1-b If necessary, narrow your focus.

Once you have settled on a question that looks promising, check to see if it is too broad, given the length of the paper you plan to write. If you suspect it is — and most writers' initial questions are — look for ways to narrow your focus as you begin researching.

Even before you visit the library, you may be able to limit the scope of your investigation. For instance, if initially you asked "Should the use of lie detectors be banned?" you might restrict your inquiry to the use of lie detectors *by private employers*. Or if at first you asked "What are the hazards of fad diets?" you might narrow your focus to the hazards of *liquid* diets.

Once inside the library, you will discover a number of ways to narrow your topic. You can read encyclopedia articles or scan the headings and subheadings in the library's on-line catalog to get a sense of your topic's natural subdivisions. For current topics, you can check the subheadings and titles in periodical indexes.

As you begin reading books and articles and become more knowledgeable, you may be able to restrict your focus even further and at the same time decide on a tentative main point. The main point of your paper, known as a *thesis,* will be an answer to the central question that you finally decide to pose. (See C1-c.)

R1-c Follow a search strategy.

A search strategy is a systematic plan for tracking down sources. To create a search strategy appropriate to your research question, you'll need to ask yourself two questions:

What kinds of sources should I consult?

In what order should I consult them?

A good search strategy usually moves from sources that give you an overview of your subject to those that supply you with more specialized information. For a historical subject you might begin with general reference works such as encyclopedias and then move to books and finally to scholarly articles. For a current subject, you might begin with magazines of general interest and end with specialized articles in scholarly journals. But be prepared to modify this strategy in light of your topic, your library resources, your level of expertise, and the amount of time you are able to spend researching. Remember that if you run into problems, a librarian will be glad to help.

Reference works

Often you'll want to begin by reading background information in a general encyclopedia, a specialized encyclopedia, or a biographical reference. Later you may need to turn to other reference works such as atlases, almanacs, or unabridged dictionaries. Many college libraries provide handouts that list their reference works, sometimes organized by academic discipline.

Books

Your library may have a computer catalog, a card catalog, a microform catalog, or some combination of these. Most libraries now have computer catalogs that allow you to search for information about books and often other materials through a terminal or personal computer. A computer catalog is a database that contains bibliographic and location information about a library's books. It can be searched by subject, author, or title.

While computer catalogs vary from library to library, most are easy to use, and a reference librarian will be available to help you if you get stuck. Look for instructions on the computer terminal's menu display or look for a help key. To begin a search, you will usually respond to a direction such as "Type in an author's name" or "Enter your subject." The computer will then display either a list of books under that author's name or subject heading or a list of subcategories from which you can choose the one closest to your topic.

Searching by subject involves the use of keywords or subject headings. The keywords may be used alone, such as *chimpanzees* or *sign language,* or they can be combined. In some systems, for example, you can use the connector *and* to narrow a search: *chimpanzees and sign language.*

If you began your search with the general subject heading *human animal communication*, you might see a screen like the one at the top of page 252. Notice that this list contains the overall

SUBJECT SEARCH: SCREEN 1

```
HU GUIDE: SUBJECT HEADING LIST              18 items retrieved by your search:
FIND SU HUMAN ANIMAL COMMUNICATION
 - - - - - - - - - - - - - - - - - - - - - - - - - - - - - - - - - - - - - - - -
 1 HUMAN ANIMAL COMMUNICATION
15 HUMAN ANIMAL COMMUNICATION --CONGRESSES
16 HUMAN ANIMAL COMMUNICATION --DATA PROCESSING
17 HUMAN ANIMAL COMMUNICATION --FOLKLORE
18 HUMAN ANIMAL COMMUNICATION --RESEARCH --CONGRESSES




 - - - - - - - - - - - - - - - - - - - - - - - - - - - - - - - - - - - - - - - -
OPTIONS:  INDEX (or I 5 etc) to see list of items      HELP
                                                       START - search options
          REDO - edit search                           QUIT - exit database
COMMAND?
```

SUBJECT SEARCH: SCREEN 2

```
HU INDEX: LIST OF ITEMS RETRIEVED           18 items retrieved by your search:
FIND SU HUMAN ANIMAL COMMUNICATION
 - - - - - - - - - - - - - - - - - - - - - - - - - - - - - - - - - - - - - - - -
HUMAN ANIMAL COMMUNICATION
 1 adams task calling animals by name /hearne vicki 1946/ 1986 bks
 2 animals are equal an exploration of animal conciousn /hall rebec/ 1980 bks
 3 apes men and language /linden eugene/ 1976 bks
 4 aping language /wallman joel/ 1992 bks
 5 butterfly revelations /swanson henry f 1923/ 1979 bks
 6 communication between man and dolphin the possibilit /lilly john/ 1987 bks
 7 education of koko /patterson francine/ 1981 bks
 8 gavagai or the future history of the animal language /premack da/ 1986 bks
 9 hund und mensch eine semiotische analyse ihrer kommu /fleischer/ 1987 bks
10 language in primates perspectives and implications/ 1983 bks
11 nim /terrace herbert s 1936/ 1979 bks
12 silent partners the legacy of the ape language exper /linden eug/ 1986 bks
13 speaking of apes a critical anthology of two way com/ 1980 bks
14 teaching sign language to chimpanzees/ 1989 bks
 - - - - - - - - - - - - - - - - - - - - - - - - - -  (CONTINUES)  - - - - - - - - -
OPTIONS: DISPLAY 1 (or D 5 etc) to see a record        HELP
         GUIDE                    MORE - next page     START - search options
         REDO - edit search                            QUIT - exit database
COMMAND?
```

SUBJECT SEARCH: SCREEN 3

```
HU LONG DISPLAY page 1 of 1              Item 7 of 18 retrieved by your search:
FIND SU HUMAN ANIMAL COMMUNICATION
------------------------------------- HU HOLLIS# AEK5177 /bks
        AUTHOR: Patterson, Francine.
         TITLE: The education of Koko / Francine Patterson and Eugene Linden.
       EDITION: 1st ed.
     PUB. INFO: New York : Holt, Rinehart and Winston, c1981.
   DESCRIPTION: xiv, 224 p. : ill. ; 24 cm.
         NOTES: Includes index.
                Bibliography: p. 215-216.

      SUBJECTS: *S1 Gorilla--Psychology.
                *S2 Human-animal communication.
                *S3 Sign language.
       AUTHORS: *A1 Patterson, Francine.
                *A2 Linden, Eugene.

      LOCATION: Gutman Education: QL737.P96 P37

---------------------------------------------------------------
OPTIONS: DISPLAY SHORT                          NEXT - next item      HELP
         LOCATION                               PREVIOUS - prev item  INDEX
         HELP COMMANDS      TRACE *S1 (etc)      QUIT - exit database  REDO
COMMAND?
```

---

subject category as well as four subcategories. If you selected the overall subject category, you would see a screen like the one at the bottom of page 252. This screen gives you a choice of a number of titles. If a title looks useful, you can call up a search screen that displays the complete record of the book (see the top of this page). Usually you can command the computer to print out this record, which includes bibliographic information and the location of the book. You will need the bibliographic information — author, title, publisher, and place and date of publication — if you decide to use the book in your paper (see R1-d and R2-a.) In the sample record, the location of the book appears after the bibliographic information. It includes the building where the book may be found and the call number, the book's address on the shelf.

Periodicals

Periodicals are publications issued at regular intervals, such as magazines, newspapers, and scholarly or technical journals. To track down useful articles, consult a magazine index, a newspaper index, or one of the many specialized indexes to scholarly or technical journals.

Some periodical indexes are in print form; others are databases that can be read at a computer terminal. You search for articles in the database just as you look for books in the library's com-

COMPUTER INDEX RECORD WITH ABSTRACT

SilverPlatter 3.1   Journal Articles (1/74-12/86)

                                                                    9 of 15

TI: Can an ape create a sentence?
AU: Terrace,-H.-S.;Petitto,-L.A.;Sanders,-R.J.;Bever,-T.G.
IN: Columbia U
JN: Science; 1979 Nov Vol 206(4421)891-902
AB: Recent demonstrations that chimpanzees and gorillas can communicate with
humans via arbitrary "words" raise the issue of whether the ability to create
and understand sentences is uniquely human. To answer this question, more than
19,000 multisign utterances of an infant chimpanzee (Nim) were analyzed for
syntactic and semantic regularities. Lexical regularities were observed in the
case of 2-sign combinations: particular signs (e.g., more) tended to occur in a
particular position. These regularities could not be attributed to
memorization or to position habits, suggesting that they were structurally
constrained. That conclusion, however, was invalidated by videotape analyses,
which showed that most of Nim's utterances were prompted by his teacher's prior
utterance and that Nim interrupted his teachers to a much larger extent than a
child interrupts an adult's speech. Signed utterances of other apes (as shown
on films) showed similar nonhuman patterns of discourse. (PsycLIT Database
Copyright 1981 American Psychological Assn, all rights reserved)
AN: 65-00553

---

puter catalog, by typing the author, title, or subject keywords.
Bibliographic records appear on the screen; sometimes an abstract
or even the full text of an article can be printed.

Most libraries provide a list of the periodicals they own. This
list tells you the form in which the periodical has been preserved:
on microfilm, on microfiche, in bound volumes, or in unbound files.
It also tells you which years and volumes of the periodical the library owns. In some libraries, all of this information appears on
the screen of a computer index.

Other library sources

A library's holdings are not limited to reference works, books, and
periodicals. Your library may have pamphlets, usually located in a
large file cabinet known as the *vertical file,* or rare and unpublished manuscripts in a special collection. Holdings might also include records, tapes, and compact discs; films, filmstrips, videos,
and interactive videodiscs; drawings, paintings, engravings, and
slides.

If your research topic is especially complex or unusual, you
may need greater resources than your library offers. In such cases,

talk to a librarian about interlibrary loan, a process in which one library borrows materials from another. This procedure can take several weeks for books, but magazine articles are commonly sent by fax in less than a week.

Sources beyond the library

For some topics, you may want to look beyond the library for information. Many organizations, both public and private, willingly mail literature in response to a phone call or a letter. The *Encyclopedia of Associations* lists organizations by their special interests, such as environment or family planning, and provides titles of their publications. Consider also the possibility of learning more about your subject through interviews or experiments that you conduct yourself.

R1-d Read selectively; maintain a working bibliography.

Even after you have narrowed your focus, your search for useful research materials may supply you with many more books and articles than you have time to read, so you will need to be selective. As you consult the library's catalog and its periodical indexes, take down bibliographic information only for sources that are clearly relevant to your research question, especially if you are pressed for time.

The information you take down about your sources, called a *working bibliography,* includes all of the details you will need later, when you compile the list of works cited that will appear at the end of your paper. For books, you will need the following information:

Call number

All authors; any editors or translators

Title and subtitle

Edition (if not the first)

Publishing information: city, publishing company, and date

At many libraries, you do not need to copy down this information; instead you can print it out from a computer terminal.

For periodical articles, you need the following information, which most computer indexes will print for you:

All authors of the article

Title and subtitle of the article

Title of the magazine, journal, or newspaper

Date and page numbers

Volume and issue numbers, if relevant

NOTE: For the exact bibliographic form to be used in the final paper, see M2 if you have been asked to use MLA documentation. If you have been asked to use another style of documentation, such as APA style or endnotes, see section A.

SAMPLE BIBLIOGRAPHY CARD FOR A BOOK

> QL737.P96   L57   1986
>
> Linden, Eugene. Silent Partners: The
>   Legacy of the Ape Language
>   Experiments. New York: Times, 1986.

SAMPLE BIBLIOGRAPHY CARD FOR A PERIODICAL

> Lewin, Roger. "Look Who's Talking Now."
>   New Scientist 29 April 1991: 49-52.

R1-e As you read, take notes systematically. Avoid unintentional plagiarism.

Systematic notes will make it clear to you later, as you are drafting your paper, just which words and phrases belong to your sources and which are your own. This is a crucial matter, for if any language from your sources finds its way into your final draft without quotation marks and proper documentation, you will be guilty of plagiarism, a serious academic offense. (See also R2-b.)

You can take notes in various ways, as long as they are accurate, but many researchers find that 3″ × 5″ note cards work best. You can write one note on each card and then shuffle and reshuffle the cards to experiment with the organization of your paper. Put the last name of the author of your source in the upper right corner of the card, and put a subject label in the upper left corner.

As you take notes, decide on the best way to preserve the information in a particular source: summarizing, paraphrasing, or quoting. Be sure to include exact page references next to the information, since you will need the page numbers later if you use the information in your paper.

Note cards that summarize

Summarizing is the best kind of preliminary note taking because it is the fastest. A summary condenses information, perhaps reducing a chapter to a short paragraph or a paragraph to a single sentence. A summary should be written in your own words; if you use apt phrases from the source, put them in quotation marks.

Here is a passage from an original source read by one student, Karen Shaw, as she researched an essay on apes and language. Following the passage is Shaw's note card summarizing it.

ORIGINAL SOURCE
Public and scientific interest in the question of apes' ability to use language first soared some 15 years ago when Washoe, a chimpanzee raised like a human child by R. Allen Gardner and Beatrice Gardner of the University of Nevada, learned to make hand signs for many words and even seemed to be making short sentences.

Since then researchers have taught many chimpanzees and a few gorillas and orangutans to "talk" using the sign language of deaf humans, plastic chips or, like Kanzi, keyboard symbols. Washoe, Sarah, a chimpanzee trained by David Premack of the University of Pennsylvania, and Koko, a gorilla trained by the psychologist Francine Patterson, became media stars.
— Eckholm, "Pygmy," p. B7

SUMMARY

> *Types of Language   Eckholm, "Pygmy"*
>
> *The ape experiments began in the 1970s with Washoe, who learned sign language. In later experiments some apes learned to communicate using plastic chips or symbols on a keyboard. (p. B7)*

Note cards that paraphrase

Like a summary, a paraphrase is written in your own words; but whereas a summary reports significant information in fewer words than the source, a paraphrase retells the information in roughly the same number of words. If you retain occasional choice phrases from the source, put quotation marks around them so that you'll know later which phrases are your own.

You will discover that it is amazingly easy to borrow too much language from a source as you paraphrase. Do not allow this to happen. You are guilty of plagiarism if you half-copy the author's sentences — either by mixing the author's well-chosen phrases with your own without quotation marks or by plugging your synonyms into the author's sentence structure. (For examples of this kind of plagiarism, see R2-b.)

To prevent unintentional borrowing, resist the temptation to look at the source while you are paraphrasing. Keep the source close by — to check for accuracy — but don't try to paraphrase with the source's sentences in front of you. You should also follow this advice while drafting your paper.

As you read the note card on page 259, which paraphrases the first paragraph of Shaw's original source (see p. 257), notice that the language is significantly different from that in the original. Working with this note card, Shaw was in no danger of unintentional plagiarism.

PARAPHRASE

> *Washoe   Eckholm, "Pygmy"*
>
> *A chimpanzee named Washoe, trained in the early '70s by U. of Nevada professors R. Allen and Beatrice Gardner, learned words in the sign language of the deaf and may even have created short sentences. (p. B7)*

Note cards that quote

A quotation consists of the exact words from a source. On your note cards, put all quoted material in quotation marks; do not trust yourself to remember later which words, phrases, and passages you have quoted and which are your own. When you quote, be sure to copy the words of your source exactly, including punctuation and capitalization.

Below is an example of a note card containing a quotation from Shaw's original source (p. 257).

QUOTATION

> *Washoe   Eckholm, "Pygmy"*
>
> *Washoe, trained by R. Allen and Beatrice Gardner, "learned to make hand signs for many words and even seemed to be making short sentences." (p. B7)*

Alternatives to note cards

Not every researcher uses note cards. For short research projects, some writers prefer to photocopy important material and underline or highlight key ideas, sometimes color coding the highlighted passages to reflect subdivisions of the topic. In the margins they may write personal comments or cross-references to other sources. Photocopying has the obvious advantage of saving time and labor. For extensive research projects, however, the technique is of limited value since there is no way of physically sorting the highlighted passages into separate batches of information.

A second alternative to note cards, the use of computer software, overcomes this disadvantage. With the appropriate software, you can type notes as you read, coding them to reflect the subdivisions of your topic; you can then print the notes in sorted batches. Although software programs can save time, their advantages should not be oversold. Any style of note taking demands that you read carefully, analyze what you read, and record information with care.

R2

Citing sources; avoiding plagiarism

In a research paper, you will be drawing on the work of other writers, and you must document their contributions by citing your sources. In research writing, sources are cited for two reasons: to alert readers to the sources of your information and to give credit to the writers from whom you have borrowed words and ideas. To borrow another writer's language or ideas without proper acknowledgment is a form of dishonesty known as plagiarism.

R2-a Use a consistent system for citing sources, such as the MLA style of in-text citations. (See M1 and M2 for important details.)

Citations are required when you quote from a source, when you summarize or paraphrase a source, and when you borrow facts and ideas from a source (except for common knowledge). (See R2-b.)

The various academic disciplines use their own editorial styles for citing sources. Most English instructors prefer the Modern Language Association's system of in-text citations. Here, very briefly, is how an MLA in-text citation usually works:

1. The source is introduced by a signal phrase that names its author.
2. The source is followed by a page number in parentheses.
3. At the end of the paper, a list of works cited (arranged alphabetically according to the authors' last names) gives complete publishing information about the source.

SAMPLE IN-TEXT CITATION

According to Eugene Linden, some psychologists have adopted the oddly unscientific attitude that "the idea of the language capacity of apes is so preposterous that it should not be investigated at all" (11).

SAMPLE ENTRY IN THE LIST OF WORKS CITED

Linden, Eugene.   <u>Silent Partners: The Legacy of the Ape Language Experiments</u>.   New York: Times, 1986.

Handling an MLA citation is not always this simple. When the author is not named in a signal phrase, for example, the parentheses must include the author's last name along with the page number. For a detailed discussion of this and other variations, see M1.

If your instructor has asked you to use the APA style of in-text citation, consult A1. If your instructor prefers footnotes or endnotes, consult A2. For a list of style manuals used in a variety of disciplines, see A3.

R2-b Avoid plagiarism.

Your research paper is a collaboration between you and your sources. To be fair and ethical, you must acknowledge your debt to the writers of these sources. If you don't, you are guilty of plagiarism, a serious academic offense.

Three different acts are considered plagiarism: (1) failing to cite quotations and borrowed ideas, (2) failing to enclose borrowed language in quotation marks, and (3) failing to put summaries and paraphrases in your own words.

Citing quotations and borrowed ideas

You must of course cite all direct quotations. You must also document any ideas borrowed from a source: paraphrases of sentences, summaries of paragraphs or chapters, statistics and little-known facts, and tables, graphs, or diagrams.

The only exception is common knowledge — information that your readers could find in any number of general sources because it is commonly known. For example, the current population of the United States is common knowledge in such fields as sociology and economics; Freud's theory of the unconscious is common knowledge in the field of psychology.

As a rule, when you have seen certain information repeatedly in your reading, you don't need to document it. However, when information has appeared in only one or two sources or when it is controversial, you should document it. If a topic is new to you and you are not sure what is considered common knowledge or what is a matter of controversy, ask someone with expertise. When in doubt, cite the source.

Enclosing borrowed language in quotation marks

To indicate that you are using a source's exact phrases or sentences, you must enclose them in quotation marks unless they have been set off from the text by indenting. (See R3-b.) To omit the quotation marks is to claim — falsely — that the language is your own. Such an omission is plagiarism even if you have cited the source.

ORIGINAL SOURCE

No animal has done more to renew interest in animal intelligence than a beguiling, bilingual bonobo named Kanzi, who has the grammatical abilities of a 2½-year-old child and a taste for movies about cavemen.

— Eugene Linden, "Animals," p. 57

PLAGIARISM

According to Eugene Linden, no animal has done more to renew interest in animal intelligence than a beguiling, bilingual bonobo named Kanzi, who has the grammatical abilities of a 2 1/2-year-old child and a taste for movies about cavemen (57).

BORROWED LANGUAGE IN QUOTATION MARKS

According to Eugene Linden, "No animal has done more to renew interest in animal intelligence than a beguiling, bilingual bonobo named Kanzi, who has the grammatical abilities of a 2 1/2-year-old child and a taste for movies about cavemen" (57).

Putting summaries and paraphrases in your own words

When you summarize or paraphrase, it is not enough to name the source; you must restate the source's meaning using your own language. (See also R1-e.) You are guilty of plagiarism if you half-copy the author's sentences — either by mixing the author's well-chosen phrases without using quotation marks or by plugging your own synonyms into the author's sentence structure. The following paraphrases are plagiarized — even though the source is cited — because their language is too close to that of the original source.

ORIGINAL VERSION
If the existence of a signing ape was unsettling for linguists, it was also startling news for animal behaviorists.
— Davis, *Eloquent Animals,* p. 26

UNACCEPTABLE BORROWING OF PHRASES

The existence of a signing ape unsettled linguists and startled animal behaviorists (Davis 26).

UNACCEPTABLE BORROWING OF STRUCTURE

If the presence of a sign-language-using chimp was disturbing for scientists studying language, it was also surprising to scientists studying animal behavior (Davis 26).

To avoid plagiarizing an author's language, resist the temptation to look at the source while you are summarizing or paraphrasing. Close the book, write from memory, and then open the book to check for accuracy. This technique prevents you from being captivated by the words on the page.

ACCEPTABLE PARAPHRASES

```
When they learned of an ape's ability to use sign lan-
guage, both linguists and animal behaviorists were
taken by surprise (Davis 26).
```

```
According to Flora Davis, linguists and animal behav-
iorists were unprepared for the news that a chimp
could communicate with its trainers through sign lan-
guage (26).
```

R3

Integrating quotations

If you include too many quotations in a research essay, readers form the impression that you cannot think for yourself. Use quotations only when a source is particularly clear or expressive or when it is important to let the debaters of an issue explain their positions in their own words. Except for this infrequent need for quotations, use your own words to summarize or paraphrase your sources and to explain your own ideas.

When you choose to use quotations, make sure that they are integrated smoothly into the text of your paper. Readers should be able to move from your own words to the words you quote without feeling a jolt.

R3-a Use signal phrases.

Avoid dropping quotations into the text without warning; instead, provide clear signal phrases, usually including the author's name, to prepare readers for the quotation.

DROPPED QUOTATION

```
Although the bald eagle is still listed as an endan-
gered species, its ever-increasing population is very
```

encouraging. "The bald eagle seems to have stabilized its population, at the very least, almost everywhere" (Sheppard 96).

QUOTATION WITH SIGNAL PHRASE

Although the bald eagle is still listed as an endangered species, its ever-increasing population is very encouraging. According to ornithologist Jay Sheppard, "The bald eagle seems to have stabilized its population, at the very least, almost everywhere" (96).

To avoid monotony, try to vary your signal phrases. The following models suggest a range of possibilities.

In the words of researcher Herbert Terrace, ". . ."

As Flora Davis has noted, ". . ."

The Gardners, Washoe's trainers, point out that ". . ."

". . . ," claims linguist Noam Chomsky.

Psychologist H. S. Terrace offers an odd argument for this view: ". . ."

Terrace answers these objections with the following analysis: ". . ."

When your signal phrase includes a verb, choose one that is appropriate in the context. Is your source arguing a point, making an observation, reporting a fact, drawing a conclusion, refuting an argument, or stating a belief? By choosing an appropriate verb, such as one on the following list, you can make your source's stance clear.

acknowledges	comments	endorses	reasons
adds	compares	grants	refutes
admits	confirms	illustrates	rejects
agrees	contends	implies	reports
argues	declares	insists	responds
asserts	denies	notes	suggests
believes	disputes	observes	thinks
claims	emphasizes	points out	writes

It is not always necessary to quote full sentences from a source. At times you may wish to borrow only a phrase or to weave part of a source's sentence into your own sentence structure.

> Bruce Bower reports that Kanzi practices "simple gram-
> matical ordering rules," such as putting actions be-
> fore objects (140).

> Perhaps the best summation of the current state of ape
> language studies comes from biologist Robert Seyfarth,
> who writes that the line separating humans from other
> animals "remains hazily drawn, somewhere between the
> word and the sentence" (18).

R3-b Set off long quotations.

When you quote more than four typed lines of prose or more than three lines of poetry, set off the quotation by indenting it ten spaces from the left margin. (See P6-b.) Use the normal right margin and do not single-space.

Long quotations should be introduced by an informative sentence, usually followed by a colon. Quotation marks are unnecessary because the indented format tells readers that the words are taken directly from the source.

> Desmond describes how Washoe tried signing to the
> other apes when the Gardners returned her to an ape
> colony in Oklahoma:
>
>> One particularly memorable day, a snake
>> spread terror through the castaways on the
>> ape island, and all but one fled in panic.
>> This male sat absorbed, staring intently at
>> the serpent. Then Washoe was seen running
>> over signing to him "come, hurry up." (42)

Notice that at the end of an indented quotation the parenthetical citation goes outside the final period.

R3-c Use the ellipsis mark and brackets to indicate changes you make in a quotation.

Two useful marks of punctuation, the ellipsis mark and brackets, allow you to keep quoted material to a minimum and to integrate it smoothly into your text.

The ellipsis mark

To condense a quoted passage, you can use the ellipsis mark (three periods, with spaces between) to indicate that you have omitted words. The sentence that remains must be grammatically complete.

```
In a recent New York Times article, Erik Eckholm

reports that "a 4-year-old pygmy chimpanzee . . . has

demonstrated what scientists say are the most human-

like linguistic skills ever documented in another

animal" (A1).
```

The writer has omitted the words *at a research center near Atlanta,* which appeared in the original.

When you want to omit a full sentence or more, use a period before the three ellipsis dots.

```
According to Wade, the horse Clever Hans "could

apparently count by tapping out numbers with his

hoof. . . . Clever Hans owes his celebrity to his

master's innocence. Von Osten sincerely believed he

had taught Hans to solve arithmetical problems"

(1349).
```

Ordinarily, do not use an ellipsis mark at the beginning or at the end of a quotation. Your readers will understand that the quoted material is taken from a longer passage. The only exception occurs when you have omitted words at the end of the final quoted sentence.

Obviously you should not use an ellipsis mark to distort the meaning of your source.

Brackets

Brackets (square parentheses) allow you to insert words of your own into quoted material, perhaps to explain a confusing reference or to keep a sentence grammatical in your context.

> Robert Seyfarth reports that "Premack [a scientist at the University of Pennsylvania] taught a seven-year-old chimpanzee, Sarah, that the word for 'apple' was a small, plastic triangle" (13).

If your typewriter has no brackets, ink them in by hand.

M

MLA
Documentation

M

MLA Documentation

Directory to MLA in-text citations (M1)

Directory to MLA list of works cited (M2)

BOOKS

In academic research papers and in any other writing that borrows information from sources, the borrowed information — quotations, summaries, paraphrases, and any facts or ideas that are not common knowledge — must be clearly documented. (See also R2-a.)

The various academic disciplines use their own editorial styles for citing sources and for listing the works that have been cited. The style described in this section is that of the Modern Language Association (MLA), contained in the *MLA Handbook for Writers of Research Papers* 4th ed., 1995), which recommends that citations be given in the text of the paper rather than in footnotes or endnotes. If your instructor prefers footnotes or endnotes or the American Psychological Association (APA) style of in-text citation, flip to the next tabbed section, Alternative Styles of Documentation, where you will also find a list of style manuals.

M1

MLA in-text citations

The Modern Language Association's in-text citations are made with a combination of signal phrases and parenthetical references. A signal phrase indicates that something drawn from a source (such as a quotation, summary, or paraphrase) is about to be used; usually the signal phrase includes the author's name. The parenthetical reference includes at least a page number.

Citations in parentheses should be as concise as possible but complete enough so that readers can find the source in the list of works cited at the end of the paper, where works are listed alphabetically by authors' last names. The following models illustrate the form for the MLA style of citation.

AUTHOR NAMED IN A SIGNAL PHRASE Ordinarily, you should introduce the material being cited with a signal phrase that includes the author's name. In addition to preparing readers for the source, the signal phrase allows you to keep the parenthetical citation brief.

Flora Davis reports that a chimp at the Yerkes Primate Research Center "has combined words into new sentences that she was never taught" (67).

The signal phrase — "Flora Davis reports" — provides the name of the author; the parenthetical citation gives the page number where the quoted sentence may be found. By looking up the author's last name in the list of works cited, readers will find complete information about the work's title, publisher, and date of publication.

Notice that the period follows the parenthetical citation. For the MLA technique for handling quotations that end in a question mark or an exclamation point, see P6-f.

AUTHOR NOT NAMED IN A SIGNAL PHRASE If the signal phrase does not include the author's name (or if there is no signal phrase), the author's last name must appear in parentheses along with the page number.

    Although the baby chimp lived only a few hours, Washoe

    signed to it before it died (Davis 42).

TWO OR MORE WORKS BY THE SAME AUTHOR If your list of works cited includes two or more works by the same author, include the title of the work either in the signal phrase or in abbreviated form in the parenthetical reference.

    In Eloquent Animals, Flora Davis reports that a chimp

    at the Yerkes Primate Research Center "has combined

    words into sentences that she was never taught" (67).

    Flora Davis reports that a chimp at the Yerkes Primate

    Research Center "has combined words into sentences

    that she was never taught" (Eloquent 67).

The title of a book should be underlined, as in the examples. The title of an article from a periodical should be put in quotation marks.

In the rare case when both the author and a short title must be given in parentheses, the citation should appear as follows:

    Although the baby chimpanzee lived only for a few

    hours, Washoe signed to it before it died (Davis,

    Eloquent 42).

TWO OR THREE AUTHORS If your source has two or three authors, name them in the signal phrase or include them in the parenthetical reference.

> Patterson and Linden agree that the gorilla Koko ac-
> quired language more slowly than a normal speaking
> child (83-90).

FOUR OR MORE AUTHORS   If your source has four or more authors, include only the first author's name followed by "et al."
(Latin for "and others") in the signal phrase or in the parenthetical
reference.

> The study was extended for two years, and only after
> results were duplicated on both coasts did the authors
> publish their results (Doe et al. 137).

CORPORATE AUTHOR   Name the corporate author in the signal
phrase or in the parentheses.

> The Internal Revenue Service warns businesses that de-
> ductions for "lavish and extravagant entertainment"
> are not allowed (43).

UNKNOWN AUTHOR   If the author is not given, either use the
complete title in a signal phrase or use a short form of the title in
the parentheses.

> The UFO reported by the crew of a Japan Air Lines
> flight remains a mystery. Radar tapes did not confirm
> the presence of another craft ("Strange Encounter" 26).

AUTHORS WITH THE SAME LAST NAME   If your list of works cited includes works by two or more authors with the same last name, include the first name of the author you are citing in the signal
phrase or parenthetical reference.

> Both Lucy and Koko have been reported to lie (Adrian
> Desmond 201).

A MULTIVOLUME WORK   If your paper cites more than one volume
of a multivolume work, you must indicate in the parentheses
which volume you are referring to.

> Terman's studies of gifted children reveal a pattern
> of accelerated language acquisition (2: 279).

If your paper cites only one volume of a multivolume work, you will include the volume number in the list of works cited at the end of the paper and will not need to include it in the parentheses.

A NOVEL, A PLAY, OR A POEM   In citing literary sources, include information that will enable readers to find the passage in various editions of the work. For a novel, put the page number first and then, if possible, indicate the part or chapter in which the passage can be found.

> Fitzgerald's narrator captures Gatsby in a moment of
> isolation: "A sudden emptiness seemed to flow now from
> the windows and the great doors, endowing with com-
> plete isolation the figure of the host" (56; ch. 3).

For a verse play, list the act, scene, and line numbers. Use arabic numerals unless your instructor prefers roman numerals.

> In his famous advice to the players, Hamlet defines the
> purpose of theater, "whose end, both at the first and
> now, was and is, to hold, as 'twere, the mirror up to
> nature" (3.2.21-23).

For a poem, cite the part (if there are a number of parts) and the line numbers.

> When Homer's Odysseus came to the hall of Circe, he
> found his men "mild / in her soft spell, fed on her
> drug of evil" (10.209-11).

A WORK IN AN ANTHOLOGY   Put the name of the author of the work (not the editor of the anthology) in the signal phrase or in the parentheses.

> At the end of Kate Chopin's "The Story of an Hour,"
> Mrs. Mallard drops dead upon learning that her husband
> is alive. In the final irony of the story, doctors re-
> port that she has died of a "joy that kills" (25).

AN INDIRECT SOURCE   When a writer's or speaker's quoted words appear in a source written by someone else, begin the citation with the abbreviation "qtd. in."

> "We only used seven signs in his presence," says
>
> Fouts. "All of his signs were learned from the other
>
> chimps at the laboratory" (qtd. in Toner 24).

AN ENTIRE WORK   To cite an entire work, use the author's name in a signal phrase or a parenthetical reference.

> Patterson and Linden provide convincing evidence for
>
> the speech-making abilities of nonhuman primates.

TWO OR MORE WORKS   You may want to cite more than one source to document a particular point. Separate the citations with a semicolon.

> With intensive training, the apes in this study learned
>
> over 200 signs or signals (Desmond 229; Linden 173).

Multiple citations can be distracting to readers, however, so the technique should not be overused. If you want to alert readers to several sources that discuss a particular topic, consider using a bibliographic note instead (see M3).

A WORK WITHOUT PAGE NUMBERS   You may omit the page number if a work has no page numbers or if a work is only one page long or is organized alphabetically (as with encyclopedias). Some electronic sources use paragraph numbers instead of page numbers. For such sources, use the abbreviation "par." or "pars." in the parentheses: (Smith, par. 4).

M2

MLA list of works cited

A list of works cited, which appears at the end of your paper, gives full publishing information for each of the sources you have cited in the paper. Start on a new page and title your list "Works Cited." Then list in alphabetical order all the sources that you have cited in the paper. Unless your instructor asks for them, sources not actually cited in the paper should not be given in this list, even if you have read them.

Alphabetize the list by the last names of the authors (or editors); if a work has no author or editor, alphabetize by the first word of the title other than *a, an,* or *the.*

Do not indent the first line of each entry in the list of works cited but indent any additional lines five spaces. This technique highlights the names by which the list has been alphabetized. (For a sample list of works cited, see pages 302–03.)

The following models illustrate the forms that the Modern Language Association (MLA) recommends for works cited entries.

Books

BASIC FORMAT FOR A BOOK   For most books, arrange the information into three units, each followed by a period and one space (unless your instructor prefers two spaces): (1) the author's name, last name first; (2) the title and subtitle, underlined; and (3) the place of publication, the publisher, and the date.

```
Tompkins, Jane. West of Everything: The Inner Life of

    Westerns. New York: Oxford UP, 1992.
```

The information is taken from the title page and the copyright page. You may use a short form of the publisher's name as long as it is easily identifiable; omit terms such as *Press, Inc.,* and *Co.* except when naming university presses (Harvard UP, for example). If several copyright dates are given, use the most recent one.

TWO OR THREE AUTHORS   Name the authors in the order in which they are presented on the title page; reverse the name of only the first author.

```
Rico, Barbara, and Sandra Mano. American Mosaic:

    Multicultural Readings in Context. Boston:

    Houghton, 1991.
```

The names of three authors are separated by commas.

```
Bentley, Nicolas, Michael Slater, and Nina Burgis. The

    Dickens Index. New York: Oxford UP, 1990.
```

FOUR OR MORE AUTHORS   Cite only the first author, name reversed, followed by "et al." (Latin for "and others").

```
Medhurst, Martin J., et al. Cold War Rhetoric:

    Strategy, Metaphor, and Ideology. New York:

    Greenwood, 1990.
```

EDITORS   After the name or names, use the abbreviation "ed." for "editor" or "eds." for "editors."

```
Anaya, Rodolfo, and Francisco Lomeli, eds. Aztlán:

    Essays on the Chicano Homeland. Albuquerque:

    Academia-El Norte, 1989.
```

AUTHOR WITH AN EDITOR   Begin with the author and title, followed by "Ed." and the name of the editor. Use "Ed." (for "Edited by") for one or more editors.

```
Franklin, Benjamin. The Autobiography and Other

    Writings. Ed. Kenneth Silverman. New York:

    Penguin, 1986.
```

TRANSLATION   List the entry under the name of the author, not the translator. After the title, write "Trans." (for "Translated by") and the name of the translator.

```
Eco, Umberto. Foucault's Pendulum. Trans. William

    Weaver. San Diego: Harcourt, 1989.
```

CORPORATE AUTHOR   List the entry under the name of the corporate author, even if it is also the name of the publisher.

```
Fidelity Investments. Mutual Brokerage Services

    Handbook. Boston: Fidelity Investments, 1993.
```

UNKNOWN AUTHOR   Begin with the title. Alphabetize the entry by the first word of the title other than *a, an,* or *the.*

```
The Times Atlas of the World. 9th ed. New York: Times,

    1992.
```

TWO OR MORE WORKS BY THE SAME AUTHOR   If your list of works cited includes two or more works by the same author, use the author's name only for the first entry. For subsequent entries use three hyphens followed by a period. The three hyphens must stand for exactly the same name or names as in the preceding entry. List the titles in alphabetical order.

Gordon, Mary. <u>Good Boys and Dead Girls and Other</u>

<u>Essays</u>. New York: Viking, 1991.

---. <u>The Other Side</u>. New York: Viking, 1989.

EDITION OTHER THAN THE FIRST Include the number of the edition after the title.

Lindemann, Erika. <u>A Rhetoric for Writing Teachers</u>. 2nd

ed. New York: Oxford UP, 1987.

MULTIVOLUME WORK Include the number of volumes before the city and publisher, using the abbreviation "vols."

<u>Mark Twain: Collected Tales, Sketches, Speeches, and</u>

<u>Essays</u>. 2 vols. New York: Library of America,

1992.

If your paper cites only one of the volumes, write the volume number before the city and publisher and write the total number of volumes in the work after the date.

<u>Mark Twain: Collected Tales, Sketches, Speeches, and</u>

<u>Essays</u>. Vol. 2. New York: Library of America,

1992. 2 vols.

ENCYCLOPEDIA OR DICTIONARY List the author of the entry (if any), the entry heading or title, the title of the encyclopedia or dictionary, the edition number (if any), and the date of the edition.

"Croatia." <u>The New Encyclopaedia Britannica:</u>

<u>Micropaedia</u>. 1991.

Volume and page numbers are not necessary because the entries are arranged alphabetically and therefore are easy to locate.

If a reference work is not well known, provide full publishing information as well.

WORK IN AN ANTHOLOGY Begin with the author and title of the selection; then give the title and the editor of the anthology. After the publishing information, give the page numbers on which the selection appears.

Synge, J. M. "On an Anniversary." <u>The New Oxford Book</u>

<u>of Irish Verse</u>. Ed. Thomas Kinsella. Oxford:

Oxford UP, 1986. 318.

If an anthology gives original publishing information for a selection, you may cite that information first. Follow with "Rpt. in," the title, editor, and publishing information for the anthology, and the page numbers on which the selection appears.

> Rodriguez, Richard. "Late Victorians." Harper's Oct.
>
> 1990: 57-66. Rpt. in The Best American Essays
>
> 1991. Ed. Joyce Carol Oates. New York: Ticknor,
>
> 1991. 119-34.

TWO OR MORE WORKS FROM THE SAME ANTHOLOGY   If you wish, you may cross-reference two or more works from the same anthology. Provide a separate entry for the anthology with complete publication information.

> Kinsella, Thomas, ed. The New Oxford Book of Irish
>
> Verse. Oxford: Oxford UP, 1986.

Then list an entry for each selection from the anthology by author and title of the selection with a cross-reference to the anthology. The cross-reference should include the last name of the editor of the anthology and the page numbers in the anthology on which the selection appears.

> Colum, Padraic. "An Old Woman of the Roads." Kinsella
>
> 321-22.
>
> Synge, J. M. "On an Anniversary." Kinsella 318.

FOREWORD, INTRODUCTION, PREFACE, OR AFTERWORD   If in your paper you quote from one of these elements, begin with the name of the writer of that element. Then identify the element being cited, followed by the title of the book, the author, and the editor, if any. After the publishing information, give the page numbers on which the foreword, introduction, preface, or afterword appears.

> Murray, Charles. Foreword. Unfinished Business: A
>
> Civil Rights Strategy for America's Third
>
> Century. By Clint Bolick. San Francisco: Pacific
>
> Research Inst. for Public Policy, 1990. ix-xiii.

BOOK WITH A TITLE WITHIN ITS TITLE   If the book title contains a title normally underlined, neither underline the internal title nor place it in quotation marks.

> Abbott, Keith. <u>Downstream from</u> Trout Fishing in
>
> America<u>: A Memoir of Richard Brautigan</u>. Santa
>
> Barbara: Capra, 1989.

If the title within the title is normally enclosed within quotation marks, retain the quotation marks and underline the entire title.

> Faulkner, Dewey R. <u>Twentieth Century Interpretations</u>
>
> <u>of "The Pardoner's Tale."</u> Englewood Cliffs:
>
> Spectrum-Prentice, 1973.

BOOK IN A SERIES Before the publishing information, cite the series name followed by the series number, if any.

> Laughlin, Robert M. <u>Of Cabbages and Kings: Tales from</u>
>
> <u>Zinacantán</u>. Smithsonian Contributions to Anthro-
>
> pology 23. Washington: Smithsonian, 1977.

REPUBLISHED BOOK After the title of the book, cite the original publication date followed by the current publishing information. If the republished book contains new material, such as an introduction or afterword, include that information after the original date.

> McClintock, Walter. <u>Old Indian Trails</u>. 1926. Foreword
>
> William Least Heat Moon. Boston: Houghton, 1992.

PUBLISHER'S IMPRINT If a book was published by an imprint of a publishing company, cite the name of the imprint followed by a hyphen and the publisher's name. An imprint name usually precedes the publisher's name on the title page.

> Oates, Joyce Carol. <u>(Woman) Writer: Occasions and</u>
>
> <u>Opportunities</u>. New York: Abrahams-Dutton, 1988.

Articles in periodicals

ARTICLE IN A MONTHLY MAGAZINE In addition to the author, the title of the article, and the title of the magazine, list the month and year and the page numbers on which the article appears. Abbreviate the names of months except May, June, and July.

> Lukacs, John. "The End of the Twentieth Century."
>
> <u>Harper's</u> Jan. 1993: 39-58.

If the article had appeared on pages 39–40 and 60–62, you would write "39+" (not "39–62").

ARTICLE IN A WEEKLY MAGAZINE   Handle articles in weekly (or biweekly) magazines as you do those for monthly magazines, but give the exact date of the issue, not just the month and year.

> Schiff, Stephen. "Muriel Spark between the Lines." New
>
>   Yorker 24 May 1993: 36-43.

ARTICLE IN A JOURNAL PAGINATED BY VOLUME   Many professional journals continue page numbers throughout the year instead of beginning each issue with page 1; at the end of the year, all of the issues are collected in a volume. Interested readers need only the volume number, the year, and the page numbers to find a particular article.

> Segal, Gabriel. "Seeing What Is Not There."
>
>   Philosophical Review 98 (1989): 189-214.

ARTICLE IN A JOURNAL PAGINATED BY ISSUE   If each issue of the journal begins with page 1, you need to indicate the number of the issue. Simply place a period after the number of the volume, followed by the number of the issue.

> Johnson, G. J. "A Distinctiveness Model of Serial
>
>   Learning." Psychological Review 98.2 (1991): 204-
>
>   17.

ARTICLE IN A DAILY NEWSPAPER   Begin with the author, if there is one, followed by the title of the article. Next give the name of the newspaper, the date, the section letter or number, and the page number.

> Sun, Lena H. "Chinese Feel the Strain of a New
>
>   Society." Washington Post 13 June 1993: A1+.

If the section is marked with a number rather than a letter, handle the entry as follows:

> Greenhouse, Linda. "Justices Plan to Delve Anew into
>
>   Race and Voting Rights." New York Times 11 July
>
>   1993, sec. 1: 1+.

If an edition of the newspaper is specified on the masthead, name the edition after the date and before the page reference: eastern ed., late ed., natl. ed., and so on.

UNSIGNED ARTICLE IN A NEWSPAPER OR MAGAZINE   Use the same form you would use for an article in a newspaper or a weekly or monthly magazine, but begin with the article title.

> "Radiation in Russia." U.S. News and World Report
>
>   9 Aug. 1993: 40-42.

EDITORIAL IN A NEWSPAPER   Cite an editorial as you would an article with an unknown author, adding the word "Editorial" after the title.

> "Gays and the Military." Editorial. Boston Globe
>
>   13 July 1993: 14.

LETTER TO THE EDITOR   Cite the writer's name, followed by the word "Letter" and the publishing information for the newspaper or magazine in which the letter appears.

> Benston, Graham. Letter. Opera Now May 1993: 12.

BOOK OR FILM REVIEW   Cite first the reviewer's name and the title of the review, if any, followed by the words "Rev. of" and the title and author or director of the work reviewed. Add the publishing information for the publication in which the review appears.

> Kermode, Frank. "Criticism without Machinery." Rev. of
>
>   Literary Reflections, by R. W. B. Lewis. New York
>
>   Times Book Review 11 July 1993: 16.
>
> Holden, Stephen. "A Union of Convenience across a
>
>   Cultural Divide." Rev. of The Wedding Banquet,
>
>   dir. Ang Lee. With Winston Chao, May Chin, and
>
>   Mitchell Lichtenstein. Goldwyn, 1993. New York
>
>   Times 4 Aug. 1993: C18.

CD-ROMs and Online Databases

Research material is available in electronic form on CD-ROM (compact disc) from vendors such as SilverPlatter and UMI-

Proquest and online from computer services or networks such as
Dialog, Nexis, and the Internet. In citations for electronic sources,
you give the same publishing information as for other sources and
in addition give pertinent information about the electronic source.
You may find that some of the information about an electronic
source, such as the name of the vendor, is not available. If so, you
may omit this information.

CD-ROM ISSUED PERIODICALLY   CD-ROM databases that are produced periodically (monthly or quarterly, for example) may contain
previously published material, such as journal or newspaper
articles, or material that has not been previously published,
such as reports. In either case, cite such material as you would a
printed source, followed by the title of the database (underlined), the medium (CD-ROM), the name of the company producing the CD-ROM, and the date of electronic publication.

Sawyer, Kathy. "Oceanography: Rising Tide Lifts

Warming Case." Washington Post 12 Dec. 1994: A2.

InfoTrac: National Newspaper Index. CD-ROM.

Information Access. Jan. 1995.

Gauch, Patricia Lee. "A Quest for the Heart of

Fantasy." New Advocate 7.3 (1994): 159-67. ERIC.

CD-ROM. SilverPlatter. Dec. 1994.

CD-ROM ISSUED IN A SINGLE EDITION   Some works on CD-ROM,
such as dictionaries and encyclopedias, are released in single editions that are not updated periodically. Treat such sources as you
would a book, but give the medium (CD-ROM) before the publishing information.

The Oxford English Dictionary. 1st ed. CD-ROM. Oxford:

Oxford UP, 1987.

"O'Keeffe, Georgia." The 1995 Grolier Multimedia

Encyclopedia. CD-ROM. Danbury: Grolier, 1995.

ONLINE MATERIAL FROM A COMPUTER SERVICE   Computer services
such as Dialog, CompuServe, America Online, and Nexis provide a
variety of databases that may be revised continually or periodically. For material from such a source, cite the publication information given in the source, the title of the database (underlined),
the medium (Online), and the name of the computer service. In ad-

dition, because it is often not possible to determine when material has been entered or updated in the service's database, give the date on which you accessed the material.

Bass, Alison. "Women Just as Spatial as Men." Boston Globe 22 Feb. 1993, 3rd ed.: 25. Boston Globe-File 631. Online. Dialog. 6 Feb. 1995.

Mann, Charles C., and Mark L. Plummer. "Empowering Species." Atlantic Monthly Feb. 1995. Atlantic Monthly Online. Online. America Online. 16 Feb. 1995.

ONLINE MATERIAL FROM A COMPUTER NETWORK   A computer network such as the Internet provides access to material such as journal articles, newsletters, and even entire books. For such material, cite whatever publication information is given in the electronic source, using the format for citing a journal article or book. Give the number of pages or paragraphs, followed by "p." (or "pp.") or "par." (or "pars."); if neither is specified, use "n. pag." for "no pagination." In addition, give the title of the database (underlined), the medium (Online), the computer network, and the date you accessed the material. If your instructor wants you to specify the electronic address of the source, place it after the word "Available" at the end of your citation.

Spetalnick, Terrie. "Privacy in the Electronic Community." EDUCOM Review 28.3 (1993): n. pag. Online. Internet. 7 Feb. 1995. Available: gopher.cic.net.

Wells, H. G. The War of the Worlds. 1898. Online. U of Minnesota Lib. Internet. 5 Feb. 1995. Available: gopher.micro.umn.edu.

Other sources

GOVERNMENT PUBLICATION   Treat the government agency as the author, giving the name of the government followed by the name of the agency.

United States. Natl. Endowment for the Humanities. Study Grants for College and University Teachers. Washington: GPO, 1993.

PAMPHLET   Cite a pamphlet as you would a book.

United States. Dept. of the Interior. Natl. Park

  Service. Ford's Theatre and the House Where

  Lincoln Died. Washington: GPO, 1989.

PUBLISHED DISSERTATION   Cite a published dissertation as you would a book, but after the title add the word "Diss.," the institution name, and the year the dissertation was written.

Healey, Robert F. Eleusinian Sacrifices in the

  Athenian Law Code. Diss. Harvard U, 1961. New York:

  Garland, 1990.

UNPUBLISHED DISSERTATION   Begin with the author's name, followed by the dissertation title in quotation marks, the word "Diss.," the name of the institution, and the year the dissertation was written.

Fedorko, Kathy Anne. "Edith Wharton's Haunted House:

  The Gothic in Her Fiction." Diss. Rutgers U, 1987.

ABSTRACT OF A DISSERTATION   Give the author's name, the dissertation title in quotation marks, and the abbreviation *DA* or *DAI* (for *Dissertation Abstracts* or *Dissertation Abstracts International*), followed by the volume number, date, and page number. Add the name of the institution at the end.

Berkman, Anne Elizabeth. "The Quest for Authenticity:

  The Novels of Toni Morrison." DAI 48 (1988): 2059A.

  Columbia U.

PUBLISHED PROCEEDINGS OF A CONFERENCE   Cite published conference proceedings as you would a book, adding information about the conference after the title.

Howell, Benita J., ed. Cultural Heritage Conservation

  in the American South. Proc. of Southern Anthro-

  pological Society. Tampa, 1988. Athens: U of

  Georgia P, 1990.

WORK OF ART   Cite the artist's name, followed by the title of the artwork, usually underlined, and the institution and city in which the artwork can be found.

```
Cassatt, Mary.  At the Opera.  Museum of Fine Arts,

     Boston.
```

MUSICAL COMPOSITION   Cite the composer's name, followed by the title of the work. Underline the title of an opera, a ballet, or a composition identified by name, but do not underline or use quotation marks around a composition identified by number or form.

```
Copland, Aaron.  Appalachian Spring.

Shostakovich, Dmitri.  Quartet no. 1 in C, op. 49.
```

PERSONAL LETTER   To cite a letter you have received, begin with the writer's name and add the phrase "Letter to the author," followed by the date. For a letter received via electronic mail, use the designation "E-mail."

```
Cipriani, Karen. Letter to the author. 25 Apr. 1993.

Gray, William A. E-mail to the author. 26 Jan. 1995.
```

LECTURE OR PUBLIC ADDRESS   Cite the speaker's name, followed by the title of the lecture (if any) in quotation marks, the organization sponsoring the lecture, the location, and date.

```
Quinn, Karen. "John Singleton Copley's Watson and the

     Shark." Museum of Fine Arts. Boston. 1 July 1993.
```

PERSONAL INTERVIEW   To cite an interview that you conducted, begin with the name of the person interviewed. Then write "Personal interview," followed by the date of the interview.

```
Harrison, Patricia. Personal interview. 19 Feb. 1993.
```

PUBLISHED INTERVIEW   Name the person interviewed, followed by the word "Interview" and the publication in which the interview was printed. If the interview has a title, put it in quotation marks after the interviewee's name and do not use the word "Interview."

```
Quindlen, Anna. Interview. Commonweal 14 Feb. 1992: 9-13.
```

RADIO OR TELEVISION INTERVIEW   Name the person interviewed, followed by the word "Interview." Then give the title of the program, underlined, and identifying information about the broadcast.

```
Holm, Celeste. Interview. Fresh Air. Natl. Public Radio.

     WBUR, Boston.  28 June 1990.
```

FILM OR VIDEOTAPE Begin with the title. For a film, cite the director and the names of the lead actors or narrator; for a videotape, give the word "Videotape" followed by the director and the names of the lead actors or narrator. End with the distributor and year and any other pertinent information, such as running time.

Much Ado about Nothing. Dir. Kenneth Branagh.

    With Emma Thompson, Kenneth Branagh, Denzel

    Washington, Michael Keaton, and Keanu Reeves.

    Goldwyn, 1993.

Through the Wire. Videotape. Dir. Nina Rosenblum.

    Narr. Susan Sarandon. Fox/Lorber Home Video,

    1990. 77 min.

RADIO OR TELEVISION PROGRAM List the information about the program in this order: the title of the program, underlined; the writer ("By"), director ("Dir."), narrator ("Narr."), producer ("Prod."), or main actors ("With"), if relevant; the network; the local station on which you heard or saw the program, followed by the city; and the date the program was broadcast. If a television episode or radio segment has a title, the order is as follows: episode or segment title in quotation marks; writer, director, narrator, and so on; title of the program, underlined; network; local station and city; and date of broadcast.

Coração Brasileiro. WMBR, Boston. 1 Aug. 1993.

"This Old Pyramid." With Mark Lehner and Roger

    Hopkins. Nova. PBS. WGBH, Boston. 4 Aug. 1993.

LIVE PERFORMANCE OF A PLAY Begin with the title of the play, followed by the author. Then include specific information about the live performance: the director, the major actors, the theater company and its location, and the date of the performance.

The Sisters Rosensweig. By Wendy Wasserstein. Dir.

    Daniel Sullivan. With Jane Alexander, Christine

    Estabrook, and Madeline Kahn. Barrymore, New

    York. 11 July 1993.

RECORD, TAPE, OR CD Begin with the composer (or author, if the recording is spoken), followed by the title of the piece. Next list pertinent artists (for instance, the conductor, the pianist, or the reader). End with the company label, the catalog number, and the date.

> Verdi, Giuseppe. <u>Falstaff</u>. With Tito Gobbi, Elisabeth
>
> Schwarzkopf, Nan Merriman, and Fedora Barbieri.
>
> Cond. Herbert von Karajan. Philharmonica Orch.
>
> and Chorus. EMI, 7 49668 2, 1988.

CARTOON Begin with the cartoonist's name, the title of the cartoon (if it has one) in quotation marks, the word "Cartoon," and the publishing information for the publication in which the cartoon appears.

> Chast, Roz. "Are You All Right?" Cartoon. <u>New Yorker</u> 5
>
> July 1993: 65.

MAP OR CHART Cite a map or chart as you would a book with an unknown author. Underline the title of the map or chart and add the word "Map" or "Chart" following the title.

> <u>Spain/Portugal</u>. Map. Paris: Michelin, 1992.

COMPUTER SOFTWARE Begin with the author of the program (if known), the title of the program, underlined, and the words "Computer software." Then name the distributor and the year of publication. At the end of the entry you may add other pertinent information, such as the computer for which the program is designed or the form of the program.

> <u>Encarta</u>. Computer software. Microsoft, 1992. PC-DOS
>
> 3.1, Windows, 386SX, CD-ROM.

M3

Content and bibliographic notes (optional)

Content and bibliographic notes are optional; do not include them unless you have a legitimate need for them. Content notes provide additional information that would interrupt the flow of the paper yet is important enough to include. Bibliographic notes refer readers to sources that contain information about the topic at hand; sometimes they comment on sources.

Such notes may be either footnotes, which appear at the foot of the page, or endnotes, which appear at the end of the paper, just before the list of works cited. For either style, notes are numbered consecutively throughout the paper. The text of the paper contains a raised arabic numeral that corresponds to the number of the note.

Content note

TEXT

In spite of claims made for the apes, however, some researchers have questioned whether the apes really learn signs or whether they merely imitate or respond to the cues of their trainers.[1]

NOTE

[1] The most famous example of cuing involves a horse named Clever Hans. The horse's owner sincerely thought that Clever Hans could solve mathematical problems, tapping out the answers with his foot. In fact, the horse was responding to the involuntary jerks of the owner's head at the point when the correct number of taps had been reached.

Bibliographic note

TEXT

The apes' achievements cannot be explained away as the simple results of conditioning or unconscious cuing by trainers.[1]

NOTE

[1] For a discussion of the cuing of animals, see Wade 1349-51.

CAUTION: Content and bibliographic notes should not be confused with notes used as an alternative to parenthetical in-text citations (see A2).

M4

Sample research paper: MLA style

On the following pages is a research paper written by Karen Shaw, a student in a college composition class. Shaw's paper is documented with the MLA style of in-text citations and list of works cited (see M1 and M2). Annotations in the margins of the paper draw your attention to features of special interest.

In preparing her final manuscript, Shaw consulted the MLA guidelines in D2-a of this book. Shaw included a separate title page because her instructor requested one.

Title is centered
about one-third
down the page.

Between the Word and the Sentence:

Apes and Language

Writer's name is
centered near the
middle of the page.

Karen Shaw

The name and
section number of
the course, the
professor's name,
and the date are
centered near the
bottom of the
page.

English 101, Section 30

Dr. Robert Barshay

1 November 1994

Between the Word and the Sentence:

Apes and Language

One afternoon, Koko the gorilla, who was often bored with language lessons, stubbornly and repeatedly signaled "red" in American Sign Language when asked the color of a white towel. She did this even though she had identified the color white many times before. At last the gorilla plucked a bit of red lint from the towel and showed it to her trainer (Patterson and Linden 80-81). At Yerkes Primate Center, chimpanzees Sherman and Austin, who had been taught symbols for foods and tools, were put in separate rooms. To obtain food in different containers, one chimp had to ask the other for a tool, such as a key or a wrench, by projecting symbols onto a screen using a computer. After some experimentation, the chimpanzees succeeded 97 percent of the time (Marx 1333). These and hundreds of similar scenes played out over the last twenty-five years demonstrate that the great apes (gorillas, orangutans, and chimpanzees) resemble humans in language abilities far more than researchers once thought. And evidence is mounting, despite opposition from some linguists and psychologists, that the most intelligent of the apes--pygmy chimpanzees--can understand and perhaps even create sentences.

Although apes lack the vocal ability to produce human sounds, they have acquired vocabularies

Writer's name and page number are typed 1/2" from top of each page.

Title is centered and double-spaced.

Citation with author's name and page number in parentheses.

Thesis states writer's conclusions about the ape language experiments.

Shaw 2

in American Sign Language (Ameslan) and in
artificial languages. Vocabularies ranging from
100 to 200 signs or symbols have been reported for
the gorillas Koko and Michael; for the orangutan
Chantek; and for numerous chimpanzees, including
Washoe, Nim, Lana, Sherman, Austin, and Kanzi.

The apes' acquisition of these vocabularies
is not in dispute, but some researchers have questioned whether the apes are truly learning the
signs and symbols. These critics suggest that the
apes may be merely imitating their trainers or responding to cues. Psychologist H. S. Terrace, the
chief trainer of a chimp named Nim, is one of the
most formidable of the skeptics because he was
once a believer. Ultimately Terrace concluded
that in many cases "the teacher's signs had
prompted Nim's signs" (75). Terrace argued that
cuing had also played a large role in Beatrice
Gardner's training of Washoe.

While it is possible that in these early
studies many of the apes' signs were in response
to cues, Terrace and other critics failed to prove
that all of them were. Even as early as 1979,
psychologists Alan and Beatrice Gardner were performing double-blind experiments that prevented
any possibility of cuing (Sebeok and Umiker-Sebeok
81-82). Terrace criticizes these experiments
without mentioning the double-blind technique, an
attack that seems unfair.

Author is named
in signal phrase;
page number is
put in parentheses
at end of
quotation.

The writer
interprets the
evidence; she
doesn't just
report it.

Perhaps the most convincing evidence that the apes have not been simply responding to cues is that they have used signs or symbols spontaneously among themselves. Francine Patterson's gorillas Koko and Michael sign to one another, with Michael occasionally using signs that he could have learned only from Koko. "Even more intriguing," write Patterson and Linden, "is his variation of the tickle sign depending on whom he is conversing with" (176).

For variety, the signal phrase is placed between parts of the quotations.

The most dramatic instances of spontaneous signing have involved Washoe. In 1976, she had a baby, and although the baby chimp lived only a few hours, Washoe signed to it before it died (Davis 42). Later, another baby chimpanzee placed in Washoe's care mastered more than 50 signs in Ameslan without help from humans (Toner). When the Gardners returned Washoe to an ape colony in Oklahoma, she desperately signaled to humans from whom she was separated by a moat, and from the start she signed to other apes. Adrian Desmond vividly describes Washoe's efforts to converse:

The writer supports her point with examples from a variety of sources.

No page number is needed for Toner because the article is one page long.

> Frustrated by lack of conversational-
> ists, she [Washoe] even tried talking to
> dogs. . . . One particularly memorable
> day, a snake spread terror through . . .
> the ape island, and all but one fled in
> panic. Then Washoe was seen running over
> signing to him "come, hurry up." (42)

Quotation longer than four lines is indented ten spaces; quotation marks are omitted; no period is used after citation.

Brackets indicate words not in the original source; ellipsis dots indicate words deleted from the original source.

Shaw   4

In addition to learning signs and using them
spontaneously, apes have used language creatively.
Koko has signed "finger bracelet" to describe a
ring and "bottle match" for a cigarette lighter
(Patterson and Linden 146). The Gardners' Lucy is
reported to have called an onion "cry fruit" and a
radish "cry hurt food" (Desmond 40). And the pygmy
chimpanzee Kanzi has punched symbols for "campfire"
and "TV" to ask to see <u>Quest for Fire</u>, a film about
early primates discovering fire (Eckholm, "Kanzi" C3).

Apes who invent creative names are not simply
learning by rote. They are adapting language for
their own purposes. And those purposes, it turns
out, may even include lying and joking. In a recent personal interview, Professor Esther Robbins,
who worked with Francine Patterson's gorilla
Michael for seven months, pointed out how difficult
it is to verify such uses of language quantita-
tively. What counts as language is "a very gray
area," she says. "But you <u>know</u> that animal, and
there is very definitely communication, even lying
and joking."

Although the great apes have demonstrated
significant language skills, one central question
remains: Can they be taught to use that uniquely
human language tool we call grammar, to learn the
difference, for instance, between "ape bite human"
and "human bite ape"? In other words, can an ape
create a sentence?

Citation includes
short title because
two works by
Eckholm appear in
the list of works
cited.

Use of a personal
interview as a
source.

A clear transition
prepares readers
for the next major
point.

Shaw 5

Apes have used multisign sequences, but until recently there was little convincing evidence that the combinations displayed a grasp of grammar. Many of the sequences seemed confusing and repetitious, such as Nim's longest sequence: "give orange me give eat orange me eat orange give me eat orange give me you" (Terrace et al. 895). Currently, however, E. Sue Savage-Rumbaugh's studies on the pygmy chimpanzee Kanzi are making even the skeptics take notice. Young Kanzi had played in the lab while his mother was being tutored in a language of symbols, and when he was two and a half, his mother was sent away for breeding. "To the scientists' amazement," writes Erik Eckholm, "he had been learning symbols out of the corner of his eye. He hit the symbol for apple, then proved he knew what he was saying by picking an apple from an assortment of foods" ("Kanzi" C2).

Citation of a work with four or more authors.

Impressed by Kanzi's ability to pick up language without explicit training, Savage-Rumbaugh decided to replace rote learning with "a more naturalistic approach": Kanzi would learn language much the way human children do (Lewin 50). Consequently, Kanzi's linguistic development has taken place not in a laboratory but in a fifty-five-acre forest, which he roams in the company of his caretakers. During games of tag and hide-and-seek and other childhood activities, Kanzi communicates with his caregivers on a computerized keyboard

Shaw 6

equipped with a voice synthesizer. A word is spoken each time Kanzi touches a symbol on the board.

Evidence of Kanzi's linguistic progress
was published in 1991, when Kanzi was ten. The
results show that he can understand grammatically
complex spoken English and that he seems to be developing a primitive grammar. In their studies of
Kanzi and his half sister Mulika, Savage-Rumbaugh
and members of her team have taken great care to
avoid cuing. Lewin reports that spoken instructions to Kanzi were "delivered by someone out of
his sight" and that the other team members "could
not hear the instructions and so could not cue
Kanzi, even unconsciously" (51). When Kanzi correctly responded to sentences like "Can you put
the raisins in the bowl?" his caretakers made the
instructions more difficult. For example, in response to the question "Can you go to the colony
room and get the telephone?" Kanzi brought back
the telephone even though there were other objects
in the room.

Most surprising is Kanzi's apparent grasp of
grammar. The first grammatical rule that Kanzi began to display was to put action before object (as
in "hide peanut" and "grab Kanzi"), a pattern
probably picked up from his caregivers. In 1985,
Eckholm reported that Kanzi's "two and three word
statements are often made without prompting, sys-

Citation appears
after the quotation
mark and before
the period.

tematically add useful information and represent his own creative responses to novel situations" ("Pygmy" B7). In the first month of study, Kanzi showed no understanding of grammatical ordering, but gradually he began to pick it up. Patricia Marks Greenfield and E. Sue Savage-Rumbaugh point out that this developmental trend "was also found for human children at the two-word stage" (559).

Citation of a work with two authors.

At times Kanzi deviated from the grammar of his keepers and began to develop his own patterns, an ability that may be more impressive than picking up rules from keepers. Without prompting, Kanzi began to combine gestures and symbols, usually pointing to the symbol first. For example, Ann Gibbons reports that when Kanzi wanted to visit the lab's dog, "he would point to the symbol for dog, then make a gesture for 'go'" (1561). Perhaps even more significant is the pattern that Kanzi developed on his own in combining various symbols. According to Gibbons, "When he gave an order combining two symbols for action--such as 'chase' and 'hide'--it was important to him that the first action--'chase'--be done first" (1561). Kanzi's consistency in combining symbols suggests that he has at least a rudimentary grasp of grammar.

If Kanzi and other pygmy chimpanzees continue to develop grammatical patterns, the implications for the study of human evolution could be profound.

Shaw 8

A quotation set
off from the text
is clearly intro-
duced.

Anthropologist Richard Leakey and coauthor Roger
Lewin pose the issue like this:

> Is spoken language merely an extension
> and enhancement of cognitive capacities
> to be found among our ape relatives? Or
> is spoken language a unique human char-
> acteristic completely separate from any
> cognitive abilities in apes? (240)

Leakey and Lewin believe that there is a continuity in linguistic ability between apes and humans. Linguist Noam Chomsky believes the opposite. Chomsky describes the entire ape language
field as gripped by "sentimental confusion" and
dismisses the studies on Kanzi with a flippant
analogy: "To maintain that Kanzi has language
ability is like saying a man can fly because he

Citation of an
indirect source
(words quoted in
another source).

can jump in the air" (qtd. in Booth). This is
certainly strong language from a man who, in the
words of Ann Gibbons, has not even "seen the new
data--and doesn't care to" (1521).

The writer
addresses opposing
arguments.

Skeptics such as Chomsky seem to be applying
a double standard when they compare apes' linguistic abilities to those of young human children.
As Savage-Rumbaugh puts it, "When children make up
novel words it is called lexical innovation, but
when chimpanzees do the same thing it is called
ambiguous" (qtd. in Lewin 51). The double standard issue is unlikely to be resolved any time

Shaw   9

soon, however, because the methodologies used in studies of human children are different from--and possibly less rigorous than--those used in the ape language studies.

Certainly no one expects any chimpanzee to perform linguistically far beyond the level of a very young human child. After all, a chimpanzee's brain is only one-third the size of our own. But the brains of the ancestors of Homo sapiens at some point were of similar size. Surely it makes more sense that an animal with whom we share 99 percent of our genetic makeup would at least have the inklings in its brain of the ability to commu-nicate in language. And surely the ability to communicate in language in our human ancestors came before language itself. Maybe I am "senti-mental," to use Chomsky's word, but when I read about Kanzi's achievements, it is difficult not to believe that there is some commonality of abili-ties.

No citation is needed for "common knowledge" — facts mentioned in many general reference works.

The writer ends with her own stand on the controversy.

Shaw 10

Works Cited

Booth, William. "Monkeying with Language: Is Chimp

　　　Using Words or Merely Aping Handlers?"

　　　Washington Post 29 Oct. 1990: A3.

Davis, Flora. *Eloquent Animals: A Study in Animal*

　　　Communication. New York: Coward, 1978.

Desmond, Adrian. *The Ape's Reflexion*. New York:

　　　Wade-Dial, 1979.

Eckholm, Erik. "Kanzi the Chimp: A Life in

　　　Science." *New York Times* 25 June 1985, local

　　　ed.: C1+.

---. "Pygmy Chimp Readily Learns Language Skill."

　　　New York Times 24 June 1985, local ed.: A1+.

Gibbons, Ann. "Déjà Vu All Over Again: Chimp-

　　　Language Wars." *Science* 251 (1991): 1561-

　　　62.

Greenfield, Patricia Marks, and E. Sue Savage-

　　　Rumbaugh. "Grammatical Combination in *Pan*

　　　paniscus: Processes of Learning and Invention

　　　in the Evolution and Development of

　　　Language." *"Language" and Intelligence in*

　　　Monkeys and Apes: Comparative Developmental

　　　Perspectives. Ed. Sue Taylor Parker and

　　　Kathleen Rita Gibson. Cambridge: Cambridge

　　　UP, 1990. 540-78.

Leakey, Richard, and Roger Lewin. *Origins*

　　　Reconsidered: In Search of What Makes Us

　　　Human. New York: Doubleday, 1992.

List of works cited begins on a separate page.

Heading, centered, is typed 1" from top of page.

List is alphabetized by authors' last names.

First line of an entry is typed at left margin; subsequent lines are indented five spaces.

Double-spacing is used throughout.

Lewin, Roger. "Look Who's Talking Now." <u>New</u>
       <u>Scientist</u> 29 Apr. 1991: 49-52.

Marx, Jean L. "Ape-Language Controversy Flares
       Up." <u>Science</u> 207 (1980): 1330-33.

Patterson, Francine, and Eugene Linden. <u>The</u>
       <u>Education of Koko</u>. New York: Holt, 1981.

Robbins, Esther. Personal interview. 17 May 1993.

Sebeok, Thomas A., and Jean Umiker-Sebeok.
       "Performing Animals: Secrets of the Trade."
       <u>Psychology Today</u> Nov. 1979: 78-91.

Terrace, H. S. "How Nim Chimpsky Changed My Mind."
       <u>Psychology Today</u> Nov. 1979: 65-76.

Terrace, H. S., et al. "Can an Ape Create a
       Sentence?" <u>Science</u> 206 (1979): 891-902.

Toner, Mike. "Loulis, the Talking Chimp." <u>National</u>
       <u>Wildlife</u> Feb.-Mar. 1986: 24.

A

Alternative
Styles of
Documentation

A

Alternative Styles of Documentation

Directory to APA in-text citations (A1-a)

Directory to APA references (A1-b)

Most English and humanities classes use the Modern Language Association (MLA) style of documentation that is described in the previous tabbed section, MLA Documentation. Section A surveys two alternative styles of documentation commonly required in other disciplines. In the social sciences, you will usually be asked to use the American Psychological Association (APA) style (see A1). In history and in some other humanities classes, you may be asked to use footnotes or endnotes (see A2). For a list of style manuals in a variety of disciplines, see A3.

Always use the style of documentation recommended by your instructor.

A1

APA style

The American Psychological Association (APA) recommends an author/date style of in-text citations. These citations refer readers to a list of references at the end of the paper.

A1-a APA in-text citations

The APA's in-text citations provide at least the author's last name and the date of publication. For direct quotations, a page number is given as well.

NOTE: In the models that follow, notice that APA style requires the use of the past tense or present perfect tense in signal phrases introducing material that has been cited: *Smith reported, Smith has argued.* (See G2-f.)

BASIC FORMAT FOR A QUOTATION   Ordinarily, introduce the quotation with a signal phrase that includes the author's last name followed by the date of publication in parentheses. Put the page number (preceded by "p.") in parentheses at the end of the quotation.

```
As Davis (1978) reported, "If the existence of a
signing ape was unsettling for linguists, it was also
startling news for animal behaviorists" (p. 26).
```

When the author's name does not appear in the signal phrase, place the author's last name, the date, and the page number in parentheses at the end of the quotation. Use commas between items in the parentheses: (Davis, 1978, p. 26).

BASIC FORMAT FOR A SUMMARY OR A PARAPHRASE   For a summary or a paraphrase, include the author's last name and the date either in a signal phrase or in parentheses at the end.

According to Davis (1978), when they learned of an

ape's ability to use sign language, both linguists and

animal behaviorists were taken by surprise.

When they learned of an ape's ability to use sign

language, both linguists and animal behaviorists were

taken by surprise (Davis, 1978).

NOTE: A page number is not required, but you should provide one if it would help your readers find a specific page in a long work.

A WORK WITH TWO AUTHORS   Name both authors in the signal phrase or parentheses each time you cite the work. In the parentheses, use "&" between the authors' names; in the signal phrase, use "and."

Patterson and Linden (1981) agreed that the gorilla

Koko acquired language more slowly than a normal

speaking child.

Koko acquired language more slowly than a normal

speaking child (Patterson & Linden, 1981).

A WORK WITH THREE TO FIVE AUTHORS   Identify all authors in the signal phrase or the parentheses the first time you cite the source.

The study noted a fluctuating divorce rate in

Middletown between the 1920s and the 1970s (Caplow,

Bahr, Chadwick, Hill, & Williamson, 1982).

In subsequent citations, use the first author's name followed by "et al." in either the signal phrase or the parentheses.

> While the incidence of wife abuse may not be higher
> than in the past, the researchers found that women are
> more willing to report it (Caplow et al., 1982).

A WORK WITH SIX OR MORE AUTHORS   Use only the first author's name followed by "et al." in all citations.

> Communes in the late 1960s functioned like extended
> families, with child-rearing responsibilities shared
> by all adult members (Berger et al., 1971).

UNKNOWN AUTHOR   If the author is not given, either use the complete title in a signal phrase or use the first two or three words of the title in the parenthetical citation.

> The UFO reported by the crew of a Japan Air Lines flight
> remains a mystery. Radar tapes did not confirm the
> presence of another craft ("Strange Encounter," 1987).

If "Anonymous" is specified as the author, treat it as if it were a real name: (Anonymous, 1987). In the list of references, also use the name Anonymous as author.

CORPORATE AUTHOR   If the author is a government agency or other corporate organization with a long and cumbersome name, spell out the name the first time you use it in a citation, followed by an abbreviation in brackets. In later citations, simply use the abbreviation.

> **FIRST CITATION:**   (National Institute of Mental Health
>   [NIMH], 1995).
>
> **LATER CITATIONS:**   (NIMH, 1995).

TWO OR MORE WORKS IN THE SAME PARENTHESES   When your parenthetical citation names two or more works, put them in the same order that they appear in the list of references, separated by semicolons: (Berger et al., 1971; Smith, 1995).

AUTHORS WITH THE SAME LAST NAME   To avoid confusion, use initials with the last names if your list of references contains two or more authors with the same last name.

> Research by J. A. Smith (1994) revealed that. . . .

PERSONAL COMMUNICATION Unpublished personal communications should be cited by initials, last name, and precise date.

> L. Smith (personal communication, October 12, 1995)
>
> predicted that government funding of this type of
>
> research will end soon.

Do not include personal communications in your list of references.

A1-b APA references (bibliographic list)

In APA style, the alphabetical list of works cited is entitled "References." The general principles are as follows.

1. Invert *all* authors' names and use initials instead of first names. With two or more authors, use an ampersand (&) rather than the word "and." Separate the names with commas.

2. Use all authors' names; do not use "et al."

3. Place the date of publication in parentheses immediately after the last author's name.

4. Underline titles and subtitles of books; capitalize only the first word of the title and subtitle (as well as all proper nouns).

5. Do not place titles of articles in quotation marks, and capitalize only the first word of the title and subtitle (and all proper nouns). Capitalize names of periodicals as you would capitalize them ordinarily (see S3-c). Underline the volume number of periodicals.

6. Use the abbreviation "p." (or "pp." for plural) before page numbers of newspaper articles and works in anthologies, but do not use it before page numbers of articles appearing in magazines and scholarly journals.

7. You may use a short form of the publisher's name as long as it is easily identifiable.

8. Alphabetize your list by the last name of the author (or editor); if there is no author or editor, alphabetize by the first word of the title other than *a, an,* or *the.*

9. Unless your instructor suggests otherwise, do not indent the first line of an entry but indent any additional lines five spaces. This technique, known as a "hanging indent," is used for final copy: student papers and actual journal articles. (For manuscripts submitted to journals, APA requires paragraph-style indents that are then converted to hanging indents.)

Books

BASIC FORMAT FOR A BOOK

Schaller, G. B. (1993). The last panda. Chicago:

   University of Chicago Press.

TWO OR MORE AUTHORS

Eggan, P. D., & Kauchall, D. (1992). Educational

   psychology: Classroom connections. New York:

   Merrill.

Caplow, T., Bahr, H. M., Chadwick, B. A., Hill, R., &

   Williamson, M. H. (1982). Middletown families:

   Fifty years of change and continuity.

   Minneapolis: University of Minnesota Press.

CORPORATE AUTHOR   When the author is an organization, the publisher is often the same organization. In such a case, give the publisher's name as "Author."

Fidelity Investments. (1993). Fidelity Brokerage

   Services handbook. Boston: Author.

UNKNOWN AUTHOR

The Times atlas of the world (9th ed.). (1992). New

   York: Times Books.

EDITORS

Fox, R. W., & Lears, T. J. J. (Eds.). (1993). The

   power of culture: Critical essays in American

   history. Chicago: University of Chicago Press.

TRANSLATION

Miller, A. (1990). The untouched key: Tracing

   childhood trauma in creativity and

   destructiveness (H. & H. Hannum, Trans.). New

   York: Doubleday. (Original work published 1988)

EDITION OTHER THAN THE FIRST

Cavanaugh, J. C. (1993). Adult development and aging
(2nd ed.). Pacific Grove, CA: Brooks/Cole.

WORK IN AN ANTHOLOGY

Ochs, E., & Schieffelin, B. (1984). Language
acquisition and socialization: Three
developmental stories. In R. Schweder & R. Levine
(Eds.), Culture theory: Essays in mind, self, and
emotion (pp. 276-320). New York: Cambridge
University Press.

TWO OR MORE WORKS BY THE SAME AUTHOR Use the author's name
for first and subsequent entries. Arrange the entries by date, the
earliest first.

Davis, F. (1973). Inside intuition: What we know
about nonverbal communication. New York: McGraw-
Hill.

Davis, F. (1978). Eloquent animals: A study in animal
communication. New York: Coward, McCann &
Geoghegan.

Articles in periodicals

ARTICLE IN A JOURNAL PAGINATED BY VOLUME

Block, N. (1992). Begging the question: Against
phenomenal consciousness. Behavioral and Brain
Sciences, 15, 205-206.

ARTICLE IN A JOURNAL PAGINATED BY ISSUE

Searle, J. (1990). Is the brain a digital computer?
Proceedings of the American Philosophical
Association, 64(3), 21-37.

ARTICLE IN A MAGAZINE

Caputo, R. (1993, August). Tragedy stalks the Horn of
    Africa. National Geographic, 184, 88-121.

ARTICLE IN A DAILY NEWSPAPER

Goleman, D. (1993, July 13). New treatments for autism
    arouse hope and skepticism. The New York Times,
    pp. C1, C11.

LETTER TO THE EDITOR

Fuller, K. S. (1993). The issue of ivory [Letter to
    the editor]. Audubon, 95(4), 12.

REVIEW

Blaut, J. M. (1993). [Review of the book Global
    capitalism: Theories of societal development].
    Science & Society, 57(1), 106-107.

TWO OR MORE WORKS BY THE SAME AUTHOR IN THE SAME YEAR   Cite
the works according to the usual style, and arrange them alphabetically by title. Add lowercase letters beginning with "a," "b," and
so on within the parentheses immediately following the year.

Eckholm, Erik. (1985a, June 25). Kanzi the chimp: A
    life in science. The New York Times, pp. C1, C3.

Eckholm, Erik. (1985b, June 24). Pygmy chimp readily
    learns language skill. The New York Times, pp.
    A1, B7.

Other sources

MATERIAL FROM AN INFORMATION SERVICE OR A DATABASE   Cite the
material as you would any other material, including all publishing
information. At the end of the citation add the name of the service
(such as ERIC) and the number the service assigns to the material.

Horn, P. (1989). The Victorian governess. History
of Education, 18, 333-344. (ERIC Document
Reproduction Service No. EJ 401 533)

DISSERTATION ABSTRACT

Pellman, J. L. (1988). Community integration: Its
influence on the stress of widowhood (Doctoral
dissertation, University of Missouri, 1988).
Dissertation Abstracts International, 49, 2367.

GOVERNMENT DOCUMENT

U.S. Bureau of the Census. (1989). Statistical
abstract of the United States (109th ed.).
Washington, DC: U.S. Government Printing Office.

PROCEEDINGS OF A CONFERENCE

Waterhouse, L. H. (1982). Maternal speech patterns and
differential development. In C. E. Johnson &
C. L. Thew (Eds.), Proceedings of the Second
Annual International Study of Child Language (pp.
442-454). Washington, DC: University Press of
America.

COMPUTER PROGRAM

Notebuilder [Computer software]. (1993). Palo Alto,
CA: Pro/Tem.

VIDEOTAPE

National Geographic Society (Producer). (1987). In the
shadow of Vesuvius [Videotape]. Washington, DC:
National Geographic Society.

A1-c Sample paper: APA style

On the following pages is a research paper written by Karen Shaw, a student in a psychology class. Shaw's assignment was to write a "review of the literature" paper documented with the APA style of citations and references. Shaw received permission from her instructor to review the literature written by psychologists studying the linguistic abilities of apes, a topic she had previously investigated in an English class (see pages 292–303). Shaw's two papers are quite different both in approach and in their styles of documentation.

In preparing her final manuscript, Shaw followed the APA guidelines in D2-b of this book. She did not include an abstract because her instructor did not require one.

Short title and
page number.

Apes and Language:

A Review of the Literature

Karen Shaw

Psychology 110, Section 2

Professor Verdi

April 4, 1995

Full title, writer's
name, name and
section number of
the course,
instructor's name,
and date, all
centered and
double-spaced.

Short title and
page number.

Full title, centered.

Apes and Language:

A Review of the Literature

Over the past twenty-five years, researchers
have demonstrated that the great apes (chimpanzees,
gorillas, and orangutans) resemble humans in
language abilities more than had been thought
possible. Just how far that resemblance extends,
however, has been a matter of some controversy.
Researchers agree that the apes have acquired
fairly large vocabularies in American Sign Language
and in artificial languages, but they have
drawn quite different conclusions in addressing
the following questions:

The writer sets up
her organization in
the introduction.

1. How spontaneously have apes used
    language?

2. How creatively have apes used language?

3. Can apes create sentences?

4. What are the implications of the ape
    language studies?

Headings,
centered, help
readers follow the
organization.

This review of the literature on apes and language
focuses on these four questions.

How Spontaneously Have Apes Used Language?

A signal phrase
names all four
authors and gives
the date in
parentheses.

In an influential article, Terrace, Petitto,
Sanders, and Bever (1979) argued that the apes
in language experiments were not using language
spontaneously, that they were merely imitating
their trainers, responding to conscious or
unconscious cues. Terrace and his colleagues at

Columbia University had trained a chimpanzee, Nim, in American Sign Language, so their skepticism about the apes' abilities received much attention. In fact, funding for ape language research was sharply reduced following publication of their 1979 article "Can an Ape Create a Sentence?"

In retrospect, the conclusions of Terrace et al. seem to have been premature. Although some of the early ape language studies had not been rigorously controlled to eliminate cuing, even as early as 1979 R. A. Gardner and B. T. Gardner were conducting double-blind experiments that prevented any possibility of cuing (Sebeok & Umiker-Sebeok, 1979). Since 1979, researchers have diligently guarded against cuing. For example, Lewin (1991) reported that instructions for pygmy chimpanzee Kanzi were "delivered by someone out of his sight," with other team members wearing earphones so that they "could not hear the instructions and so could not cue Kanzi, even unconsciously" (p. 51).

There is considerable evidence that apes have signed to one another spontaneously, without trainers present. Like many of the apes studied, gorillas Koko and Michael have been observed signing to one another (Patterson & Linden, 1981). At Central Washington University the baby chimpanzee Loulis, placed in the care of an older,

Because the authors of the work are not named in the signal phrase, their names appear in parentheses, along with the date.

For quotations, a page number preceded by "p." appears in parentheses.

An ampersand links the names of two authors in parentheses.

signing chimpanzee, mastered more than fifty
signs in American Sign Language without help
from humans. "We only used seven signs in his
presence," said psychologist Roger Fouts. "All
of his signs were learned from the other chimps
in the laboratory" (Toner, 1986, p. 24).

The extent to which chimpanzees spontaneously
use language may depend on their training.
Terrace trained Nim using the behaviorist
technique of operant conditioning, so it is not
surprising that many of Nim's signs were cued.
Many other researchers have used a conversational
approach that parallels the process by which human
children acquire language. In an experimental
study, O'Sullivan and Yeager (1989) contrasted the
two techniques, using Terrace's Nim as their
subject. They found that Nim's use of language was
significantly more spontaneous under conversational
conditions.

How Creatively Have Apes Used Language?

There is considerable evidence that apes have
invented creative names. One of the earliest and
most controversial examples involved the Gardners'
chimpanzee Washoe. Washoe, who knew the signs for
"water" and "bird," once signed "water bird" when
in the presence of a swan. Terrace et al. (1979)
suggested that there was "no basis for concluding
that Washoe was characterizing the swan as a 'bird

The word *and*
links the names
of two authors
in the signal
phrase.

When this article
was first cited, all
four authors were
named. In
subsequent
citations of a work
with three to five
authors, "et al." is
used after the first
author's name.

that inhabits water.'" Washoe may simply have been "identifying correctly a body of water and a bird, in that order" (p. 895).

Other examples are not so easily explained away. The pygmy chimpanzee Kanzi has requested particular films by combining symbols in a creative way. For instance, to ask for Quest for Fire, a film about early primates discovering fire, Kanzi began to use symbols for "campfire" and "TV" (Eckholm, 1985). And the gorilla Koko has a long list of creative names to her credit: "elephant baby" to describe a Pinocchio doll, "finger bracelet" to describe a ring, "bottle match" to describe a cigarette lighter, and so on (Patterson & Linden, 1981, p. 146). If Terrace's analysis of the "water bird" example were applied to the examples just mentioned, it would not hold. Surely Koko did not first see an elephant and then a baby before signing "elephant baby"--or a bottle and a match before signing "bottle match."

Can Apes Create Sentences?

The early ape language studies offered little proof that apes could combine symbols into grammatically ordered sentences. Apes strung together various signs, but the sequences were often random and repetitious. Nim's series of sixteen signs is a case in point: "give orange me give eat orange me eat orange give me eat orange

The writer interprets the evidence; she doesn't just report it.

give me you" (Terrace et al., 1979, p. 895). The
Gardners were impressed by Washoe's multisign
sequences, seeing in them the beginnings of some
grasp of grammar, but their findings have been
disputed. In one frequently cited film sequence,
Washoe's teacher placed a baby doll in a cup.
Washoe signed "baby in baby in my drink," a series
of signs that seemed to make grammatical sense.
Terrace et al. noted, however, that Washoe had
previously been drilled in similar patterns and
that the teacher had pointed to the objects.

Recent studies with pygmy chimpanzees at the
Yerkes Primate Center in Atlanta are breaking new
ground. Kanzi, a pygmy chimpanzee trained by
E. S. Savage-Rumbaugh, seems to understand simple
grammatical rules about lexigram order. For
instance, Kanzi learned that in two-word
utterances action precedes object, an ordering
also used by human children at the two-word stage.

The writer draws
attention to an
important article.

In a major new article reporting on their
research, Greenfield and Savage-Rumbaugh (1990)
wrote that Kanzi rarely "repeated himself or
formed combinations that were semantically
unrelated" (p. 556).

More important, Kanzi began on his own to
create certain patterns that may not exist in
English but can be found among deaf children and
in other human languages. For example, Kanzi used

his own rules when combining action symbols. Lexigrams that involved an invitation to play, such as "chase," would appear first; lexigrams that indicated what was to be done during play ("hide") would appear second. Kanzi also created his own rules when combining gestures and lexigrams. He would use the lexigram first and then gesture, a practice often followed by young deaf children (Greenfield & Savage-Rumbaugh, 1990, p. 560).

The writer gives a page number for this summary because the article is long.

What Are the Implications of the Ape Language Studies?

Kanzi's linguistic abilities are so impressive that they may help us understand how humans came to acquire language. Pointing out that 99% of our genetic material is held in common with the chimpanzees, Greenfield and Savage-Rumbaugh (1990) have suggested that something of the "evolutionary root of human language" can be found in the "linguistic abilities of the great apes" (p. 540). Noting that apes' brains are similar to those of our human ancestors, Leakey and Lewin (1992) argued that in ape brains "the cognitive foundations on which human language could be built are already present" (p. 244).

The suggestion that there is a continuity in the linguistic abilities of apes and humans has created much controversy. Linguist Noam Chomsky has strongly asserted that language is a unique

The writer presents a balanced view of the philosophical controversy.

human characteristic (Booth, 1990). Terrace has continued to be skeptical of the claims made for the apes, as have Petitto and Bever, coauthors of the 1979 article that caused such skepticism earlier (Gibbons, 1991). However, according to Lewin (1991), "Many psychologists are extremely impressed with Kanzi and the implications of the observations" (p. 52).

The tone of the conclusion is objective.

Although the ape language studies continue to generate controversy, researchers have shown over the past twenty-five years that the gap between the linguistic abilities of apes and humans is far less dramatic than was once believed.

References

Booth, W. (1990, October 29). Monkeying with language: Is chimp using words or merely aping handlers? The Washington Post, p. A3.

Eckholm, E. (1985, June 25). Kanzi the chimp: A life in science. The New York Times, pp. C1, C3.

Gibbons, A. (1991). Déjà vu all over again: Chimp-language wars. Science, 251, 1561-1562.

Greenfield, P. M., & Savage-Rumbaugh, E. S. (1990). Grammatical combination in Pan paniscus: Processes of learning and invention in the evolution and development of language. In S. T. Parker & K. R. Gibson (Eds.), "Language" and intelligence in monkeys and apes: Comparative developmental perspectives (pp. 540-578). Cambridge: Cambridge University Press.

Leakey, R., & Lewin, R. (1992). Origins reconsidered: In search of what makes us human. New York: Doubleday.

Lewin, R. (1991, April 29). Look who's talking now. New Scientist, 130, 49-52.

O'Sullivan, C., & Yeager, C. P. (1989). Communicative context and linguistic competence: The effect of social setting on a chimpanzee's conversational skill.

The list of references appears on a separate page.

The heading is centered.

List is alphabetized by authors' last names.

In student papers the first line of an entry is typed at left margin; subsequent lines are indented five spaces.

Double-spacing is used throughout.

In R. A. Gardner, B. T. Gardner, & T. E. Van
Cantfort (Eds.), Teaching sign language to
chimpanzees (pp. 269-279). Albany: SUNY
Press.

Patterson, F., & Linden, E. (1981). The education
of Koko. New York: Holt, Rinehart & Winston.

Sebeok, T. A., & Umiker-Sebeok, J. (1979,
November). Performing animals: Secrets of the
trade. Psychology Today, 13, 78-91.

Terrace, H. S., Petitto, L. A., Sanders, R. J., &
Bever, T. G. (1979). Can an ape create a
sentence? Science, 206, 891-902.

Toner, M. (1986, February-March). Loulis, the
talking chimp. National Wildlife, 24, 24.

A2

Footnotes or endnotes

Although the *MLA Handbook* treats in-text citations as its preferred style (see M1), it also lists footnotes or endnotes as an acceptable alternative.

Notes provide complete publishing information, either at the bottom of the page (footnotes) or at the end of the paper (endnotes). A raised arabic numeral in the text indicates that a quotation, paraphrase, or summary has been borrowed from a source; to find the publishing information for that source, readers consult the footnote or endnote with the corresponding number. Notes are numbered consecutively throughout the paper.

TEXT

For instance, Lana once described a cucumber as "banana which is green."[9]

NOTE

[9] Flora Davis, <u>Eloquent Animals: A Study in Animal Communication</u> (New York: Coward, 1978) 300.

A2-a First reference to a source

The first time you cite a source in your paper, the note should include the full publishing information for that work as well as the page number of the specific quotation, paraphrase, or summary. The following examples cover the formats that are most frequently encountered.

Books

BASIC FORMAT FOR A BOOK

[1] Jane Tompkins, <u>West of Everything: The Inner Life of Westerns</u> (New York: Oxford UP, 1992) 22.

TWO OR THREE AUTHORS

^{2} Barbara Rico and Sandra Mano, American Mosaic: Multicultural Readings in Context (Boston: Houghton, 1991) 121.

FOUR OR MORE AUTHORS

^{3} Martin J. Medhurst et al., Cold War Rhetoric: Strategy, Metaphor, and Ideology (New York: Greenwood, 1990) 52.

EDITORS

^{4} Rodolfo Anaya and Francisco Lomeli, eds., Aztlán: Essays on the Chicano Homeland (Albuquerque: Academia-El Norte, 1989) 65.

TRANSLATION

^{5} Umberto Eco, Foucault's Pendulum, trans. William Weaver (San Diego: Harcourt, 1989) 234.

CORPORATE AUTHOR

^{6} Fidelity Investments, Fidelity Brokerage Services Handbook (Boston: Fidelity Investments, 1993) 5.

UNKNOWN AUTHOR

^{7} The Times Atlas of the World, 9th ed. (New York: Times, 1992) 135.

EDITION OTHER THAN THE FIRST

^{8} Erika Lindemann, A Rhetoric for Writing Teachers, 2nd ed. (New York: Oxford UP, 1987) 23.

MULTIVOLUME WORK

^{9} Mark Twain: Collected Tales, Sketches, Speeches, and Essays, vol. 2 (New York: Library of America, 1992) 98.

10 "Croatia," The New Encyclopaedia Britannica: Micropaedia, 1991.

WORK IN AN ANTHOLOGY

11 J. M. Synge, "On an Anniversary," The New Oxford Book of Irish Verse, ed. Thomas Kinsella (Oxford: Oxford UP, 1986) 318.

Articles in periodicals

ARTICLE IN A MONTHLY MAGAZINE

12 John Lukacs, "The End of the Twentieth Century," Harper's Jan. 1993: 41.

ARTICLE IN A JOURNAL PAGINATED BY VOLUME

13 Gabriel Segal, "Seeing What Is Not There," Philosophical Review 98 (1989): 200.

ARTICLE IN A JOURNAL PAGINATED BY ISSUE

14 G. J. Johnson, "A Distinctiveness Model of Serial Learning," Psychological Review 98.2 (1991): 208.

ARTICLE IN A DAILY NEWSPAPER

15 Lena H. Sun, "Chinese Feel the Strain of a New Society," Washington Post 13 June 1993: A1.

UNSIGNED ARTICLE IN A NEWSPAPER OR MAGAZINE

16 "Radiation in Russia," U.S. News and World Report 9 Aug. 1993: 41.

EDITORIAL IN A NEWSPAPER

17 "Gays and the Military," editorial, Boston Globe 13 July 1993: 14.

LETTER TO THE EDITOR

[18] Graham Benston, letter, Opera Now May 1993: 12.

BOOK REVIEW

[19] Frank Kermode, "Criticism without Machinery," rev. of Literary Reflections, by R. W. B. Lewis, New York Times Book Review 11 July 1993: 16.

Other sources

GOVERNMENT PUBLICATION

[20] United States, Natl. Endowment for the Humanities, Study Grants for College and University Teachers (Washington: GPO, 1993) 3.

PAMPHLET

[21] United States, Dept. of the Interior, Natl. Park Service, Ford's Theatre and the House Where Lincoln Died (Washington: GPO, 1989) 1.

PUBLISHED DISSERTATION

[22] Robert F. Healey, Eleusinian Sacrifices in the Athenian Law Code, diss., Harvard U, 1961 (New York: Garland, 1990) 36.

UNPUBLISHED DISSERTATION

[23] Kathy Anne Fedorko, "Edith Wharton's Haunted House: The Gothic in Her Fiction," diss., Rutgers U, 1987, 59.

ABSTRACT OF A DISSERTATION

[24] Anne Elizabeth Berkman, "The Quest for Authenticity: The Novels of Toni Morrison," DAI 48 (1988): 2059A (Columbia U).

LECTURE OR PUBLIC ADDRESS

[25] Karen Quinn, "John Singleton Copley's Watson and the Shark," Museum of Fine Arts, Boston, 1 July 1993.

PERSONAL INTERVIEW

[26] Patricia Harrison, personal interview, 19 Feb. 1993.

PUBLISHED INTERVIEW

[27] Anna Quindlen, interview, Commonweal 14 Feb. 1992: 10.

COMPUTER SOFTWARE

[28] Encarta, computer software, Microsoft, 1992, PC-DOS 3.1, Windows, 386SX, CD-ROM.

MATERIAL FROM AN INFORMATION SERVICE OR A DATABASE

[29] Pamela Horn, "The Victorian Governess," History of Education 18 (1989): 335 (ERIC EJ 401 533).

FILM OR VIDEOTAPE

[30] Through the Wire, videotape, dir. Nina Rosenblum, narr. Susan Sarandon, Fox/Lorber Home Video, 1990 (77 min.)

TELEVISION OR RADIO PROGRAM

[31] "This Old Pyramid," with Mark Lehner and Roger Hopkins, Nova, PBS, WGBH, Boston, 4 Aug. 1993.

LIVE PERFORMANCE OF A PLAY

[32] The Sisters Rosensweig, by Wendy Wasserstein, dir. Daniel Sullivan, with Jane Alexander, Christine Estabrook, and Madeline Kahn, Barrymore, New York, 11 July 1993.

RECORD, TAPE, OR CD

> [33] Giuseppe Verdi, <u>Falstaff</u>, with Tito Gobbi, Elisabeth Schwarzkopf, Nan Merriman, and Fedora Barbieri, cond. Herbert von Karajan, Philharmonia Orch. and Chorus, EMI, 7 49668 2, 1988.

A2-b Subsequent references to a source

Subsequent references to a work that has already been cited in a note should be given in shortened form. You need to give only enough information so that the reader can identify which work you are referring to — usually the author's last name and a page number. The abbreviations *ibid.* and *op. cit.* are no longer used.

> [34] Tompkins 85.
> [35] Rico and Mano 23.
> [36] <u>Times Atlas</u> 99.

If you are using more than one work by one author or two works by authors with the same last name, cite the author's last name and a shortened title.

> [37] Gordon, <u>Good</u> 135.
> [38] Gordon, <u>Other</u> 34.

When you use notes as your method of documentation, you may not need a list of works cited, since complete publishing information is given in the notes themselves. Some professors prefer, however, that you include an alphabetized list of the works cited in the paper or a bibliography of the works you consulted, whether or not they were cited. If you do include a list of works cited or a bibliography, use the MLA style described in M2.

A3

List of style manuals

A Writer's Reference describes three commonly used systems of documentation: MLA in-text citations, used in English and the humanities (see M1 and M2); APA in-text citations, used in psychology and the social sciences (see A1); and footnotes or endnotes, an MLA alternative (see A2). Following is a list of style manuals used in a variety of disciplines.

BIOLOGY

Council of Biology Editors. *CBE Style Manual: A Guide for Authors, Editors, and Publishers in the Biological Sciences.* 5th ed. Bethesda: CBE, 1983.

CHEMISTRY

Dodd, Janet S., ed. *The ACS Style Guide: A Manual for Authors and Editors.* Washington: American Chemical Soc., 1986.

ENGLISH AND THE HUMANITIES (SEE M1 AND M2.)

Gibaldi, Joseph, and Walter S. Achtert, *MLA Handbook for Writers of Research Papers.* 4th ed. New York: Modern Language Association of America, 1995.

GEOLOGY

Cochran, Wendell, Peter Fenner, and Mary Hills, eds. *Geowriting: A Guide to Writing, Editing, and Printing in Earth Science.* Alexandria, VA: American Geological Inst., 1984.

GOVERNMENT DOCUMENTS

Garner, Diane L. *The Complete Guide to Citing Government Information Resources: A Manual for Writers and Librarians.* Rev. ed. Bethesda: Congressional Information Service, 1993.

United States. Government Printing Office. *Style Manual.* Washington: GPO, 1984.

JOURNALISM

Associated Press Staff. *Associated Press Stylebook and Libel Manual.* Reading, MA: Addison, 1992.

LAW

The Bluebook: A Uniform System of Citation. Comp. editors of *Columbia Law Review* et al. 15th ed. Cambridge: Harvard Law Review, 1991.

LINGUISTICS

Linguistic Society of America. "LSA Style Sheet." Published annually in the December issue of the *LSA Bulletin.*

MATHEMATICS

American Mathematical Society. *A Manual for Authors of Mathematical Papers.* Rev. ed. Providence: AMS, 1990.

MEDICINE

Iverson, Cheryl, et al. *American Medical Association Manual of Style.* 8th ed. Baltimore: Williams and Wilkins, 1989.

MUSIC

Holoman, D. Kern, ed. *Writing about Music: A Style Sheet from the Editors of* 19th-Century Music. Berkeley: U of California P, 1988.

PHYSICS

American Institute of Physics. *AIP Style Manual*. 4th ed. New York: AIP, 1990.

PSYCHOLOGY AND THE SOCIAL SCIENCES (SEE A1.)

American Psychological Association. *Publication Manual of the American Psychological Association*. 4th ed. Washington: APA, 1994.

SCIENCE AND TECHNICAL WRITING

Rubens, Philip, ed. *Science and Technical Writing: A Manual of Style*. New York: Holt, 1992.

B

Basic Grammar

Index

B

Basic Grammar

B1

Parts of speech

The parts of speech are a system for classifying words. There are eight parts of speech: noun, pronoun, verb, adjective, adverb, preposition, conjunction, and interjection. Many words can function as more than one part of speech. For example, depending on its use in a sentence, the word *paint* can be a noun (*The paint is wet*) or a verb (*Please paint the ceiling next*).

B1-a Nouns

A noun is the name of a person, place, thing, or an idea. Nouns are often but not always signaled by an article (*a, an, the*).

> The *cat* in *gloves* catches no *mice.*

> *Repetition* does not transform a *lie* into *truth.*

Nouns sometimes function as adjectives modifying other nouns.

> You can't make a *silk* purse out of a *sow's* ear.

Nouns are classified for a variety of purposes. When capitalization is the issue, we speak of *proper* versus *common* nouns (see S3-a). If the problem is one of word choice, we may speak of *concrete* versus *abstract* nouns (see W4-b). Most nouns come in *singular* and *plural* forms; *collective* nouns may be either singular or plural (see G1-e and G3-a). *Possessive* nouns require an apostrophe (see P5-a).

B1-b Pronouns

A pronoun is a word used in place of a noun. Usually the pronoun substitutes for a specific noun, known as its *antecedent.*

> When the *wheel* squeaks, *it* is greased.

Although most pronouns function as substitutes for nouns, some can function as adjectives modifying nouns.

This hanging will surely be a lesson to me.

Most of the pronouns in English are listed in this section.

PERSONAL PRONOUNS   Personal pronouns refer to specific persons or things.

Singular: I, me, you, she, her, he, him, it

Plural: we, us, you, they, them

POSSESSIVE PRONOUNS   Possessive pronouns indicate ownership.

Singular: my, mine, your, yours, her, hers, his, its

Plural: our, ours, your, yours, their, theirs

INTENSIVE AND REFLEXIVE PRONOUNS   Intensive pronouns emphasize a noun or another pronoun (The senator *herself* met us at the door). Reflexive pronouns name a receiver of an action identical with the doer of the action (Paula cut *herself*).

Singular: myself, yourself, himself, herself, itself

Plural: ourselves, yourselves, themselves

RELATIVE PRONOUNS   Relative pronouns introduce subordinate clauses functioning as adjectives (The man *who robbed us* was never caught). In addition to introducing the clause, the relative pronoun, in this case *who,* points back to a noun or pronoun that the clause modifies (*man*). (See B3-e.)

who, whom, whose, which, that

DEMONSTRATIVE PRONOUNS   Demonstrative pronouns identify or point to nouns. Frequently they function as adjectives (*This* chair is my favorite), but they may also function as noun equivalents (*This* is my favorite chair).

this, that, these, those

INDEFINITE PRONOUNS Indefinite pronouns refer to nonspecific persons or things. Most are always singular (*everyone, each*); some are always plural (*both, many*); a few may be singular or plural (see G1-d).

all, another, any, anybody, anyone, anything, both, each, either, everybody, everyone, everything, few, many, neither, nobody, none, no one, nothing, one, several, some, somebody, someone, something

RECIPROCAL PRONOUNS Reciprocal pronouns refer to individual parts of a plural antecedent (By turns, we helped *each other* through college).

each other, one another

NOTE: Pronouns cause a variety of problems for writers. See Pronoun-antecedent agreement (G3-a), Pronoun reference (G3-b), Case of nouns and pronouns (G3-c), and Case of *who* and *whom* (G3-d).

B1-c Verbs

The verb of a sentence usually expresses action (*jump, think*) or being (*is, become*). It is composed of a main verb (MV) possibly preceded by one or more helping verbs (HV).

MV
The best fish *swim* near the bottom.

HV   MV
A marriage *is* not *built* in a day.

Notice that words can intervene between the helping and the main verb (*is* not *built*).

Helping verbs

There are twenty-three helping verbs in English: forms of *have, do,* and *be,* which may also function as main verbs; and nine modals, which function only as helping verbs. The forms of *have, do,* and *be* change form to indicate tense; the nine modals do not.

FORMS OF *HAVE, DO,* AND *BE*

have, has, had

do, does, did

be, am, is, are, was, were, being, been

MODALS

can, could, may, might, must, shall, should, will, would

The phrase *ought to* is often classified as a modal as well.

Main verbs

The main verb of a sentence is always the kind of word that would change form if put into these test sentences:

BASE FORM	Usually I (*walk, ride*).
PAST TENSE	Yesterday I (*walked, rode*).
PAST PARTICIPLE	I have (*walked, ridden*) many times before.
PRESENT PARTICIPLE	I am (*walking, riding*) right now.
***-S* FORM**	Usually he/she/it (*walks, rides*).

If a word doesn't change form when slipped into these test sentences, you can be certain that it is not a main verb. For example, the noun *revolution,* though it may seem to suggest an action, can never function as a main verb. Just try to make it behave like one (*Today I revolution . . . Yesterday I revolutioned . . .*) and you'll see why.

When both the past-tense and the past-participle forms of a verb end in *-ed,* the verb is regular (*walked, walked*). Otherwise, the verb is irregular (*rode, ridden*). (See G2-a.)

The verb *be* is highly irregular, having eight forms instead of the usual five: the base form *be;* the present-tense forms *am, is,* and *are;* the past-tense forms *was* and *were;* the present participle *being;* and the past participle *been.*

Helping verbs combine with the various forms of main verbs to create tenses. For a survey of tenses, see G2-f.

NOTE: Some verbs are followed by words that look like prepositions but are so closely associated with the verb that they are a part of its meaning. These words are known as *particles.* Common verb-particle combinations include *bring up, call off, drop off, give in, look up, run into,* and *take off.*

A lot of parents *pack up* their troubles and *send* them *off* to camp.
— Raymond Duncan

NOTE: Verbs cause many problems for writers. See Subject-verb agreement (G1); Other problems with verbs, including verb forms, tense, mood, and voice (G2); and ESL problems with verbs (T2).

B1-d Adjectives and articles

An adjective is a word used to modify, or describe, a noun or pronoun. An adjective usually answers one of these questions: Which one? What kind of? How many?

the *lame* elephant [Which elephant?]

rare valuable old stamps [What kind of stamps?]

sixteen candles [How many candles?]

Adjectives usually precede the words they modify. However, they may also follow linking verbs, in which case they describe the subject. (See B2-b.)

Good medicine always tastes *bitter*.

Articles, sometimes classified as adjectives, are used to mark nouns. There are only three: the definite article *the* and the indefinite articles *a* and *an*.

A country can be judged by *the* quality of its proverbs.

NOTE: Writers sometimes misuse adjectives (see G4). Speakers of English as a second language may have trouble placing adjectives correctly (see T3-d); they may also encounter difficulties with articles (see T1).

B1-e Adverbs

An adverb is a word used to modify a verb (or verbal), an adjective, or another adverb. It usually answers one of these questions: When? Where? How? Why? Under what conditions? To what degree?

Pull *gently* at a weak rope. [Pull how?]

Read the best books *first*. [Read when?]

Adverbs modifying adjectives or other adverbs usually intensify or limit the intensity of the word they modify.

Be *extremely* good, and you will be *very* lonesome.

The negators *not* and *never* are classified as adverbs.

NOTE: Writers sometimes misuse adverbs (see G4). Speakers of English as a second language may have trouble placing adverbs correctly (see T3-d).

B1-f Prepositions

A preposition is a word placed before a noun or pronoun to form a phrase modifying another word in the sentence. The prepositional phrase nearly always functions as an adjective or as an adverb. (See B3-a.)

The road *to hell* is paved *with good intentions*.

To hell functions as an adjective modifying the noun *road; with good intentions* functions as an adverb, modifying the verb *is paved*.

There are a limited number of prepositions in English. The most common are included in the following list.

about	beneath	for	out	to
above	beside	from	outside	toward
across	besides	in	over	under
after	between	inside	past	underneath
against	beyond	into	plus	unlike
along	but	like	regarding	until
among	by	near	respecting	unto
around	concerning	next	round	up
as	considering	of	since	upon
at	despite	off	than	with
before	down	on	through	within
behind	during	onto	throughout	without
below	except	opposite	till	

Some prepositions are more than a word long. *Along with, as well as, in addition to, instead of, next to,* and *up to* are common examples.

NOTE: Except for certain idiomatic uses (see W4-e), prepositions cause few problems for native speakers of English. For second-language speakers, however, prepositions can cause considerable difficulty (see T2-d and T3-f).

B1-g Conjunctions

Conjunctions join words, phrases, or clauses, and they indicate the relation between the elements joined.

COORDINATING CONJUNCTIONS Coordinating conjunctions connect grammatically equal elements. (See E1-b and E6.)

and, but, or, nor, for, so, yet

CORRELATIVE CONJUNCTIONS Correlative conjunctions are pairs of conjunctions that connect grammatically equal elements. (See E1-b.)

either . . . or, neither . . . nor, not only . . . but also, whether . . . or, both . . . and

SUBORDINATING CONJUNCTIONS Subordinating conjunctions introduce subordinate clauses and indicate their relation to the rest of the sentence. (See B3-e.)

after, although, as, as if, because, before, even though, if, in order that, rather than, since, so that, than, that, though, unless, until, when, where, whether, while

CONJUNCTIVE ADVERBS Conjunctive adverbs are adverbs used to indicate the relation between independent clauses. (See G6-b and P3-b.)

accordingly, also, anyway, besides, certainly, consequently, conversely, finally, furthermore, hence, however, incidentally, indeed, instead, likewise, meanwhile, moreover, nevertheless, next, nonetheless, otherwise, similarly, specifically, still, subsequently, then, therefore, thus

NOTE: The ability to distinguish between conjunctive adverbs and coordinating conjunctions will help you avoid comma splices and make punctuation decisions (see G6, P1-a, and P3-b). The ability to recognize subordinating conjunctions will help you avoid sentence fragments (see G5).

B1-h Interjections

Interjections are words used to express surprise or emotion (*Oh! Hey! Wow!*).

B2

Parts of sentences

Most English sentences flow from subject to verb to any objects or complements. *Predicate* is the grammatical term given to the verb plus its objects, complements, and modifiers.

B2-a Subjects

The subject of a sentence names who or what the sentence is about. The simple subject is always a noun or a pronoun; the complete subject consists of the simple subject (SS) and all of its modifiers.

┌──COMPLETE SUBJECT──┐
SS
The purity of a revolution usually lasts about two weeks.

┌────COMPLETE SUBJECT────┐
SS
Historical books that contain no lies are extremely tedious.

COMPLETE
SUBJECT
┌─SS─┐
In every country, *the sun* rises in the morning.

To find the complete subject, ask Who? or What?, insert the verb, and finish the question. What usually lasts about two weeks?

The purity of a revolution. What are extremely tedious? *Historical books that contain no lies.* What rises in the morning? *The sun* [not *In every country, the sun*].

To find the simple subject, strip away all modifiers in the complete subject. This includes single-word modifiers such as *the* and *historical,* phrases such as *of a revolution,* and subordinate clauses such as *that contain no lies.*

A sentence may have a compound subject containing two or more simple subjects joined with a coordinating conjunction such as *and* or *or.*

ss   ss
Much industry and little conscience make us rich.

In imperative sentences, which give advice or commands, the subject is an understood *you.*

[You] Hitch your wagon to a star.

Although the subject ordinarily comes before the verb, occasionally it does not. When a sentence begins with *There is* or *There are* (or *There was* or *There were*), the subject follows the verb. The word *There* is an expletive in such constructions, an empty word serving merely to get the sentence started.

ss
There is *no substitute for victory.*

Sometimes a writer will invert a sentence for effect.

ss
Happy is *the nation that has no history.*

In questions, the subject frequently appears in an unusual position, sandwiched between parts of the verb.

ss
Do *married men* make the best husbands?

NOTE: The ability to recognize the subject of a sentence will help you edit for a variety of problems such as sentence fragments (G5), subject-verb agreement (G1), and case of nouns and pronouns (G3-c). If English is not your native language, see also T3-a and T3-b.

B2-b Verbs, objects, and complements

Section B1-c explains how to identify verbs. A sentence's verb(s) may be classified as linking, transitive, or intransitive, depending on the kinds of objects or complements the verb can (or cannot) take.

Linking verbs and subject complements

Linking verbs (V) take subject complements (SC), words or word groups that complete the meaning of the subject (S) by either renaming it or describing it.

```
┌──────────S──────────┐   V   ┌─────────SC──────────┐
```
The quarrels of friends are the opportunities of foes.

```
┌─S─┐ V ┌─SC─┐
```
Love is blind.

When the simple subject complement renames the subject, it is a noun or pronoun, such as *opportunities;* when it describes the subject, it is an adjective, such as *blind.*

Linking verbs are usually a form of *be: be, am, is, are, was, were, being, been.* Verbs such as *appear, become, feel, grow, look, make, prove, remain, seem, smell, sound,* and *taste* are linking when they are followed by a word group that names or describes the subject.

Transitive verbs and direct objects

Transitive verbs take direct objects (DO), words or word groups that complete the meaning of the verb by naming a receiver of the action. The simple direct object is always a noun or a pronoun.

```
┌──────S──────┐   V   ┌─────────DO─────────┐
```
The little snake studies the ways of the big serpent.

Transitive verbs usually appear in the active voice, with the subject doing the action and a direct object receiving the action. Active-voice sentences can be transformed into the passive voice, with the subject receiving the action instead.

ACTIVE VOICE The early bird sometimes catches the early worm.

PASSIVE VOICE The early worm is sometimes caught by the early bird.

What was once the direct object (*the early worm*) has become the subject in the passive-voice transformation, and the original subject appears in a prepositional phrase beginning with *by*. The *by* phrase is frequently omitted in passive-voice constructions: *The early worm is sometimes caught.* (See also G2-h.)

Transitive verbs, indirect objects, and direct objects

The direct object of a transitive verb is sometimes preceded by an indirect object (IO), a noun or pronoun telling to whom or for whom the action of the sentence is done.

┌S┐ ┌V┐   IO ┌DO┐   S ┌—V—┐   IO ┌—DO—┐
You show [to] me a hero, and I will write [for] you a tragedy.

Transitive verbs, direct objects, and object complements

The direct object of a transitive verb is sometimes followed by an object complement (OC), a word or word group that completes the direct object's meaning by renaming or describing it.

┌———S———┐ V ┌DO┐ ┌————————OC————————┐
Some people call a spade an agricultural implement.

┌S┐ V ┌———DO———┐┌OC┐
Love makes all hard hearts gentle.

When the object complement renames the direct object, it is a noun or pronoun, such as *implement*. When it describes the direct object, it is an adjective, such as *gentle*.

Intransitive verbs

Intransitive verbs take no objects or complements. They may or may not be followed by adverbial modifiers.

S   V
Money talks.

```
      s     v
All roads lead to Rome.
```

Nothing receives the actions of talking and leading in these sentences, so the verbs are intransitive. Intransitive verbs are often followed by adverbial modifiers. In the second sentence, for example, *to Rome* is a prepositional phrase functioning as an adverb modifying *lead*.

NOTE: The dictionary will tell you whether a verb is transitive or intransitive. Some verbs have both transitive and intransitive functions.

>   TRANSITIVE   Sandra flew her Cessna over the canyon.
>
>   INTRANSITIVE   A bald eagle flew overhead.

In the first example, *flew* has a direct object that receives the action: *her Cessna*. In the second example, the verb is followed by an adverb (*overhead*), not by a direct object.

B3

Subordinate word groups

Subordinate word groups cannot stand alone. They function only within sentences, usually as adjectives, adverbs, or nouns.

B3-a Prepositional phrases

A prepositional phrase begins with a preposition such as *at, by, for, from, in, of, on, to,* or *with* (see B1-f) and ends with a noun or a noun equivalent. The noun or noun equivalent is known as the object of the preposition.

Prepositional phrases nearly always function as adjectives or as adverbs. When functioning as an adjective, a prepositional phrase appears immediately following the noun or pronoun it modifies.

Variety is the spice *of life*.

When functioning as an adverb, a prepositional phrase may or may not appear next to the verb it modifies.

Do not judge a tree *by its bark*.

B3-b Verbal phrases

A verbal is a verb form that does not function as the verb of a clause. Verbals include infinitives (the word *to* plus the base form of the verb), present participles (the *-ing* form of the verb), and past participles (the form of the verb usually ending in *-d, -ed, -n, -en,* or *-t*) (see B1-c).

Verbals can take objects, complements, and modifiers to form verbal phrases. These phrases are classified as participial, gerund, and infinitive.

Participial phrases

Participial phrases always function as adjectives. Their verbals are either present participles or past participles.

Being a philosopher, I have a problem for every solution.

Truth *kept in the dark* will never save the world.

Gerund phrases

Gerund phrases always function as nouns: usually as subjects, subject complements, direct objects, or objects of the preposition. Their verbals are present participles.

Justifying a fault doubles it.

Kleptomaniacs can't help *helping themselves*.

Infinitive phrases

Infinitive phrases, usually constructed around *to* plus the base form of the verb (*to call, to drink*), can function as adjectives, adverbs, or nouns. When functioning as a noun, an infinitive phrase usually plays the role of subject, subject complement, or direct object.

We do not have the right *to abandon the poor*.

He cut off his nose *to spite his face*.

To side with truth is noble.

B3-c Appositive phrases

Appositive phrases describe nouns or pronouns. In form they are nouns or noun equivalents.

Politicians, *acrobats at heart,* can sit on a fence and yet keep both ears to the ground.

B3-d Absolute phrases

An absolute phrase modifies a whole clause or sentence, not just one word. It consists of a noun or noun equivalent usually followed by a participial phrase.

His words dipped in honey, the senator mesmerized the crowd.

B3-e Subordinate clauses

Subordinate clauses are patterned like sentences, having subjects and verbs and sometimes objects or complements, but they function within sentences as adjectives, adverbs, or nouns. They cannot stand alone as complete sentences.

Adjective clauses

Adjective clauses modify nouns or pronouns, usually answering the question Which one? or What kind of? They begin with a relative pronoun (*who, whom, whose, which,* or *that*) or a relative adverb (*when* or *where*).

The arrow *that has left the bow* never returns.

Adverb clauses

Adverb clauses modify verbs, adjectives, or other adverbs, usually answering one of these questions: When? Where? Why? How? Under what conditions? To what degree? They begin with a subordinating conjunction (*after, although, as, as if, because, before, even though, if, in order that, rather than, since, so that, than, that, though, unless, until, when, where, whether, while*).

When the well is dry, we know the worth of water.

Venice would be a fine city *if it were only drained*.

Noun clauses

Noun clauses function as subjects, objects, or complements. They usually begin with one of the following words: *how, that, which, who, whoever, whom, whomever, what, whatever, when, where, whether, whose, why.*

Whoever gossips to you will gossip of you.

B4

Sentence types

Sentences are classified in two ways: according to their structure (simple, compound, complex, and compound-complex) and according to their purpose (declarative, imperative, interrogative, and exclamatory).

B4-a Sentence structures

Depending on the number and types of clauses they contain, sentences are classified as simple, compound, complex, or compound-complex.

Clauses come in two varieties: independent and subordinate. An independent clause contains a subject and predicate, and it either stands alone or could stand alone. A subordinate clause also contains a subject and predicate, but it functions within a sentence as an adjective, an adverb, or a noun; it cannot stand alone.

SIMPLE SENTENCE   A simple sentence is one independent clause with no subordinate clauses.

┌────────── INDEPENDENT CLAUSE ──────────┐
Without music, life would be a mistake.

COMPOUND SENTENCE   A compound sentence is composed of two or more independent clauses with no subordinate clauses. The independent clauses are usually joined with a comma and a coordinating conjunction (*and, but, or, nor, for, so, yet*) or with a semicolon.

┌──── INDEPENDENT CLAUSE ────┐   ┌──── INDEPENDENT CLAUSE ────┐
One arrow is easily broken, but you can't break a bundle of ten.

COMPLEX SENTENCE   A complex sentence is composed of one independent clause with one or more subordinate clauses.

┌─── SUBORDINATE ───┐
       CLAUSE
If you scatter thorns, don't go barefoot.

COMPOUND-COMPLEX SENTENCE   A compound-complex sentence contains at least two independent clauses and at least one subordinate clause. The following sentence contains two independent clauses, each of which contains a subordinate clause.

┌──── IND CLAUSE ────┐   ┌──── IND CLAUSE ────┐
     ┌─SUB CLAUSE─┐   ┌─SUB CLAUSE─┐
Tell me what you eat, and I will tell you what you are.

B4-b Sentence purposes

Writers use declarative sentences to make statements, imperative sentences to issue requests or commands, interrogative sentences to ask questions, and exclamatory sentences to make exclamations.

DECLARATIVE	The echo always has the last word.
IMPERATIVE	Love your neighbor.
INTERROGATIVE	Are second thoughts always wisest?
EXCLAMATORY	I want to wash the flag, not burn it!

(Continued from page iv)

Jane Brody, from *Jane Brody's Nutrition Book.* Copyright © 1981 by Jane E. Brody. Reprinted by permission of W. W. Norton & Company, Inc.

Roger Caras, from "What's a Koala?" Copyright 1983 by Roger Caras. First appeared in *Geo* Magazine, May 1983. Reprinted by permission of Roberta Pryor, Inc.

Bruce Catton, from "Grant and Lee: A Study in Contrasts," *The American Story.* Earl Schenck Miers, editor. © 1956 by Broadcast Music, Inc. Reprinted by permission of the U.S. Capitol Historical Society.

Earl Conrad, from *Harriet Tubman.* Reprinted by permission of Paul S. Eriksson, Publisher.

Emily Dickinson, from "The Snake," *The Poems of Emily Dickinson,* Thomas H. Johnson, Ed. Cambridge, Mass.: The Belknap Press of Harvard University Press. Copyright 1951, © 1955, 1979, 1983 by the President and Fellows of Harvard College.

Erik Eckholm, from "Pygmy Chimp Readily Learns Language Skill," *The New York Times.* Copyright © 1985 by The New York Times Company.

Jane Goodall, from *In the Shadow of Man.* Copyright © 1971 by Hugo and Jane van Lawick-Goodall. Published by Houghton Mifflin Company.

Stephen Jay Gould, from "Were Dinosaurs Dumb?" *The Panda's Thumb: More Reflections in Natural History.* Copyright © 1980 by Stephen Jay Gould. Reprinted by permission of W. W. Norton & Company, Inc.

Hillary Hauser, from "Exploring a Sunken Realm in Australia." *National Geographic,* January 1984. Reprinted by permission of the National Geographic Society.

Richard Hofstadter, from *America at 1750: A Social Portrait.* Copyright © 1971 by Beatrice K. Hofstadter, executrix of the estate of Richard Hofstadter. Published by Alfred A. Knopf, Inc.

Philip Kopper, "How to Open an Oyster." Copyright © 1979 by Philip Kopper. Published by Times Books, a division of Quadrangle/The New York Times Book Co., Inc., from *The Wild Edge: Life and Lore of the Great Atlantic Beachers* by Philip Kopper.

Margaret Mead, from "New Superstitions for Old," *A Way of Seeing.* Published by William Morrow & Company, Inc.

Gloria Naylor, from *Linden Hills.* Copyright © 1985 by Gloria Naylor. Published by Houghton Mifflin Company.

Anne Rudloe and Jack Rudloe, from "Electric Warefare: The Fish That Kill with Thunderbolts." *Smithsonian* Magazine, August 1993. © Anne Rudloe and Jack Rudloe.

Lewis Thomas, from "On Societies as Organisms," *The Lives of a Cell.* Copyright © 1974 by Lewis Thomas. All rights reserved. Published by Viking Penguin, Inc.

Margaret Visser, from *Much Depends on Dinner* by Margaret Visser. Published by Grove Press.

Olivia Vlahos, from *Human Beginnings.* Published by Viking Penguin Inc. Reprinted by permission of the author.

Index

Special Help for ESL Students

Correction Symbols

Numbers refer to sections of this book.

abbr	faulty abbreviation S4		**om**	omitted word E2
ad	misuse of adverb or adjective G4		**p**	error in punctuation
agr	faulty agreement G1, G3-a		$\wedge$	comma P1
appr	inappropriate language W3		**no ,**	no comma P2
			;	semicolon P3
awk	awkward		**:**	colon P4
cap	capital letter S3		$\vee$	apostrophe P5
case	error in case G3-c, G3-d		**" "**	quotation marks P6
coh	coherence C3-d		**. ?**	period, question mark, exclamation point, dash, parentheses, brackets, ellipsis, slash P7
coord	faulty coordination E6-b		**!**	
cs	comma splice G6		**— ( )**	
dev	inadequate development C3-b		**[ ] . . .**	
			/	
dm	dangling modifier E3-e		**par, ¶**	new paragraph C3-e
-ed	error in -*ed* ending G2-d		**pass**	ineffective passive W4-c, G2-h
exact	inexact language W4		**ref**	error in pronoun reference G3-b
frag	sentence fragment G5			
fs	fused sentence G6		**-s**	error in -*s* ending G2-c
ESL	ESL trouble spot T1, T2, T3		**shift**	distracting shift E4
			sp	misspelled word S1
gl/us	see glossary of usage W1		**sub**	faulty subordination E6-c, E6-d
hyph	error in use of hyphen S2		**sxt**	sexist language W3-e
irreg	error in irregular verb G2-a		**t**	error in verb tense G2-f
			trans	transition needed C3-d
ital	italics (underlining) S6		**var**	lack of variety in sentence structure E6-a, E6-b, E7
jar	jargon W3-a			
lc	use lowercase letter S3		**vb**	verb error G2
mixed	mixed construction E5		**w**	wordy W2
mm	misplaced modifier E3-b		**wc**	word choice W3, W4
mood	error in mood G2-g		**//**	faulty parallelism E1
ms	manuscript form D2		$\wedge$	insert
nonst	nonstandard usage W3-c		**x**	obvious error
num	error in use of numbers S5		**#**	insert space
			$\bigcirc$	close up space

Contents